THIS LOVING
DARKNESS

UNIVERSITY OF HULL PUBLICATIONS

THIS LOVING DARKNESS

DARKNESS

The Cinema and
Spanish Writers
1920–1936

C. B. MORRIS

Published for the UNIVERSITY OF HULL *by the*
OXFORD UNIVERSITY PRESS
1980

Oxford University Press, Walton Street, Oxford OX2 6DP

OXFORD LONDON GLASGOW
NEW YORK TORONTO MELBOURNE WELLINGTON
KUALA LUMPUR SINGAPORE JAKARTA HONG KONG TOKYO
DELHI BOMBAY CALCUTTA MADRAS KARACHI
NAIROBI DAR ES SALAAM CAPE TOWN

Published in the United States by
Oxford University Press, New York

© University of Hull 1980

British Library Cataloguing in Publication Data

Morris, Cyril Brian
  This loving darkness.
  1. Spanish literature – 20th century – History
and criticism
  2. Moving-pictures and literature
  I. Title II. University of Hull
  860'.9'0062   PQ6041   80-40340

  ISBN 0–19–713440–8

Set, printed and bound in Great Britain by
Fakenham Press Limited, Fakenham, Norfolk

For Carmen,
who built my dream-house,
and for
Venessa, Julian and Paul,
who share it with us.

ACKNOWLEDGEMENTS

B Y a happy chance, this book was written within a hundred miles of Hollywood thanks to the invitation extended to me by the late Professor Jorge de Sena to spend the academic year 1977–8 as Visiting Professor in his Department at the University of California, Santa Barbara. I am grateful to the United States–United Kingdom Educational Commission for recommending the award of a Fulbright-Hays Travel Grant. Through its award of a Faculty Fellowship in European Studies, the Leverhulme Trust enabled me to undertake in Spain in 1974 the fundamental research for my book. A number of people generously provided information and material; Professor Dru Dougherty gave me valuable insights into Valle-Inclán; Mrs Nancy Mémbrez relayed to me a key piece of information about García Lorca and New York; Emeritus Professor K. S. Reid let me draw on his expert knowledge of Ortega y Gasset; Professor Katherine M. Sibbald sent me an early article by Jorge Guillén; and Ms Elizabeth R. Ziman, of the University of London Library, kindly searched for and sent me some illuminating material about New York and Coney Island. My pursuit of the elusive comic Charles Bowers benefited greatly from the assistance of Mr Kevin Brownlow; Mr Paul Myers, of the Lincoln Center, and Ms Barbara J. Humphrys, of the Library of Congress. I am indebted to Don Rafael Alberti for allowing me to quote from his works; to Doña Isabel García Lorca for authorizing my quotations from her brother's works; and to the Fondo de Cultura Económica, Mexico, for allowing me to quote from Cernuda's poetry. Two special debts remain to be acknowledged: the first to my secretary, Miss Jill Hodgson, serene, efficient, indispensable; the second to my wife, Carmen, constant in her encouragement, constructive in her criticisms; without her this book would not have been written.

January 1980   C.B.M.

CONTENTS

INTRODUCTION

A GIFT OF THE GODS

El cinema se me antoja un
espléndido regalo de los dioses . . .*
Benjamín Jarnés (1936)

IN 1916 the young Spanish readers of the children's magazine
Los Muchachos were offered instructions on how to build 'Un
cine sencillo'.[1] To judge from the imprint left by the cinema on
Spanish literature during the subsequent twenty years, many
fledgling writers followed those instructions, or absorbed in
1915 'Secretos del cine'.[2] The name of Ricardo Acevedo does
not appear among the ranks of adult Spanish writers who
responded creatively to the appeal and stimulus of the cinema,
but by publishing in *Los Muchachos* at the age of twelve a story
entitled 'En el cine', he succumbed to the whimsical fantasies of
slapstick comedy and recounted them with the candour and
zaniness which were to be refined by Lorca and Alberti some
ten years later.[3] The bicycle on which young Ricardo's cinematic hero 'Tontolín' bowled over people and evaded the pursuing
police will be followed by the bicycle on which Buster Keaton
takes a ride in Lorca's *El paseo de Buster Keaton* (1928) and
commemorated in the words Alberti put into Harold Lloyd's
mouth in his poem 'Harold Lloyd, estudiante' (1929):

Sígueme por el aire en bicicleta.†

Ricardo Acevedo's elders were no more able – or willing – to
escape the pervasive influence of the cinema, whose presence
made itself felt in magazines of varying cultural levels and
political persuasions; the steady polarization of Spanish political life and the increasing menacing social unrest of the early
1930s separate Mauricio Bacarisse's apolitical essays published

* The cinema seems to me to be a splendid gift of the gods . . .
† Follow me through the air on your bicycle.

in *España* in 1920 and 1921 and the overtly sectarian, slanted attacks on the 'capitalist' cinema which appeared in the left-wing magazine *Octubre* in 1933.[4] During the years preceding the Civil War the cinema was credited in Spain with many virtues and indicted for many vices; films thrilled and inspired many, and disgusted and appalled others. Those who were passionately excited by the cinema could join one of the clubs which spread throughout Spain after the founding in Madrid in 1928 of the pioneering Cineclub Español. Those who were equally passionate in their opposition to the cinema could ventilate their hostility in critical essays, satirical attacks, and strident, pious calls for censorship and banning. The very fact that there echoed during the 1920s and 1930s a chorus of voices raised vehemently against the cinema reveals the importance its detractors attributed to it and their awareness that it was, whether they liked it or not, an essential strand in the literary and social fabric of Spain.

The mark left on Spanish literature by the cinema is obvious for all to see in Lorca's *El paseo de Buster Keaton*, or in Alberti's poems to silent cinema comics and actors, or in Francisco Ayala's story 'Polar estrella' (1928). In Spanish literature of the 1920s and 1930s cinemas and their stars are so evident and ubiquitous that critics need little vision to declare firstly that 'the cinema is one of the agglutinants of the Generation of 1927', or contend, without elaboration, that the cinema 'had an intense influence on the techniques of the novel, the theatre, and even poetry'.[5] Although such statements abound, what is lacking is a study firstly of the climate of passionate support and vigorous opposition in which Spanish writers wrote, and then of the various ways in which those writers translated into literature the ideas, techniques, and images they derived from watching films.

The history of the Spanish film industry has been fully documented by Juan Antonio Cabero in his *Historia de la cinematografía española* (1949). More recently, Luis Gómez Mesa has examined the debt the Spanish cinema owes to Spanish literature in *La literatura española en el cine nacional 1907–1977* (1978). Although the cinema has spawned a vast critical literature, only a minute proportion of it is devoted to its relationship with literature. Studies such as George Bluestone's

Novels into Film (1957) and Robert Richardson's *Literature and Film* (1969) are stimulating and refreshing attempts to plot a route through a relatively uncharted area. Neither critic, however, turns his eyes even once towards Spain, and students of Spanish literature have to accept at face value Richardson's claim that 'the film has had important repercussions in literature and has even been in some ways a major influence on modern writing.'[6] His contention is particularly true of Spanish literature of the 1920s and 1930s, and certainly neither English nor French literature of the same period reveals the same breadth and depth of response. The Surrealists may have celebrated the cinema as 'la mise en œuvre du hasard',[7] but it was Spanish writers who put that theory into practice with most enthusiasm, imagination, and resourcefulness.

Enthusiasm is no guarantee of quality, and whereas the cinema generated some sensitive, deep, and original literature, it also inspired some frankly feeble and absurd pieces, which demonstrated clearly that to compose a good poem or a good story about the cinema it was necessary to be a good poet or a good story-writer. It would be easy, but gratuitously unfeeling, to compile an anthology—or, to borrow a waggish neologism from a magazine of the 1920s, a *tontología*—of Spanish poems about the cinema that are pretentious, or linguistically gauche, or lushly sentimental, or superficial; Spanish poets were certainly not immune from the coy diction and sentimental archness found in the following tribute penned to Lillian Gish by an American versifier:

> A fairy's gifts were on her cradle shed—
>   This Pierrette of the screen, whose happy wit
>   And dainty store of fancy exquisite,
> Seems fragrant of old gardens, quaintly spread
> With tangled blooms of roses, white and red;
>   As with swift gleams of joy or sadness lit
>   Her winsome, little, wistful gestures flit
> Thru pictures by her grace dream-garlanded.[8]

The choice of the cinema or a star as a theme was no guarantee of instant fame, and the cinema's probing capacity to bring out the worst and the best in writers explains why Alberti's poems of *Yo era un tonto y lo que he visto me ha hecho dos tontos* speak to us more confidently and with deeper feeling after fifty

years than, say, Guillermo de Torre's poems about the cinema
in *Hélices* (1918–22). Why this is so will, I hope, be established
in those chapters—4, 5, and 6—in which I consider the mark
left by the cinema on Spanish poets. In Chapter 7 I examine the
imprint of the cinema on prose fiction. The lack of a chapter
devoted specifically to the theatre may raise a few eyebrows,
but, as I shall stress in Chapter 3, it was the genre most resistant
to the influence of the cinema. I shall therefore consider the
theatre's debt, represented almost exclusively by the plays of
Ramón del Valle-Inclán, in conjunction with the literary
debates and controversies provoked by the cinema. The first
two chapters will be concerned with the conflicting feelings—of
enthusiasm and hostility—aroused by films in the 1920s and
1930s.

Two chapters—5 and 6—will be devoted to three poets:
Rafael Alberti, Luis Cernuda, and Federico García Lorca. Page
references to their works will be embedded in the text and will
be to the following editions:

Alberti, *Poesías completas* (Buenos Aires, 1961)

Luis Cernuda, *La realidad y el deseo*, 3rd ed. (Mexico, 1958)

García Lorca, *Obras completas*, 2 vols., 20th ed. (Madrid,
1977).

I have provided a prose translation of the quotations from
Spanish poems, plays, novels, and stories. I have rendered
directly into English all other Spanish quotations.

I

THE DREAM-HOUSE

Enter the dream-house, brothers and sisters, leaving
Your debts asleep; your history at the door:
This is the home for heroes, and this loving
Darkness a fur you can afford.
                    Cecil Day Lewis, *Overtures to Death*

THERE is an excellent example of Laurie Lee's gift of reliving
an experience and making us share it with him in *As I Walked
Out One Midsummer Morning*; his recollection of watching a
film in the open air in Segovia recaptures the excitement felt by
a guileless audience before an artless film:

After a supper of beans and mutton, served in a cloud of wood-
smoke, I was invited out into the plaza to watch a midnight ciné. Here,
once again, the aqueduct came into use, with a cotton sheet strung
from one of its pillars, on to which a pale beam of light, filtering from
an opposite window, projected an ancient and jittery melodrama.
Half the town, it seemed, had turned out for the show, carrying foot-
stools and little chairs, while children swarmed on the rooftops and
hung in clusters from the trees, their dark heads shining like elder-
berries.
    The film's epic simplicity flickered across the Roman wall, vague
and dim as a legend, but each turn of the plot was followed with gusto,
people jumping up and down in their seats, bombarding the distant
shadows with advice and warning, mixed with occasional shouts of
outrage. The appearance of the villain was met by darts and stones,
the doltish hero by exasperation, while a tide of seething concern was
reserved for the plight of the heroine who spent a vigorously distress-
ful time. During most of the film she hung from ropes in a tower,
subject to the tireless affronts of the villain, but when the hero finally
bestirred himself and disembowelled the villain with a knife, the
audience was satisfied and went to bed.[1]

As we shall see in later chapters, the cardboard characters and
crudely melodramatic plots of many early films also left their

mark on a number of Spanish writers. In its improvised simplicity, the cotton sheet draped across a pillar of the Segovia
aqueduct had one thing in common with the cinema screens
installed in Madrid in the Hotel Ritz and the Palacio de la
Prensa, where the Cineclub Español held some of its sessions:
they derived from one room in Carrera de San Jerónimo 34,
Madrid, where on 15 May 1896 a Mr Promio set up with the
'Cinematógrafo Lumière' the first makeshift cinema in Spain.[2]

The 'ancient and jittery melodrama' reflected on the sheet
and the challengingly innovative films projected on the screens
linked the simple-minded and the sophisticated, the illiterate
and the intellectuals, arousing in them a range of emotional
responses embracing the screams of horror caused by Buñuel's
Un chien andalou, the foot-stamping provoked by *The Jazz
Singer*, and the candid delight aroused in illiterate peasants
whose eyes were opened to the wonder of moving pictures, as
María Teresa León has recalled, by the visits of Las Misiones
Pedagógicas during the Second Republic: 'How they trembled
as they watched the screen! The spectacle of those enraptured
faces as they saw the marvel of the cinema for the first time, so
moved those who could read and write that they could not
speak.'[3]

Although the inability to read the often ludicrous subtitles
was no obstacle to the enjoyment of films, it was left to those
who made their living by the pen to chronicle and evoke that
enjoyment. Rogelio Sinán's insistence in a poem published in
1929—'yo sigo en actitud de cinefante' ('I persist in my
cinephantic attitude')—categorized the lover of films with a
neologism whose gracelessness was surpassed in the same year
by Ernesto Giménez Caballero's definition of himself and
his fellow enthusiasts as 'cineasts, filmophiles, motion-
picturegoers'.[4] Blending the same linguistic resourcefulness
with a lively imagination, Giménez Caballero captured the
magnetic appeal of the cinema in the 1920s with his picturesque
description of it as 'A vampire preying on eyes. A sucker of
brains. A drinker of souls. An abductor of consciences.'[5]

The zest with which Giménez Caballero coined definitions of
the cinema is one example of 'the new emotions' which, according to Ortega y Gasset in *España invertebrada* (1921), were
'aroused by the cinema'.[6] The hypnotic, anaesthetic effect of

films was advocated as a positive ideal in 1923 by Angel Marsá, who maintained in an essay unashamedly entitled 'Elogio sentimental del cine' that films should induce a state of euphoria, which he colourfully called 'a blue chimera': 'The cinema is the supreme refuge, the sweet refuge of all one's leisure hours, the placid refuge favourable to sentimental flights towards a blue chimera.'[7] At the other extreme, Henri Klosz, the young protagonist of Ramón Gómez de la Serna's story 'El hijo surrealista' (1930), found in the cinema not a soporific but a stimulant to aggressive action. 'He was not like the youth of former times,' explained the author. 'He had seen in the cinemas the world's mouth full of light and daring.'[8]

The risk of films inciting people to violence was recognized and averted by the Republican government when it banned the showing of *The Battleship Potemkin* in Seville in 1933 during a period of agricultural unrest in Andalusia.[9] That banning could only strengthen the conviction held by some idealists that films could and should play a role in shaping and revitalizing attitudes to society, morality, and politics. Early film titles such as *The Victory of Conscience* (1917), *Moral Courage* (1917), *The Price of a Good Time* (1918), and *The Bully Who Paid* (1918) reveal a naively direct didactic purpose which was refined into cinematic masterpieces by D. W. Griffith in *The Birth of a Nation* (1914) and Erich von Stroheim in *Greed* (1923–24). In Spain in the 1930s the didactic potential, the moral usefulness of films preoccupied many people, and the cinema enjoyed the ardent support of those who saw it as a power for good and drew the fire of those who—as I shall show in the next chapter—viewed it as a breeder of corruption. The adjectives 'social' and 'educative' were applied often enough to 'cinema' in the 1930s to reveal a constant concern and a deeply-felt ambition, probably inculcated in the minds of some by the example of the Soviet government. Observing Lenin's dictum that 'of all the arts, for us the cinema is the most important', the Soviet government gave generous financial support to the cinema in its campaign to indoctrinate the population.[10]

In 1918 an English critic had maintained that 'The best and cheapest school we know is the motion picture theatre.'[11] This view reverberated in Spanish cinema magazines throughout the

1930s in such articles as 'Cinema documental y educativo' (1931), 'Laboremos por un cinema infantil-educativo' (1933), 'El cine educativo' (1934), 'Películas educativas' (1935), and 'Notas y noticias del cinema educativo' (1936).[12] The question Giménez Caballero posed in 1931—'What is educative cinema?'[13]—was deflected rather than answered by those who declared categorically that the cinema had a 'pedagogical mission', 'a great educative value', without defining that value or specifying the means by which that mission could be accomplished.[14] Gregorio Marañón's belief—expressed in 1929 in answer to the question 'What do you think of the cinema and who are your favourite stars?'—that 'The cinema is nowadays one of the best and most practical modes of instruction'[15]—was shared and voiced with equal vigour and idealistic candour by Benjamín Jarnés in 1933 and by Luis Gómez Mesa in 1936. In advocating the use of 'the art of the film as an instructive entertainment, as an educational delight', Gómez Mesa was as naïvely inspired by the Renaissance ideal—to teach by giving pleasure—as Jarnés, who had maintained three years earlier: 'The cinema should be the instrument of an educative campaign embracing people who are either uneducated or uneducable by other methods that make sterner cultural demands.'[16]

Jarnés's allusion in the same essay to the cinema's 'inescapable social duty' signals a preoccupation with the role of the cinema in society which was to exercise writers of different political colourings in the 1930s. César M. Arconada's essay 'Hacia un cinema proletario' (1933), together with Juan Piqueras's article on '"Kuhle Wampe" y el cine proletario' (1933),[17] gave to that concern with society and the cinema a precise political bias which was only hinted at in such anodyne essay titles as 'Posibilidades sociales del cinema' (1933), 'Apuntes sobre cinema social' (1933), and 'Función social del cinema' (1934).[18] The banning by a Republican government of *The Battleship Potemkin* and Buñuel's *Las Hurdes* made it difficult for films to fulfil a 'social function' if by that phrase their directors meant a challenge to accepted social values and attitudes. Arturo Casinos Guillén showed a more sober grasp of reality when he recognized in 1933 that the 'longing for social regeneration' moving some who wrote for the cinema faced two obstacles: the commercial desire for gain—represented by 'America and its dollars'—and bland apathy—embodied in 'the mass public'.[19]

There was no shortage of films to satisfy the financial aspirations of one group or to anaesthetize the other. Those who sought in the cinema an intellectual and aesthetic experience had to band together in the rarefied atmosphere of the Cineclub Español remote from the commercial cinemas whose repertoire was unashamedly and invariably lowbrow. Of the films mentioned or advertised in the magazine *Cartelera gráfica* during 1929, only a handful still command a place in our memory and in our respect: Abel Gance's *Napoléon* and *La Dame aux camélias*, Emil Jannings's *Variety* and *The Way of All Flesh*, Fritz Lang's *Metropolis*, D. W. Griffiths' *The Battle of the Sexes*. The titles of the other films mentioned in *Cartelera gráfica* during 1929 signpost a fantasy world of love, adventure, and melodrama fabricated mainly in the studios of Metro-Goldwyn Mayer; the MGM films mentioned by that magazine in 1929 include such forgettable productions as *The Actress* (*La actriz*), *Detectives* (*El representante de la ley*), *Divine Woman* (*La mujer divina*), *Rose Marie*, *Student Prince* (*El príncipe estudiante*), and *West Point* (*El cadete de West-Point*).

A complete list of films shown in Spain during the years preceding the Civil War may never be compiled. However, such magazines as *Cartelera gráfica*, *El Cine*, *Cinema*, *Films Selectos*, *La Pantalla*, and *Popular Film* do give a clear idea of the vast range of films shown in the 1,497 cinemas opened in Spain up to 1925,[20] from feebly repetitive knockabout farce to the brilliantly staged and orchestrated comedies of Chaplin and Keaton, from tearful melodramas to such profoundly allegoric observations on modern civilization as Lang's *Metropolis*. Critical responses to films displayed similar extremes in aim and in quality; whereas some writers sought to analyse a film's quality and style, many more hovered on a level of triviality as inane and jejune as studio publicity. Many stars have lent themselves to the myths invented by their studios; the renaming of Theodosia Goodman as Theda Bara—an anagram of Arab Death—was meant to transport her to a plane of fantasy which Dean Martin was to occupy some fifty years later when he married for the third time. Under a report headed 'Dean

Martin marries in cinema style', *The Times* recounted on 27 April 1973 how

Cage loads of doves fluttered among thousands of imported flowers and guests sat on pews lent by Warner Brothers and 20th Century Fox Film studios, when Dean Martin, the actor and singer, was being married in Hollywood style. . . . .

Apart from the doves, guests had to squeeze between 200 dozen white lilacs, 92 dozen white tulips—all flown in from Paris—and thousands of California blooms.

The flamboyance of this wedding ceremony conformed to the grandiose dimensions demanded by the publicity machines of an industry whose obsession with scale and statistics proved so infectious among those who wrote in the early cinema magazines that they offered their readers an inexhaustible supply of useless data; one can only wonder how many people were awe-struck in 1917 by the extraordinary calculation 'that it would require 6,742 thumbnails to cover the area of a standard size screen'.[21]

Those who sought and recorded such information took themselves seriously. The author of the essay 'Estética y ritmo de Johnny Weismuller' was as blind in 1934 to the pretentious absurdity of his title as the person who in 1928 elevated kissing to what he called 'La ciencia del beso'.[22] The 'Antología del beso' presented in the twenty-first session of the Cineclub on 9 May 1931 demonstrated the fascination exercised in Spain by a physical contact that, subject to only minimal restraints on the screen, was still controlled in real life by rigid standards of decorum.[23] Innocuous and infantile as it may seem today, the interest shown by magazines in the way stars kissed on the screen was part of the mental and moral freedom induced and inspired by films. At one extreme of this freedom was the release of deep-seated passionate impulses filmed in *L'Age d'or*, where Buñuel showed a man and a woman 'lasciviously rolling about in the mud' and later that man 'nervously kissing her breasts'.[24] At the other extreme were such earnest but unwittingly ludicrous essays as 'Los besos cinematográficos' (1927 and 1931). 'Besos cinematográficos' (1928), 'Cómo besan los ases de la pantalla. Clases e importancia de los besos' (1930), 'El beso en el cine' (1933), 'El nuevo arte del beso' (1934), and '¿Sabría usted besar para el celuloide?' (1935).[25]

Happily, the responses of Spanish writers and critics to the cinema went far deeper than the foolish question 'Would you know how to kiss for the screen?' As they display a sensitive appreciation of the cinema as an art form, the articles published in *La Gaceta Literaria* particularly follow the line of informed and intelligent interest which can be traced back to the sensible and instructive essays published in children's magazines in 1915 and 1916 on 'Secretos del cine', 'Cine sencillo', and 'Delicias del cine'.[26] As I shall show in Chapter 4, *La Gaceta Literaria* also published many poems devoted to the cinema; in so doing, it followed the example of the magazine *Grecia*, which in 1919 offered Apollinaire's 'Antes del cinema', Guillermo de Torre's 'Friso ultraísta. Film', and Pedro Garfias's 'Cinematógrafo'.[27] And by fostering in writers an interest in the cinema and giving them space in which to express it, *La Gaceta Literaria* observed the precedent set by *España*, where the poet Mauricio Bacarisse published in 1920 and 1921 a number of essays with titles as intriguing as 'Crónica de cinematógrafo. Cervantes y Julio Verne' and 'Kinéscopo. Teddy, o el héroe cómico'.[28]

La Gaceta Literaria was not, of course, the only magazine attentive to the cinema, but what distinguished it from *Hélix* (1929–30), *Gaceta de Arte* (1932–4), and *Octubre* (1933–4) was its role as the organ of the Cineclub Español, which was founded in 1928 by the magazine's director, Ernesto Giménez Caballero. Between 1 October 1928, when he issued his 'Convocatoria a los cineastas. Cineclub Español (C.E.)' (no. 43), and 15 January 1932, when he reported the 'Muerte y resurrección del Cineclub' (no. 121), *La Gaceta Literaria* faithfully chronicled the activities of the Cineclub in a series of essays, film reviews, reports of individual sessions, and accounts of lectures given by Ramón Gómez de la Serna and Pío Baroja in 1929 and by Gregorio Marañón in 1930.[29] Before founding the Cineclub Giménez Caballero had a stroke of inspiration: he invited Luis Buñuel to direct the cinema section of his magazine. A drawing of Buñuel 'Redactor' in number 25 (1 January 1928) commemorates this invitation. In enabling Buñuel to publish from 1927 essays at once informed and provocative, Giménez Caballero enabled the readers of *La Gaceta Literaria* to consider films through the eyes of a man who began his career in the cinema apprenticed to Jean Epstein. Buñuel's quotation of Epstein's canon—'dans le cinéma il n'y a pas de nature morte. Les objets ont des attitudes'—in his review of *La Dame aux camélias* transmitted to Spain a theory that Alberti and Lorca found applicable to poetry.[30] And his description of *Metropolis* as 'A marvellous ode, a new poetry for our eyes' implanted in Spain the determination of some French critics—for example, André Maurois, who wrote in 1927 of 'La Poésie du cinéma'—to provide for film criticism a poetic frame of reference and to see films as a form of visual poetry with its images and rhythms.[31]

Buñuel relayed from France not only provocative opinions but provocative films. In the person of Buñuel Giménez Caballero established a bridge between Madrid and Paris, to which Buñuel had repaired in 1924. The report on 1 February 1928 that 'Luis Buñuel, our dear colleague and director of our cinema section, has just arrived from Paris' only hints at the significance in Giménez Caballero's design of Buñuel's residence in Paris; the importance of his role was made clear seven months later in the announcement, alluding to the founding of the Cineclub, that 'Luis Buñuel, our cinematographic director, will help us—from the front line of Paris—to implement this interesting project'.[32] Buñuel was thus a key factor in aiding Giménez Caballero to realize his ambition that the Cineclub should mark 'definitive moments in the evolution of the Cinema'.[33] Buñuel was able to send to Madrid René Clair's *Entr'acte* and *Le Poème de la Tour Eiffel*, about which he wrote, referring to the noisy reception accorded *The Jazz Singer* in the second session of the Cineclub: 'I am convinced that this programme will satisfy the most demanding member of the Cineclub, and that the heel of every shoe will remain beatifically still'.[34]

Buñuel made no such waggishly bland assurance about *Un chien andalou*, and those who were shocked and stunned by it failed to realize that the shock and horror they felt were precisely what Buñuel intended, as he made clear in his remarks prior to its showing at the Cineclub on 8 December 1929. 'What I want,' he said, 'is that you do not like the film, that you protest. I should be sorry if it pleased you.'[35] In the previous February Giménez Caballero had announced in *La Gaceta*

Literaria that Buñuel and Dalí had finished the screenplay of a film 'unprecedented in the history of the cinema':

Luis Buñuel and Salvador Dalí have already finished their collaboration on the screenplay of a film whose provisional title is 'C'est
dangereux de se pencher au dedans'. We are told that it is an experiment unprecedented in the history of the cinema, as remote from the
run-of-the-mill film as from those so-called oneiric, absolute films
about objects, etc., etc. The film is the result of a series of subcon-
scious states, which can be expressed only through the cinema. It
contains a plot in which people intervene; moreover, it has subtitles
and it will be an example of a talking film. Luis Buñuel has already left
for Paris, where he will immediately begin filming it. The film will be
finished in April, and will have its first showing in the Studio del
Ursulines; from there it will go to the Cineclub of Madrid, and to the
theatre clubs of Berlin, Genoa, Prague, London, New York, etc.,
etc.[36]

There is nothing in Giménez Caballero's announcement that
prepares anyone for the jolts and surprises of a film which Juan
Piqueras described as 'so crudely and so bestially beautiful'. *Un
chien andalou* was shown in the eighth session of the Cineclub
between Epstein's *La Chute de la Maison Usher* and Jean
Renoir's *La Fille de l'eau*, and, as Juan Piqueras reported, its
'barbarous intensity' so animated the audience that *La Fille de
l'eau* came as a tame anticlimax, and the 'commotion and frenzy'
it incited in the spectators led Piqueras to report soberly that
'Then the atmosphere degenerated'.[37]

The turbulent reception given to Renoir's film, bringing with
it the threat of closure of the Cineclub by the Dirección de
Seguridad, was one event which made Giménez Caballero
summarize the history of the Cineclub as 'Three vigorous years
of life'.[38] Its activities, particularly its noisy incidents, attracted
the attention of magazines other than *La Gaceta Literaria*. In
January 1930 one magazine referred to the boisterous reaction
to *Un chien andalou* and *La Fille de l'eau* as 'scandals' when it
reported primly: 'In a salon of the Ritz, and almost behind
closed door to avoid the scandalous incidents like those during
the last session at the Royalty, the Cineclub has held its monthly
meeting, devoted to the Russian cinema.'[39] With his recollection in 1933 that 'The Cineclub fought with everyone and
everything, even with its audience,' one writer—J. G. de

Ubieta—made it clear that the Cineclub was obliged to join battle even with its own supporters, its so-called 'select and cultured membership'.[40] Having founded the Cineclub in the face of the doubts and opposition of established, older writers, Giménez Caballero and his companions had to endure what he called 'the torrent of words, even of insults, which has fallen on our heads as a result of the second session of the Cineclub'.[41]

Despite the hostility it aroused, the Cineclub can be credited with a number of solid achievements: it gave a new stimulus and direction to young Spanish writers; it fostered the mature appreciation of films; and it encouraged the founding of affiliated cinema clubs. In December 1928 *La Gaceta Literaria* reported on the proposed founding of affiliated cinema clubs in Barcelona, Gijón, Oviedo, Santander, Valladolid, Palencia, Segovia, Bilbao, San Sebastián, Vitoria, Valencia, Sevilla, Málaga, and Logroño.[42] The Cineclub also served as the prototype for other cinema clubs, such as Proa Filmófono, Cineclub F.U.E., Cineclub Proletario de los Empleados de Banca y Bolsa, 'Cinestudio 33'.[43]

The question which 'A.R.' posed in *La Gaceta Literaria* in March 1929–'Which European Cineclub attracts to its sessions the foremost literary figures of the country?'[44]—signalled proudly the rapport it achieved between cinema and literature and its success in inspiring in writers an enthusiasm for the cinema. The 'Lista de inscripciones' published in *La Gaceta Literaria* in December 1928 includes the names of Rafael Alberti, Vicente Aleixandre, Rosa Chacel, and José Díaz Fernández.[45] Films were to leave their mark on the work of all of them; Alberti in particular advertised the intimate connection he and others established between films and poetry by reciting during the interval of the sixth session of the Cineclub three of the poems that were to form part of his collection *Yo era un tonto y lo que he visto me ha hecho dos tontos*: 'Cita triste de Charlot', 'Harold Lloyd, estudiante', and 'Buster Keaton busca por el bosque a su novia, que es una verdadera vaca'.[46]

Alberti's poems to the silent cinema comics, together with Lorca's *El paseo de Buster Keaton*, demonstrate the creative impact of the silent comics and complemented the Cineclub's efforts, recorded by Piqueras in August 1929, to accomplish 'the rehabilitation of comic films'.[47] Buñuel had already described comic films in the same magazine as 'The best poems the cinema has composed', and went on to declare provocatively that 'The surrealist equivalent, in the cinema, is to be found solely in those comic films.'[48] It was thanks to *La Gaceta Literaria* and to the Cineclub that such views could be aired and that those who heeded them included some of the most sensitive, fertile, and original writers of the 1920s and 1930s. Were its achievements to be judged solely on the films it showed, the Cineclub would be assured of a place of honour in the cultural history of Spain during the 1920s and 1930s, so unerring was its choice of international films. But the list of those who spoke during the sessions of the Cineclub, while justifying Giménez Caballero's promise in 1928 that the Cineclub 'will almost always be accompanied by lectures', made it clear that the Cineclub married word and image.[49] The enthusiasm for the cinema it radiated and generated proved immune to the attacks and misgivings of enemies, who, as we shall see in the next chapter, saw in the cinema only moral danger, aesthetic poverty, and a threat to literature.

II

THE BALEFUL CINEMA

'Pero es que van tan de prisa . . .' Cierto; no nos dan
ni tiempo para pensar lo que hacen y lo que desha-
cen. ¡Es el cine, el fatídico cine!*

Miguel de Unamuno (1923)

THE promotion by Jean Harlow's studio of over three hundred
Platinum Blonde Clubs before 1932 and the consequent thirty-
five per cent increase in the sale of cosmetic peroxide justify on a
level of glossy superficiality a critic's assertion in 1926 that 'The
motion picture . . . has become . . . the most potent single factor
in modern life.'[1] Reactions to the influence exercised by the
cinema have been extreme since the industry was born: for
some that power was beneficent and healthy, for others it was
noxious and sinister. The cinema has been glorified with infantile candour and assailed by high-minded bigots. It has been
represented both as a medicine and as a disease which the
author of a medical thesis has named as *la filmophagie*.[2] When he
advocated in 1917 'The Therapeutic Value of the Movies', one
American critic – Fred. W. Phillips – prescribed the cinema as a
cure for mental and physical ills in the hyperbolic terms used by
the travelling quack to sell his elixir:

For the price of a dish of ice-cream you may travel to Europe, Africa,
or any other part of the globe. You may, like a modern Aladdin, rub a
silver dime, instead of a lamp, and be transported to any place of your
heart's content; or, if you prefer, you may be entertained for an hour
or two by one of the world's best comedians. And, in being so
entertained, you are taken away from yourself, you forget your illness,
are healed in mind, and physical health usually follows.[3]

The presence in the same magazine—*Motion Picture Classic*
—of cartoons, caricatures, and parodies of movie gossip such

* 'But they go fast . . .' True, they give us no time to think what they are doing and
what they are undoing. It is the cinema, the baleful cinema!

as 'Lillian Buffels' hobby is removing warts from pickles'[4] points to a redeeming feature of the cinema industry in general and of cinema magazines in particular: their ability to take a humorous look at themselves, to recognize their ludicrous features, and to laugh at them. Linking Mack Sennett's frenetic but crude *The Hollywood Kid* (1924) and François Truffaut's zany but polished *La Nuit Américaine* (*Day for Night*) (1973) is the humour which both directors extract from the mechanics of film-making, which provide the films' theme, framework, and *raison d'être*. With imagination and technical brilliance Keaton used the cinema and the cinema-screen in *Sherlock Junior* (1924) as the pretext and as the setting for the dreams he dreams from his projectionist's box. The same light-hearted self-scrutiny is to be found in those American, English, and Spanish magazines that owed their existence and their circulation to the cinema. In stereotyped characters and hackneyed situations cartoonists found an inexhaustible supply of targets, and an innocent sense of fun connects a group of caricatures published in an American magazine in 1928—'Very Wild Western. The Dance Hall'—, the first of 'Scenes we are sick of', published in an English magazine in 1918, and the Spanish cartoon which appeared in 1930 showing a Spanish film director finishing his film entitled *Y la vanguardia le volvió loco*.[5] With an irony devoid of malice one English critic purported in 1918 to explain to her readers 'America as seen on the Films' by ridiculing stock types and cinematic clichés; 'American business men,' she explained, 'are awfully well dressed and clean and polished up. They smoke large cigars and always bite about half of it off. They do nearly all their work by telephone and in drawing rooms, where they are helped by beautiful wives, who hate them.' She went on to point out that 'Revolvers, or 'guns' in America, are not very efficient. They are discharged heaps of times into crowds, but very few people ever get hurt.'[6] The same ironic jibe was made in the same magazine six years later when it was announced with mock solemnity that 'There were 289763 shots fired in Western dramas last year. Six of them hit the mark. What happened to the others is a complete mystery.'[7]

Revolvers, their ubiquitousness, and the futile and indiscriminate firing of them were particularly easy to make fun of, and one American critic ridiculed their ready availability with the bogusly precise calculation that in 1918 'One thousand and seventy-two revolvers have been produced from top-desk or dressing-table drawers. One revolver was taken from the second drawer.'[8]

The assaults on credulity made unwittingly by film-makers were satirized in Spain by the humorist Enrique Jardiel Poncela, who ridiculed the gap between fact and fantasy in a series of norms and canons applicable to Western films. He mocked the invulnerability of cowboy heroes with his rule that 'A shot fired treacherously at the hero never achieves more than blowing a hole through his hat.' And he explained why screen gunfights appear interminable by divulging that 'The six-shooters used by the cowboys have exactly forty-five bullets each.'[9] When Jardiel Poncela went on to specify that 'The appropriate time for kissing is twilight and the best place is the river-bank', he made fun of those situations whose predictability proved equally laughable to many others. In selecting as the subject of his cartoons 'Indispensable elements for the shooting of a film', Castanys chose in 1936 piles of crockery 'For a film of Stan Laurel and Oliver Hardy' and a guitar, cape, and torero hat 'For a national production'.[10]

A year earlier Castanys had taken a wryly critical look at American films in a series of essays unified by a satiric vision which encompassed newsreels, documentaries, film titles, and far-fetched characterizations. His inclusion among 'Unseen heroes' of 'The servant who throws tennis balls onto the centre of King Gustav of Sweden's racket' shows as little respect for status and reputation as the titles he proposed for two documentary films: *Greta Garbo's Beetle* and *Marlene Dietrich and her Wild Boar*.[11] Film titles were also the butt of his mockery in the conversation he imagined between a father and son; to the former's protest that they saw *Burning Hearts* 'just the other day', the son retorts: '– No, daddy, the film we saw the other day was *Inflammable Hearts*.'[12]

Castanys's most pungent remarks were aimed at the demands made on our credulity by characters in American films, which expect us—he charged—to believe in the inherent goodness of certain people in spite of what they do: 'Every American film wants to prove to us that a banker's daughter can go out at night, drink, smoke, marry, divorce, elope with a gangster, and at heart still be a good girl, a feather-brained little thing, but full of good intentions.'[13]

Castanys's jibes, although devoid of sharpness, are symptomatic of the discontent felt by some Spanish writers and critics in the 1920s and 1930s at the failure of many film-makers to create believable situations and characters. Although Antonio Espina aspired in *Pájaro pinto* (1927) to 'Buscar una especie de proyección imaginista sobre la blanca pantalla del libro' ('Seek a kind of projection of images on the book's white screen') and so enrich the technique and texture of his writings, he achieved little; he did no more than to present people entranced by 'La ventana del gran lienzo blanco' ('The window of the great white screen') and to highlight superficial features of films, such as the instantly recognizable distinction between 'Un hombre bonachón y tranquilo' and 'Un hombre terrible' ('A kindly, placid man' and 'A fearsome man'), both of whom belong to the gallery of 'Exemplary types'.[14] His account that a cat climbs onto the shoulder of the first and flees from the second, that a child clings to the former's legs and looks terrified at the latter from a doorway, leads to his mildly reproving and quizzically rhyming conclusion:

> Haremos mal en generalizar.
> Pero hay aquí, evidentemente, una postal popular.*[15]

Critical as Espina and Castanys were of the cinema, the fascination it exercised on them softened the blows they dealt it, which were little more than glancing and half-hearted. In his novel *Cinelandia* (1923) Ramón Gómez de la Serna put the full weight of his wit and inventiveness into his sardonic assault on Hollywood. Using the satirist's classic tools of hyperbole, caricature, and grotesque deformation, he created a world as false, as absurd as the one he parodied. The gossip of cinema magazines was both the source and the target of his observations that Elsa has 'más de mil trajes' ('more than a thousand gowns') and that everyone in Cinelandia wore 'magníficos zapatos de charol' ('magnificent patent-leather shoes').[16] It was equally easy to devise names like Venus de Plata, which is as ridiculous

---

* It would be wrong for us to generalize.
  But in this there is clearly a popular postcard.

as Theda Bara or as Hart Crane's Lottie Honeydew, 'movie queen', moving 'Towards lawyers and Nevada'; and little imagination was needed to make fun of Mary—undoubtedly Mary Pickford—as 'la mujercita vestida de blanco que personifica la inocencia en los jardines llenos de sol en que las hojas son sus lentejuelas' ('the little lady dressed in white who personifies innocence in sun-filled gardens where the leaves are the sequins of her dress').[17] But it was his own antipathy to the film industry's smothering of pain and infirmity in a tissue of legend and propaganda that led him to match—and so to indict—in a series of euphemisms the smooth fabrications of the publicity machines; in Cinelandia the blind are 'desretinados' ('deretinated'), the madhouse was called, incredibly, the Museo de la Expresión (the Museum of Expression), and death was disguised in the bland euphemism 'Se fue sin dejar su dirección' ('He went away without leaving his address').[18] The sharp edge of moral judgement is clearly seen and felt in Gómez de la Serna's remark that the bored actress 'se entrega al opio y a la morfina' ('surrenders to opium and morphine') and in the comment he imputed to Venus/Mary that it is no longer possible to believe in love 'después de ver las fábulas de nuestras películas') ('after seeing the fables contained in our films').[19]

According to Gómez de la Serna, Cinelandia presented even greater perils: its streets 'tenían los nombres de los grandes artistas de cine muertos en el ejercicio de sus funciones' ('bore the names of the great stars who died while discharging their duties'), and films about madmen were cast with 'antiguos actores de cinematógrafo que enloquecieron en medio de las extrañas y violentas aventuras de cine y por causa también del vicio que anda suelto por Cinelandia' ('former cinema actors who went mad amid the strange and violent adventures of the cinema and also because of the vice which is rife in Cinelandia').[20] With such calculatedly critical strokes, Gómez de la Serna expressed the conviction which others voiced in plain, sober statements that the cinema was harmful to people's minds, be they actors, writers, children, or the cinema-going public. In *The Day of the Locust* Nathaniel West referred tartly to the daily diet of violence offered by the cinema to those who emigrated to California:

Every day of their lives they read the newspapers and went to the movies. Both fed them on lynchings, murder, sex crimes, explosions, wrecks, love-nests, fires, miracles, revolutions, war. This daily diet made sophisticates of them. The sun is a joke. Oranges can't titillate their jaded palates.[21]

Gómez de la Serna's achievement in *Cinelandia* was to encompass in a fictional framework a range of accusations, from the charge of 'childishness' levelled by Fernando Vela in 1927 to Unamuno's grumpy belief, expressed in 1923, that 'Literature has no role to play in the cinema.'[22] This conviction had not inhibited Unamuno six years earlier from imagining in *Niebla* that 'La calle era su cinematógrafo y él [Augusto Pérez] sentíase cinematográfico, una sombra, un fantasma' ('The street was a cinema, and he felt himself to be cinematographic, a shadow, a phantom').[23] Unamuno's conviction, also expressed in 1923, that 'a writer, an authentic writer, a poet, whose tool is words, cannot write for the cinema' was shared by Gómez de la Serna, who enlivened and dramatized it in the conversation of two characters:

— ¿Así que usted no cree que una novela maestra mejora con el cine?
— De ningún modo. Queda destruída, anulada, devuelta a la noche de lo inimaginado.*[24]

In imagining that 'Las muestras de las tiendas eran deslumbrantes, efectistas y parecían una falsificación' ('The displays in the shops were dazzling, flamboyant and looked totally counterfeit'), Gómez de la Serna chose as the key to the backcloth of Cinelandia the artificiality which recurred time and time again as the main target of verbal thrusts against the cinema.[25] In describing 'a dream dump' with such detail, Nathaniel West gave *The Day of the Locust* a similar moral dimension as he presented his protagonist, Ted Hackett, watching a ten-ton truck adding another load to 'a gigantic pile of sets, flats, and props':

In the centre of the field was a gigantic pile of sets, flats, and props. While he watched, a ten-ton truck added another load to it. This was

* — So you do not think that a novelistic masterpiece improves with the cinema?
— By no means. It is destroyed, annulled, sent back to the night of the unconceived.

the final dumping-ground . . . a dream dump. And the dump grew continually, for there wasn't a dream afloat somewhere which wouldn't sooner or later turn up on it having first been made photographic by plaster, canvas, lath, and paint.[26]

Jean Cocteau's bitter comment, translated in the Tenerife newspaper *La Tarde* in 1933—'Our streets, our customs, our women have that overpowering odour and that false appearance of the cinema'—reverberated two years later in José Castellón Díaz's austere strictures published in the magazine *Nuestro Tiempo*; after his introductory charge that 'The cinema has achieved nothing more up to the present moment than to tell us false stories, to show us an artificial world which can be of no interest to anyone', he proceeded to mock Mussolini raising his arm 'in a majestically banal gesture', King George placing 'a wreath of poppies on the tomb of the unknown soldier', and concluded:

Always the same, eternally the same. And what lies behind it all? Behind it lie war, hatred, hunger, poverty, revolutions, death. The cinema is oblivious to it all, turns its back on reality and dazzles us with that world which it creates in secret complicities in order to make the masses see what they are already sick and tired of seeing and believing.[27]

Concerned as Castellón Díaz was at the falsifying web spun by the cinema, others were even more fearful of the damage films could do to the minds and morals of children. Writing in 1932 of the 'Influencia del cinema en la imaginación de los niños', Mariana Hoffmann contended gloomily that 'films for public consumption have frequently a disturbing effect on the minds and emotions of children'.[28] Her contention is corroborated by the elements of violence, injury, and punishment studding the story—called simply 'En el cine'—written in 1918 by the twelve-year-old Ricardo Acevedo, who imagined his protagonist literally scarred for life after trying vainly to emulate the antics of silent film comics:

Luisito había ido al cine con su primo Enrique y había visto una película que le llamó la atención. Un hombre, que llamaban *Tontolín*, montado en una bicicleta, atropellaba a todo el que se le ponía delante, costándole a cada uno la consiguiente caída, y aunque la Policía le perseguia no le pudo coger, pues untándose una pomada en la frente desapareció. Despertó Luisito al amanecer del siguiente día y antes de que nadie de su familia lo hiciera; con manteca y pimentón hizo un mejurge que metió en una cajita y cogiendo su triciclo salió a la calle, y como en la que habitaba había una parte muy pendiente, no consiguió más que un trompazo y estropearse la cabeza; pasó un guardia y entre él y un transeúnte le llevaron a su casa, donde, acordándose de la pomada, la sacó para untarse, lo que le valió una azotaina de sus papás.

No volvió más al cine pues le quedó una señal en la cabeza, para que se acordase.*[29]

Events recorded in 1927 apparently justify Miss Hoffmann's graver accusation levelled at the commercial cinema's pernicious influence on children: 'It disturbs their judgment, weakens their appreciation of normality, and through its prompting makes them commit criminal acts.' On 1 March 1927 the *Heraldo de Madrid* reported the escape from her home to Madrid of a fourteen-year-old girl whose only luggage was 'a pile of novels about the cinema and several photographs of famous cinema stars'. To judge from the headline of the story, those novels and photographs did to her mind what novels of chivalry did to Don Quixote's, for the newspaper diagnosed her condition in a phrase at once pompous and stern: 'Was the child Teresa González abducted? To judge from all the clues the child is cinematographically deranged'. Fifty years later an American attorney talked about 'sick, emotionally disturbed people' in remarkably similar terms when he based his defence of a fifteen-year-old youth's shooting of an eighty-two-year-old neighbour by alleging that he had been brainwashed by the violence dominating television films.[30] Pedro de Répide recounted in 1927 a series of audacious robberies perpetrated by the 'Apaches de Teruel', 'a secret terrorist society of children influenced by the cinema'. By asserting that their robberies

---

* Little Luis had gone to the cinema with his cousin Henry and had seen a film which had impressed him. A man, called *Tontolín*, seated on a bicycle, bowled over everyone who got in his way, and although the Police chased him they could not catch him, because he disappeared by rubbing an ointment on his forehead. Little Luis woke up early the following morning before anyone else in his family; with lard and paprika he made an ointment which he put into a little box and collecting his tricycle he emerged into the street, and as there was a steep part to the street where he lived, all he managed to do was to fall and hurt his head; a policeman came along and he and a passer-by carried him to his house, where, remembering the ointment, he took it out of his pocket in order to rub it on his head, all of which merited a beating from his parents.

He went no more to the cinema as a scar remained on his head as a reminder.

were inspired by 'films about thieves', Répide justified his call for the banning of 'certain subjects' when their audience is 'unprepared' to accept them: 'With films that make a direct impression on minds hardly prepared to receive it, the banning of certain subjects would undoubtedly be a great benefit.'[31]

The futility of Répide's dream of censorship was exposed almost fifty years later when an English judge used even sterner language in sentencing a youth who claimed to have been moved to violence by the film *Clockwork Orange*:

Cases like yours [Judge Bailey said to the accused] present, in my view, an unassailable argument in favour of the return as quickly as possible of some form of censorship to prevent this sort of exhibition being released on the screen or stage, which is evil in itself.

If that happens, it will be very salutary in that those salacious creatures who appear to dominate what is called show business today are compelled to earn a more respectable and honourable livelihood instead of inciting young persons to violence at the expense of their victims.[32]

The sad feature of censorship is that it can satisfy the interests only of a minority group that claims the right to decide what the majority should see. In times of war governments justify censorship by citing national security. In times of peace moral and religious standards shift so rapidly in so-called free societies that no satisfactory agreement can ever be reached on the criteria for censorship. The freedom won slowly but inexorably by film-makers to depict explicitly sexual and violent subjects has so modified and numbed moral responses that many of us today find laughable the stern belief expressed by an anonymous writer in 1917 that 'One of the prevalent evils in motion pictures of to-day is the reckless use of the eyebrow pencil', or absurdly pious the scruples felt by Monsignor Thomas F. Little, who said after sixteen years heading the League of Decency: 'I want to die in the Stations of the Cross, not looking at Gina Lollobrigida.'[33]

In a perceptive article on 'La censura cinematográfica' written after the banning in Tenerife in 1935 of Buñuel's *L'Age d'or*, R. Martínez de la Rosa pointed out acutely that 'There has fallen on the cinema the tenacious persecution of the moralists, who think they see it in the synthesis of every vice and the worst academy of manners.' Stressing that the censor 'is a moralist and not a cineast', he concluded sensibly and sombrely that 'The film is banned. And it is worse if it is not banned, because it is transformed into a lifeless mutilated body, devoid of thread or continuity.'[34]

In Spain during the 1920s and 1930s the austere code of morality enforced in the United States by the League of Decency encountered both favour and mockery; they were mentioned approvingly by Ramiro de Maeztu in 1935 when he demanded for the Catholic community the power to impose on films 'the standards of necessary morality and cleanliness'.[35] And they were censured by the left-wing magazine *Octubre* in 1933 as 'the morals of an old bourgeois spinster'. *Octubre*'s sneer was made as a postscript to Eisenstein's 'Código de conducta moral del cinema norteamericano', whose 'fundamental principles' were:

No film will be made that can damage the moral level of the public, whose sympathy must never be engaged by crime, wrongful acts, evil or sin.

The sanctity of human laws must not be mocked. Those who infringe laws must not be made attractive in the eyes of the public.[36]

In the estimation of those who contributed to *Octubre*, the observance of such principles made the 'capitalist' cinema guilty of inducing blindness and insensitivity to human misery, pain, and misfortunes, of submerging the harsh realities of suffering in a treacle of romanticization and cinematic commonplaces. 'Have you seen the war films put out by the bourgeois?' asked 'Inga' in 1933:

Have you seen a film made on the battlefront? In the first example, the soldiers are good lads who slap the thighs of the 'invaded' girls and who, when they return to the attack, converted into 'heroes', still have time to sing in the 'peace' of the trenches. In the second example, wretched, caked in mud, weary, broken, they wander about blinded, caught in the trap of patriotism as victims of human misery and grief.[37]

The indictment explicit in this contrast is that the 'bourgeois' cinema—otherwise branded as the 'capitalist' cinema, or just simply 'Hollywood'—was guilty of dishonesty, distortion, in fact of a form of censorship. As someone sheltering under the initials F.M. had charged in the first issue, the 'capitalist' cinema used cartoon films as a 'sweet opium of the senses' drugging people into indifference to orphaned children, lynched negroes or brutal policemen:

Newsreels: scenes of the world. It is not only the feature films, the mainstay of any programme, that anaesthetize consciences and stupefy the masses. According to these films, if the working man is good, well-behaved, and honest—that is, a traitor to his class, an abject slave, the boss's lackey—he will marry a millionairess after rescuing her from some idiotic bandits, and the pretty typist will become the boss's 'legitimate' wife if she yields graciously to his initial lewdnesses. The Hollywood studios are oblivious to the lynchings of negroes, or the brutal repression of the police, or the immorality of its governments. There are only enchanting princes in their world. If the imagination had an escape route, the capitalist cinema plugged it with cartoon films, a sweet opium of the senses, wonderful fairy-tales. Nor are there any suffering children in the world.

In a tirade bristling with indignation, F.M. went on to denounce the capitalist cinema for not merely drugging the public, but for brainwashing it through biased newsreels to accept as facts the popularity of Hitler and Mussolini and the inevitablity of war:

But it is clearly not enough to stupefy the crowds who day after day fill the darkened temples of the cinema. The mission is also to deceive them, to spirit away surrounding reality, to condition minds for future wars, for imminent tyrannies. Then that mission prostitutes the bright young miracle of the cinema precisely in its most interesting activity; the newsreels; the mirror of the world. . . . And according to them, the world is composed of people who acclaim Hitler, Mussolini, who smile at the bankers of Wall Street. . . .

There are no unemployed, there is no poverty, or hunger, or strikes; there are no repressions, no oppressed peoples, no bankruptcies.[38]

Curiously, when Ramiro de Maeztu—the self-styled 'son of light'[39]—made his attack on the 'immoral' cinema from the opposite extreme of the political spectrum, he had in his sights those American companies assailed by *Octubre*. Those who for different reasons were hostile to American film companies could find ample justification for their antagonism in the volume of American films imported into Spain, which was quintupled in the space of ten years, rising from 2,700,000 feet during 1923 to 12,116,637 feet in 1933; out of the 543 feature films distributed in Spain during 1928, 420 were American and only 8 were Spanish.[40] However, Maeztu's observation that 'eighty-five per cent of American film companies are in the hands of Jews' gave a distastefully anti-semitic bias and bigotedly Catholic direction to his censure. It was with obvious relish that he reminded his audience in the speech he made in Madrid during 'La semana contra el "cine" inmoral' that the spread of what he vaguely termed 'immoral films' was being staunched by 'a campaign directed by the Catholic bishops, which is already beginning to bear fruit'.[41] One distinguished victim of the Spanish bishops' crusade was *L'Age d'or*, which was to have been shown publicly during the Surrealist Exhibition in Tenerife on 16 June 1935, but which was banned by the Civil Governor in response to pressures from the Bishop of Tenerife and the Catholic newspaper *Gaceta de Tenerife*. Buñuel had already shown his ability to arouse strong feelings and passionate opposition; the students who reacted with 'broken chairs' and 'subversive shouts' to the showing of *Un chien andalou* in the University of Madrid in May 1930 set a pattern of boisterous protest which the editors of *Gaceta de Tenerife* were to distort into invective: against the film, against those who wanted to show it, and against the owner of the cinema where it was to be shown.[42]

Upholding those standards of 'moral cleanliness' which Maeztu had advocated in the previous month, *Gaceta de Tenerife* announced the banning of *L'Age d'or* with unctuous glee:

We are gratified by this gubernatorial banning, for the said film is a repulsive accumulation of religious profanations, unfit to be shown before a cultured public.
GACETA DE TENERIFE has done its duty denouncing to its readers and to the authorities the proposed showing, in the Numancia Cinema, of *L'Age d'or*, and demanding its banning as an urgent and energetic measure of moral therapy.[43]

On the same day—15 June—the liberal newspaper *La Tarde* quoted approvingly Giménez Caballero's description of *L'Age d'or* as 'the most exciting film that has so far been made', and picturesquely accused *Gaceta de Tenerife* of misleading its readers with 'lies as big as millstones, lotteries of faith, and false, brittle idols'.[44] A day later Benigno Ramos, proprietor of the Cine Numancia, retorted in a letter published in *Gaceta de Tenerife* and the Republican newspaper *Hoy* that 'This cinema has no political colouring whatsoever. Proof of that is the various lectures which have been given in it, some of them on Catholic subjects.'[45] Ramos's letter and *La Tarde*'s article were attempts to parry with dignity and common sense the salvos of abuse fired by *Gaceta de Tenerife* in its ferocious denunciation of *L'Age d'or* on 14 June:

L'Age d'or

A singularly attractive title is the one that gives us our theme for today. However, in this case the title is equivalent to the 'wolf dressed in sheep's clothing'. *L'Age d'or* is a surrealist film; it was imported by some who call themselves artists, and it is in the hands, in this city of Santa Cruz de Tenerife, of the Ateneo de Santa Cruz and *Gaceta de Arte*. Two institutions whose prestige endorses a film made expressly to induce heresy, to poison souls, to debase them, and to inspire contempt and hatred for the Catholic religion.

L'Age d'or is criminal heresy in the hands of those who have lost all sensitivity and all artistic feeling; it is the exponent of the spiritual impotence of those who have forgotten that they have a conscience. *L'Age d'or* aims to spread degeneration, the most repulsive corruption of our age. And as it could not fit on the cinema screens of the Spanish Peninsula, it comes to Santa Cruz doomed, apparently, to harvest the dross.

The management of the Numancia Cinema has lent itself as the vehicle for this degeneration. What idea does its owner have of Tenerife? And how do the Ateneo de Santa Cruz and *Gaceta de Arte* appraise the people of this city?

Such effrontery and such cynicism are beyond belief, and it is inconceivable that such a monstrous embryo could be displayed on the screen of a cinema situated amid a civilized population.

Mr. Civil Governor, we have before us the invitation which the Ateneo de Santa Cruz and the director of *Gaceta de Arte* distribute surreptitiously amid the population, to attend the (trial!) showing which will take place next Sunday, the 16th, at 11 a.m, in the Numancia Cinema. This monstrous film, about which we shall speak at greater length, has not been censored and did not manage to get shown in the Peninsula. Every conscience repudiates it, however sectarian it may be. Because it damages, Mister Governor, not only the Christian feelings of the people, but love for the family, for our ancestors, for our parents. *L'Age d'or* is the new poison which judaism, masonry, and rabid, revolutionary sectarianism want to use in order to corrupt the people.[46]

In describing *L'Age d'or* as the poison distilled by Jews, masons, and revolutionaries, *Gaceta de Tenerife* assailed the standard targets of right-wing demagogues during the 1930s. No more dignified was the sneer directed from the opposite side of the political arena by the Tenerife newspaper *El Noticiario* at 'the foul slaver of the sacristy owls'.[47] What both newspapers demonstrated in their equally distasteful and mutually cancelling invective was the power of a single film to provoke extreme reactions and heated, at times savage, debates. It is with the debates and disagreements aroused by the cinema as an art and an industry rather than by individual films that the next chapter will be concerned.

III

CINEMA, THEATRE, AND
LITERATURE: THE CONTROVERSIES

La literatura nada tiene que hacer en
el cinematógrafo . . .*
> Miguel de Unamuno (1923)

Y no puede negarse la influencia del
cine en la literatura contemporánea.†
> Benjamín Jarnés (1933)

WITH his bleak prophecy, pronounced in 1923, that 'the cinema will only ruin the minds of those writers who set themselves to pen pantomimes', Unamuno berated the cinema as an infantile frivolity injurious to the intelligence of writers.[1] Gregorio Marañón was no less militant in 1930, when he chose the members of the Cineclub as the audience for his avowals that he did not belong to 'the numerous phalanx of those who adore films and their actors' and that, so far as he was concerned, the cinema could not compete as a source of emotional experiences with either watching plays or reading books.[2] Happily for Spanish literature of the 1920s and 1930s, many writers of different ages and talents disagreed with Marañón as well as with Unamuno, whose hostility to the cinema and whose championing of literature and the theatre identified the most significant and most hard-fought controversies aroused by the cinema in Spanish literary circles during those years.

The development of the talkies and Spain's failure to create a serious film industry provoked other minor skirmishes among those who at least accepted the cinema as a fact of life. A protective and nostalgic love of silent films rather than hostility to the cinema made Francisco Ayala declare in 1929 that 'Talking films are a truculent mystification', led Jardiel Poncela in 1930 to compare talking films to 'railway disasters inside tun-

---

* Literature has no role to play in the cinema . . .
† The influence of the cinema on contemporary literature cannot be denied.

nels', and provoked Agustín Espinosa's censure in 1933 of 'the
trite verbiage of the dialogues'.[3] When Castanys drew in 1936 a
guitar, a cape, and a torero hat as 'indispensable elements' for a
Spanish film, he gave a lighthearted but unequivocally negative
answer to the question one critic had asked in 1930 about
Spanish film-makers: 'Will they ever be able to forget bullfighters and dancers and mould cinematographic stars for their
films?'[4] Less important than the contradictions manifest in the
titles of the essays Mateo Santos wrote in 1934 – '¿Dónde está el
cine español?' and 'Hay que defender el cine español'[5]—is the
author's blindness to the lack of talent, initiative, and imagination which so constricted Spain's film industry that its cinemas
were almost entirely dependent on foreign films. In reporting
'Considerable agitation for a quota system' in Spain, *The 1930
Film Daily Year Book of Motion Pictures* revealed the puny
efforts of Spanish film-makers with its report that 'out of 543
features distributed [in Spain] during 1928, 420 were American, 65 German, 20 English, 20 French, 10 Italian and 8
Spanish.' Santos clearly had cause for concern, and his question
'Where is the Spanish cinema?' was justified by the drop in
exports of Spanish films to the U.S.A. from 40,285 feet in 1927
to 1,100 feet in 1928.[6]

For those who opposed talking films or expressed concern
about the Spanish film industry, the cinema was a reality and
the anxieties they voiced were engendered by their passionate
acceptance of that reality. Neither Francisco Ayala, nor Jardiel
Poncela, nor Espinosa, nor Santos was drawn into those agonizing appraisals of the relationship between films and literature,
or of the superiority of the theatre over the cinema. The relationship between films and literature provoked a many-sided
debate; the theatre and the cinema were matched face to face in
direct combat by their backers, who generated what one critic
called 'a storm which breaks, which recedes, dies down, and
bursts again'.[7] Some of those who took part in the polemic
forced a choice between the theatre or the cinema in essays
entitled as directly as '¿Cinema o teatro?' and '¿Cine o teatro?'[8]
By selecting such titles as 'Teatro y cinema', 'Eternos rivales.
Cinema y teatro', 'El pleito eterno. ¿Cine? ¿Teatro?', 'Cine y
teatro', and 'El teatro ante el cinema',[9] other critics simulated a
reasonableness, a balance, which was more an illusion than a

fact: those who purported to assess the relative merits of cinema or theatre invariably entered the controversy with closed minds. The reasoned discussion promised by a title as unassuming as 'Dialogos de la vida moderna. El teatro y el cine' is in effect a eulogy of the cinema delivered ostensibly by a son who answers his father's reproach of 'excessive devotion to the cinema'. Although Carlos Fortuny casts the father as a 'Writer who claims to belong to the avant-garde', he gives the son—'Intelligent and educated in the modern manner'—the vision and sensitivity to defend the cinema as 'modern, instructive, spectacular, showy'. In his eulogy we see its author's conviction that the cinema belongs to youth and to the future:

It is the only spectacle I can bear to watch, dad. Bullfights seem to me to be an anachronism; boxing is a vulgarity; football, an insipid game. And as for the theatre . . . the wisest thing is to say nothing. When I watch a play I have the feeling that they are rehearsing a film . . . without people. For me the cinema is the only interesting art.[10]

Two years earlier—in 1928—Rafael Marquina had shown how futile were the arguments such as those deployed by Fortuny with his self-evident but sensible reminder that 'the theatre and the cinema are manifestly opposite things.' He was not alone in believing that 'the cinema has committed a serious mistake by resorting to the theatre for its plots.'[11] In 1916 Hugo Munsterberg had declared sternly that 'As long as the photoplays are fed by the literature of the stage, the new art can never come to its own and can never reach its new goal.'[12] One successful dramatist at least was anything but pleased with the filmed version of one of his plays; commenting on the filming of *The Skin Game*, John Galsworthy remarked in 1926: 'I arranged the scenario and we all kept faith with the stage play. Even then it was anything but satisfactory.'[13]

What set Marquina apart from other critics was his cool mind and sober language, which were absent from Lorenzo Conde's description of the influence of the theatre on the cinema as 'pernicious'.[14] In the same year—1934—another critic ranked the cinema over the theatre by describing them as 'a marvellous palace alongside a wretched hut'.[15] And in the same year, a third critic—in an essay unambiguously entitled 'Al cine español le estorban los autores teatrales'—condemned the attempt to nurture the Spanish cinema with plays as 'infusing old blood into a young body'.[16] His obvious relief on recalling that 'we were spared the storm which was forecast of films by Muñoz Seca, Arniches, Benavente, Marquina, etc.' was inspired by his anti-pathy to the habit, entrenched in the film industry in Spain, of adapting Spanish plays to the screen. The debt contracted by the Spanish cinema to the theatre is seen clearly in the filming of the Duque de Rivas's *Don Alvaro, o la fuerza del sino* (1907–10), Zorrilla's *Don Juan Tenorio* (1907–10, and again in 1921), Calderón's *El alcalde de Zalamea* (1914), Benavente's *La mal-querida* (1914), *Los intereses creados* (1918), and *La madona de las rosas* (1920); Echegaray's *El gran galeote* (1924); Moratín's *El médico a palos* (1926); the Alvarez Quinteros' *El agua en el suelo* (1933); and Arniches's *Las estrellas* (1927) and *¡Es mi hombre!* (1935).

Those who opposed the frequent recourse of Spanish film-makers to the Spanish theatre clearly had ample evidence on which to base their antagonism and pronounce their stern judgements. But so hostile were they to the theatre as a provider of cinematic subjects that they never stopped to ask themselves whether the watching of films stimulated Spanish dramatists and enriched their plays. The lack in this book of a chapter devoted to the cinema and the Spanish theatre should suggest immediately that the influence exercised by films on plays did not match either in depth or in extent the impact they made on Spanish poetry and prose fiction during the same period. Nor could they be expected to, for the theatre, a verbal art contained within a physically restricted ambit, was the genre most resist-ant to a flow of wordless images which explored space once it broke the constraints of the camera filming characters on a stage. The theatre, with the camera occupying the place of the audience, gave early films their stiff structure and their fixed perspective. As soon as D. W. Griffith liberated the camera and explored angles, distance, and perspective, films enjoyed a freedom denied to the theatre.

Any imprint left by films on Spanish plays during the 1920s and 1930s must therefore be sought in stage effects, in the emulation of cinematic techniques and angles, in reminiscences of specific films and actors, and in the dress and mannerisms of characters rather than in what they say. At the end of the first act of *Las adelfas* (1928) Manuel and Antonio Machado appealed to the actress playing their heroine Araceli rather than compose for her a precise stage direction:

Tal vez no es posible expresar con el rostro sentimientos tan complejos. Haga, sin embargo, la actriz un esfuerzo en este sentido. Piense que ante la pantalla cinematográfica se vería obligada a esta expresión muda.*[17]

Lorca's *El paseo de Buster Keaton* is composed preponderantly of stage directions. In *La zapatera prodigiosa* he directed that the three suitors spurned by the shoemaker's wife enact what he called 'casi una escena de cine' ('almost a scene from the cinema') when he made them bewail in rapid succession—in a parody of those often unwittingly absurd subtitles—'¡Ay! ¡Ay! ¡Ay!' ('Woe! Woe! Woe!') (II, pp. 284–5). In *Amor de don Perlimplín con Belisa en su jardín* Lorca's direction that 'Las perspectivas están equivocadas deliciosamente' ('The perspectives are delightfully distorted') (II, p. 344) impose on Perlimplín's dining-room the crazy angles which characterize such optically zany Expressionist films as *The Cabinet of Dr. Caligari*. In *El público* he specified that a bed spin on its axis and then directed that the light assume 'un fuerte tinte plateado de pantalla cinematográfica' ('the silvery hue of a cinema screen') (II, p. 521). In 1925 Valle-Inclán had presented in his *esperpento Las galas del difunto* a character who, sporting 'Bastón y bombín, botas con grillos en las suelas' ('A cane and a bowler hat, and boots with crickets in their soles'), modelled himself on the pertly energetic Chaplin, whose habits of scratching his buttocks and twirling his cane he also emulated.[18] Valle-Inclán also commemorated the mime of silent cinema comics in the actions of Don Filiberto, who, when the telephone rings in the seventh scene of *Luces de bohemia* (1924), 'toma la trompetilla y comienza una pantomima de cabeceos, apartes y gritos' ('picks up the ear-piece and begins a pantomime of nods, asides, and shouts').[19] Valle-Inclán's sensible insistence in 1922 that 'The cinema speaks only to our eyes,' that everything in the cinema

---

* Perhaps it is not possible to express such complex feelings with the face. However, the actress must make an effort to do so. She must think that on the cinema screen she would be obliged to adopt this silent expression.

enters 'directly through our eyes', reveals a basic understanding of and ready sympathy for the potently visual impact of silent films, which he tried to define, in a long and thoughtful stage-direction of *Las galas del difunto*:

La palabra se intuye en el gesto; el golpe de los pies, por los ángulos de la zapateta. Es un instante donde todas las cosas se proyectan colmadas de mudez. Se explican plenamente con una angustiosa evidencia visual.*[20]

Valle-Inclán's belief that on the cinema screen all things speak for themselves, possess a visual force and presence, is in total harmony with Jean Epstein's doctrine 'A l'écran, il n'y a pas de nature morte. Les objets ont des attitudes.'[21] Objects, either singly or in groupings, are an essential element of Valle-Inclán's stage-directions. The mouse which pokes its nose out of a hole in the second scene of *Luces de bohemia* is as visually appealing as the lights and faces and shadows he isolated in a series of single shots and then assembled in a sinister sequence in the ninth scene of the same play:

Remotamente, sobre el asfalto sonoro, se acompasa el trote de una patrulla de Caballería. Los focos de un auto. El farol de un sereno. El quicio de una verja. Una sombra clandestina. El rostro de albayalde de otra vieja peripatética. Diferentes sombras.†[22]

Shadows fascinated Valle-Inclán, and out of the play of light and shade he imagined some striking effects which demonstrate the potent impact left on his mind by films' stark contrast of black and white. Moonlight held a particular appeal for him; it provides a static backcloth for a rotating pattern of shadows in *Ligazón (Auto para siluetas)* (1913), where he directed that 'En el claro de luna gira su sombra la rueda del mozo afilador' ('In the moonlight the grinding wheel of the young knife-sharpener

---

* Words have to be sensed from the expression on a character's face; the sound of his footsteps must be apprehended from the angles of the soles of his shoes. It is a moment in which all objects are projected before our eyes saturated with silence. They reveal themselves as they are in all their painful, visual presence.

† In the distance, on the resonant asphalt, can be heard the rhythmic trotting of a Cavalry patrol. The headlights of a car. The lamp of a nightwatchman. The hinge of a door. A furtive shadow. The deathly white face of another wandering old woman. Other shadows.

spun its shadows').[23] And in *Luces de bohemia* it creates a symmetrical contrast of black and white as it hangs 'sobre el alero de las casas, partiendo la calle por medio' ('over the eaves of the houses, splitting the street in half').[24] The reflections of flames constitute other graphically visual effects in *La rosa de papel* (1913), where at the end of the play 'Toda la fragua tiene un reflejo de incendio' (The fire's reflections dance all over the forge') and in *El embrujado (Tragedia de tierra de Salnés)* (1913), where a group of women 'Quedan en el umbral viendo el fuego, con las llamas bailando en los ojos' ('stand in the doorway watching the fire, with the flames dancing in their eyes').[25] At times effects of light and shade are created by characters who as part of the action direct a beam of light: onto a pool of blood in *La hija del capitán* (1922), and onto shelves of books in *Luces de bohemia*, where Valle-Inclán put Zaratustra, and specifically his face, at the centre of a strikingly cinematic composition: 'La mano, calzada con mitón negro, pasea la luz por los estantes de libros. Media cara en reflejo y media en sombra.'*[26]

A gloved hand, a pool of blood, a face divided by light and shadow, shafts of light piercing the darkness: all these belong to the melodramatic apparatus of mystery serials and adventure films, which no doubt suggested to Valle-Inclán the revolvers found in *La rosa de papel* and fired in *El embrujado*.[27] Shots are also fired in *Luces de bohemia*, but what Valle-Inclán showed is not their firing but their infant victim in two scenes that recall the savage firing on the crowd in *The Battleship Potemkin:*

> Una mujer, despechugada y ronca, tiene en los brazos a su niño muerto, la sien traspasada por el agujero de una bala.
> Llega un tableteo de fusilada. El grupo se mueve en confusa y medrosa alerta. Descuella el grito ronco de la mujer, que al ruido de las descargas aprieta a su niño muerto en los brazos.†[28]

With such scenes and stage-effects Valle-Inclán aimed to take his spectators' minds beyond the theatre and lead them towards

---

* His hand, enclosed in a black mitten, sends the beam along the shelves of books. Half of his face reflected in the light and half in shadow.

† A woman, hoarse, her bosom bare, holds her dead child in her arms, his temple pierced by a bullet.

A volley of rifle shots can be heard. The group moves off in confusion and frightened expectation. Over all the noise can be heard the hoarse shout of the woman, who at the sound of the fusilade clutches her dead child in her arms.

the cinema, which is honoured as a vital force and a fertile inspiration for a dramatist. He thus enriched his own dramatic craftsmanship both visually and technically by his eager recognition of and receptivity to the cinema as 'A new Art. The new plastic art. Living beauty.'[29] Proud of his own enterprise and ingenuity, he felt confident enough to explain why 'the most ingenious work of Jacinto Benavente proves to be a failure when transposed to the cinema': for the simple reason that Benavente put things in the wrong order, placing the play before the film instead of the film before the play. As Valle-Inclán contended, 'To make films based on 'famous' plots, that is, plots of high literary merit, is equivalent—if I may use the simile—to adapting materials to the design of a building.' And, confirming the importance he attributed to objects and their visual power, he sharply indicted as 'a folly, a waste, and furthermore, an absurdity, to base a film precisely on a literary, an acoustic foundation . . .'[30]

Valle-Inclán's trenchant strictures give a special piquancy to the attack on the cinema and the defence of the theatre which Benavente put into the mouth of one of his characters in his play *Literatura*, which he staged in 1931:

Pero tampoco estoy por el cine. Y si la película es como la del otro día, mejor es que oigáis la novela por atrevida que sea . . . ¡Qué película! . . . No sé de qué pueden asustarse luego en el teatro . . .*[31]

What makes Esperanza's words an exposé of cynical double standards is the fact, surely known to some of his audience, that several of his plays had already been made into films and that he had written *La madona de las rosas* 'expressly for the cinema', as he admitted to a magazine in 1924.[32] The dramatist who thus had one of his characters pronounce disdainful remarks about films was the screenwriter who blandly acknowledged in 1924 that writing for the cinema was a game and a business:

The cinema, like the theatre, like everything else, is something of a game, at least for me. I do not hate the cinema, nor do I love it; I write for it to amuse myself, I almost venture to say as a business.[33]

* But I am not in favour of the cinema either. And if the film is like the one I saw the other day, you would do better to listen to the novel, however daring the novel may be . . . What a film! . . . I cannot imagine what the theatre has to be afraid of . . .

As a game and as a business the cinema proved irresistible to Gregorio Martínez Sierra, who was drawn—like Blasco Ibáñez, Jardiel Poncela, and Claudio de la Torre—to the lure and financial promise of Hollywood. According to a newspaper headline which appeared in 1933, 'Claudio de la Torre declares that the cinema is the best literary invention', yet in Hollywood he and Jardiel Poncela did no more than adapt the works of other writers.[34] Martínez Sierra and Blasco Ibáñez, however, adapted their own works and wrote expressly for the screen, and their activities were recounted proudly by Spanish magazines deeply impressed by their presence in Hollywood. The caption under a photograph which was published in *Arte y cinematografia* in 1924—'The distinguished novelist Vicente Blasco Ibáñez on his visit to Paramount Studios accompanied by the great actor Thomas Meighan'—contains a tone of nationalistic adulation which reverberates in the 'Champagne in honour of Martínez Sierra' given by Fox Films and reported by *Popular Film* in 1934.[35] When they talked about writing for the screen, both writers evinced a candour that was tinged with caution in Martínez Sierra and spiced with breeziness in Blasco Ibáñez; the latter's avowal in 1924 that 'no one has yet managed to become a world-famous novelist of the cinema' did not inhibit him from penning 'unpublished novels directly for the cinema'.[36] The bronze statuette of four horsemen proudly owned by Blasco Ibáñez in his Villa Fontana Rosa, near Menton,[37] suggests his awareness that his contribution to the cinema will be remembered not for such films as *Mademoiselle Midnight* and *El paraíso de las mujeres*, but for the novels he lent to and adapted for the screen, which provided ideal vehicles for Valentino's talents: *The Four Horsemen of the Apocalypse* (1921), and *Blood and Sand* (1922).

By adapting several other of his novels for the screen—for example, *Los enemigos de la mujer*, *Mare Nostrum*, and *La bodega*—Blasco Ibáñez established a precedent of circumspect self-exploitation, which Martínez Sierra eagerly followed. His recognition that 'the ideal thing is to write directly for the screen' was qualified by his honest but timorous caveat: 'but this is dangerous ... because the writer has to create.' He divulged his reluctance to create original screenplays in 1935 when he listed his achievements as 'A few plays of mine adapted for the screen—*Mamá, Primavera en otoño, La viuda romántica, Yo, tú y ella*—and a story written expressly for the screen—*La ciudad de cartón* ...'[38]

Martínez Sierra and Blasco Ibáñez were clearly indifferent to Unamuno's strictures on writing for the cinema, which had no more deterrent effect on them than on other established writers of their generation, who accepted the cinema as a reality and as a challenge. In 1927 *La Pantalla* serialized Wenceslao Fernández Florez's story 'Una aventura de cine', and in the following year Alberto Insúa's 'Los vencedores de la muerte. Película novelesca', which had reached the screen in 1927.[39] By posing in 1927 the question 'What is your opinion of the cinema?', the same magazine enabled a number of writers to publicize their views. Although breathtakingly naïve, the opinions expressed by Azorín did at least reveal a mind open to sophisticated progress beyond 'the age of story-telling' in which 'Men and things will form a world of associations and disassociations which at present the theatre and the novel only rarely approach.'[40] Armando Palacio Valdés's answer to the same question was more informed and positive, as one would expect from a writer who had permitted the filming in 1927 of his best-known novel, *La hermana San Sulpicio*.[41] Although upbraiding the cinema in terms beloved by self-righteous opponents as a 'school of thieves and assassins, an academy of wantonness', Palacio Valdés extolled it as 'a marvellous invention'—with a precise, limited function: to assist, complement, and illustrate the reading of a novel:

Cinematography is a marvellous invention which has still not achieved total effectiveness. I rate it as a powerful aid to literature, particularly to the novel. For if it is true that those readers endowed with imagination can picture scenes and passages accurately and graphically, those who lack imagination find in the cinema an adequate stimulus for enjoying the pages penned by the novelist.[42]

There is a myopic condescension in Palacio Valdés's belief that a reader devoid of imagination needs to see the filmed version of a novel in order to understand and enjoy that novel. Unlike Palacio Valdés, Pío Baroja was studiously nonchalant and inconsistent about the cinema, and the filming of his novel *Zalacaín el aventurero* in 1929 turned against himself his recipe in 1927 for 'an interesting film' as 'Some good actors and some good technicians, with any subject whatsoever'.[43] His delight at seeing on the screen 'the figures which one has imagined somehow or other, made flesh' inspired his wish in 1931: 'I wish that I could write screenplays!'[44]

The doubts and hesitations of Baroja and Palacio Valdés in no way obscure an important fact: that their acceptance of the cinema and their readiness to let their novels be adapted for the screen involved them, unwittingly or not, in the debates and disputes surrounding the cinema. As the first two chapters demonstrated, those debates swung between extremes: between the condemnatory conviction that literature paralysed and poisoned the cinema, and the passionate advocacy of certain literary works as either ideal subjects for films or 'cinematic' in conception. Attacks on what one critic called 'the gloomy literary tradition' were particularly strong in Spain during the 1930s.[45] Pérez Bellver's view, expressed in 1935, that 'the cinema gives the impression of poverty every time it has to take a plot from a literary work' reveals a composure absent from G. Gómez de la Mata's vigorous claim that 'the cinema has suffered a fateful invasion of that melodramatic pseudo-literature of cheap, street-corner magazines which authentic writers abominate.'[46] Neither critic would have taken very long to answer the question posed by an English critic in 1918: 'Should Novels be Filmed?'[47] Spaniards were certainly not the only ones to question the wisdom of filming novels; in 1928 the English critic E. W. White declared vigorously that 'For too long literature poisoned the cinema by making her the most tempting of offers of plots and titles.'[48] And in 1923 the French critic André Obey resorted to picturesquely damning metaphors by upbraiding 'la mauvaise herbe littéraire' and 'de lourds emplâtres littéraires', which allowed him to contend sternly that 'Le cinéma ne doit jamais être l'illustration animée d'une histoire écrite.'[49]

The opposite view was advocated with equal vigour by a number of Spanish critics, such as María Luisa Clement, who, rejecting the contention expressed in 1932 that 'there are few, very few novels that are adaptable to the screen', insisted that 'our literature offers a vast field of choice to those who adapt works for the cinema.'[50] Some critics went further than Clement's selection of Pérez Galdós's novel *Gloria* and José María de Pereda's novel *La Montálvez*, devising in one case a 'Retórica cinematográfica', positing in another a connexion between 'Goethe y el cinematógrafo', and in a third postulating Ariosto's *Orlando furioso* as a 'cinematographic poem' and its author as a 'peerless creator of images which succeed one another with a bold cinematographic rhythm'.[51] The critic who saw Douglas Fairbanks as an ideal Count Orlando and Wallace Beery as a good Rodomonte displayed an imagination enlivened by the cinema and stimulated by films to look afresh at literature. However, his feeble observation that 'Many are the episodes that offer all the characteristic elements of popular films, in which everything ends happily' reveals a naïve critical vision narrowed rather than broadened by films.

Happily, Spain did produce in the 1920s and 1930s writers with cooler heads, more sense, and greater detachment, who recognized that between literature and the cinema there had to be a mutually enriching two-way traffic. In choosing for his essay a title as measured as 'Literatura en el cinema y cinema en la literatura', Rafael Gil displayed a critical balance which led him to state, accurately, in 1936 that 'if up to now literature has exercised a decisive influence on the cinema, for several years the cinema has begun to influence literature.'[52] The same common sense inspired the rhetorical questions Benjamín Jarnés posed in 1933: 'What good film could not be recounted in the minutest detail? What good novel could not be made into a film?'[53] As we shall see in Chapter 7, Jarnés's own novels corroborate his claim in the same essay that 'the influence of the cinema on contemporary literature cannot be denied.' Guillermo de Torre had contended more excitedly in 1923 that 'The Cinema projects its angular beams of light and its dynamic, accelerating rhythm onto our vanguard literature.'[54] It is with that influence and those 'beams of light' that I shall be concerned in the rest of this book.

IV

SPANISH POETS

Les poètes modernes . . . veulent être les premiers
à fournir un lyrisme tout neuf à ces nouveaux
moyens d'expression qui ajoutent à l'art le mouve-
ment et qui sont le phonographe et le cinéma.
Apollinaire, 'Conférence sur l'esprit
nouveau' (1917)

ESSAY titles such as André Maurois' 'La Poésie du cinéma',
which appeared in 1927, and César M. Arconada's 'La poesía en
el cinema', which was published in 1935, reveal the desire
shared by French and Spanish critics in the 1920s and 1930s to
see films as visual poetry and to interpret them in poetic terms.[1]
In order to corroborate his claim that 'Il en est de la poésie du
cinéma comme de toute poésie', Maurois resorted to the musical
terms beloved by other French critics. His dream of 'créer . . .
comme une sorte de contrepoint d'images' was couched
in the same metaphorical language as that used by Emile
Vuillermoz, who claimed that 'Le cinéma est bien une musique
d'images.'[2]

The words *imagen, música, poesía*, and *ritmo* recurred with
equal persistence—and naïve imprecision—in essays devoted
by Spanish writers to the cinema during the same period. In
1932 J. Palau declared in an essay entitled 'Precisiones sobre el
ritmo' that 'rhythm in the cinema . . . tries to hypnotize the
spectator and to put him, thereby, in a passive state.'[3] In the
same vein, Cipriano Rivas-Cheriff spoke of films' 'persistent
inner harmony'.[4] The translation into Spanish of the enthusiastic—and idealistic—theories of Jean Cocteau and Jean Epstein
provided authoritative support for opinions defended by Spanish film-critics. Cocteau's simple equation—'Poetry of today:
the cinema'—summarized succinctly Fernando Vela's belief,
recorded in 1925, that 'The very physical apparatus of the
cinema . . . contains an elemental capacity to poeticize.'[5] And

Rafael Marquina's praise of 'the capacity images possess of psychological and poetic revelation' echoed Epstein's faith, translated in *La Gaceta Literaria* in 1928, that 'The cinema is made to narrate with images and not with words.'[6]

When Arconada stated, somewhat challengingly, in 1935 that 'If the cinema had no connexion with poetry it would not be an art', he was voicing what had come to be a critical common-place, which, although persistently connecting poetry and film, said nothing about either. He was also repeating himself; by 1935 he had clearly made no progress towards answering the questions he posed in his comments on *L'Etoile de mer*, shown in the first session of the Cineclub on 23 December 1928: 'Poetry of the cinema or poetic transformation? . . . Poetry in a book is the same as poetry in the cinema?'[7] To describe *L'Etoile de mer* as poetry, however impressive it may have seemed in a contemporary magazine, was a pretentious critical pose which others emulated; in describing the end of Chaplin's *The Circus* (1928) as an example of 'an expressive poetry full of efficacy', Marquina likewise failed to squeeze much meaning out of what had become a critical cliché.[8]

Those who saw or pretended to see poetry in films had their counterparts in those who sought the imprint of films on poetry, some of whom saw no deeper a connexion between them than that between images on the screen and images on a page. The common denominator provided by images is so self-evident that it is difficult half a century later to fathom Marquina's 'profound aesthetic emotion' on realizing in 1929 'the substantial parallel which . . . exists between the new poetry and the seventh art'.[9] If we cut our way through Guillermo de Torre's dense and florid language, we find that he had the same simple point to make, although he did make it much earlier. His essay in 1921 on 'El cinema y la novísima literatura: sus co-nexiones' vigorously postulated a similarity between American films and what he called the 'new-shaped poem':

There is an incontrovertible similarity between some American films which set out to fragment and superimpose their spatial images on their rapid projection, and the new-shaped poem which through the multiplicity of its images—the only connecting link in the theme—produces a feeling of simultaneity in the fusion and animation of spatial and temporal planes.[10]

Torre did not fulfil the promise of this provocative critical approach when he returned to the topic in 1926; instead of amplifying and enriching his original idea with deeper insights and precise illustrations, he contented himself with a weary restatement of his views and an apologetic reluctance to go into details:

It would be a long task to indicate the series of influences which the cinema is at present exercising on young minds.

I shall content myself with pointing out that that fever of image-making which is consuming the young poets, their striving to invent, to transpose, to transcend the constricting reality of the known world in order to create another universe at once more fresh and fragrant, will be free to express themselves only in the ambit of the cinema. Lyricism and photography.... The virginal cinema screen must seem to the genuine poets of our day like an enticing blackboard, on whose surface they may develop the boldest equations of their imagination.[11]

The vigour, assurance, and lexical richness of Torre's declarations are in direct contrast with the flimsiness of their content; he says nothing about what types of film induced that 'fever of images', who were the 'genuine poets of our time', what their 'most audacious equations of their imagination' represent, or how those unnamed poets translated visual stimuli into words. Torre's confident rhetoric lacked the simple focus of Juan Piqueras, who in 1929 directed his readers' gaze towards Alberti and Lorca with his unambitious comment that 'This comic facet of the cinema has recently aroused great interest in the public and, above all, in young writers.'[12] And an anonymous critic did at least look at the disposition of words on a page when he observed in 1927 that the *creacionista* poet was the one who wrote 'the most cinematographic poetry'; alluding to the disconnected images and disjointed rhythms pursued as ends in themselves by Gerardo Diego in *Imagen* (1921) and *Manual de espumas* (1923), that critic suggested perceptively that 'His lines of poetry operate on great planes in the same way that films do. To prove it take a poem, number its lines consecutively, and you will have transformed it into a screenplay.'[13] Thought-provoking as these points are, they were rare in Spanish criticism of the 1920s and 1930s. No Spanish critic was adventurous enough to follow the example of Jean Epstein, who in 1921 in his book *La Poésie d'aujourd'hui* considered 'Le Cinéma et les lettres modernes' and formulated a series of criteria for assessing the effects of films on literature. His criteria are perceptive and resourceful, and it would be easy to find in the poems of Vicente Aleixandre passages that illustrate Epstein's 'esthétique de proximité', by which 'Un déplacement de plans désole mon équilibre', as well as his 'esthétique momentanée', determined by the presence 'd'instables métamorphoses'.[14] Many passages from Lorca's *Poeta en Nueva York* could be seen as examples of Epstein's 'esthétique de succession', defined by his succinct formula 'Cinéma et lettres, tout bouge'; and the poems Alberti wrote in homage to the silent comics could serve to illustrate the 'esthétique de rapidité mentale', which Epstein exemplified by recalling that 'A la suite de quelques Douglas Fairbanks, j'ai eu des courbatures, mais point d'ennui'.[15]

We could apply to any number of Spanish poems the rest of Epstein's criteria: the 'esthétique de suggestion', the 'esthétique de sensualité', and the 'esthétique de métaphores'; but in doing so we could offer no guarantee and adduce no proof that films had been the operative influence on them. Systematic and pioneering as his terms may be, they are invalidated by their rigidity, for they concentrate exclusively on literature without considering the diversity of films or actors which could have inspired writers. And in codifying the technical repercussions of a writer's interest in the cinema, Epstein neglected his purpose, his talent, the strength of his passion, and the quality of his writings. The weakness of Epstein's criteria is that they neither pay sufficient attention to the diversity of films as sources nor do they enable us to discriminate between major and minor writers; we could thus conceivably identify the same principles in, say, Lorca's *El paseo de Buster Keaton*, a profound work written by a gifted poet on a major comic, and Carlos Vinafán's 'A Lulú Alvarez', a pedestrian poem written by an obscure versifier to a forgotten actress who did not live up to the faith he placed in her in his pious prayer:

> Gitana, gitanilla,
> que ayer en Hollywood y hoy en Sevilla
> has conquistado un puesto en la pandilla
> que a la gente divierte y maravilla.

¡Dios te guarde y te ampare y te bendiga,
ya que eres de su amor preciosa hechura
que en un arte sin límites madura
como el grano en las hojas de la espiga!*[16]

The response of Spanish poets, major and minor, to the films they saw was as varied—in matter, manner, and quality—as their tastes and talents, and as distinct as the films that caught their imagination. Those who starred in them left their mark on many Spanish poets, who advertised the inspiration and the theme of their poems with titles that are tributes to figures now forgotten or still justly famous; to pass within Alberti's *Yo era un tonto* from 'Cita triste de Charlot' to 'Charles Bower [*sic*], inventor' is to stray from memories of the familiar images and facile sentiments of *The Gold Rush* to a state of visual blankness and emotional neutrality; no reassuring mental pictures are induced by cryptic allusions, put in the mouth of a little-known comic, to films few people have seen since the 1920s. Our critical and emotional response to these two poems is therefore uneven; although Alberti's imagination was clearly engaged by the films of Bowers he saw, as we shall see in the next chapter, his tribute to him is inevitably a private experience which shuts out the reader, who cannot establish his own bridge between the poem and the films. In the same way, a versifier like Leandro Rivera Pons, in paying poetic homage to Mary Pickford and Mimí Jordán, selected two names, one of which elicits some response in many people and the other of which elicits none in many more.

The mention in the same paragraph of Rafael Alberti and Leandro Rivera Pons demonstrates that poets of all talents and statures were inspired by the cinema, and it is left to us as readers and critics to separate Alberti's sensitive and imaginative entry into the mind of Chaplin from Rivera Pons's saccharine praise of Mimí Jordán:

> Tú sola ... Azul ambiente,
> Las aguas, al pasar,

---

* Gypsy, little gypsy, who conquered yesterday in Hollywood and today in Seville a place among the group who fill people with delight and wonder. May God keep you and protect you and bless you, since you are a precious creature of His love ripening in an art that knows no limits like a seed in the ears of grain!

miraban dulcemente
tus ojos como el mar.*[17]

The gushing banality of Rivera Pons's diction exposes the superficiality of his response to a forgotten star; it is doubtful whether he knew, or cared about, who directed her films. The depth of other poets' sensitivity to the cinema can sometimes be gauged not merely by their responses to a star, but by their recognition of a director's distinctiveness and by his awareness of his purpose, personality, and style. Certain directors made a profound impression on Alberti and Lorca, but their tributes, filtered through their creative works, were less direct than the essays of critics who could champion their favourites in essays as unequivocal and enthusiastic as 'Fritz Lang, el poeta moderno de la cinematografía' and 'El genio de Eisenstein'.[18] Guillermo de Torre singled out Epstein when he quoted as the epigraph to the eighth section of *Hélices* (1918–22) the words: 'Photogénie, photogénie pure, mobilité scandée ...' Lorca followed his example in 1926, in his lecture on 'La imagen poética de Don Luis de Góngora', where he paid Epstein the compliment of ranking him with Góngora as an authority on images, and invited us at the same time to seek the relevance to his own poetry of Epstein's definition of the metaphor as 'a theorem in which one jumps directly from the hypothesis to the conclusion' (I, p. 1038). A poem of *Sobre los ángeles* shows that Alberti's attention and imagination were caught by a gripping sequence from *La Chute de la Maison Usher* (1925) in which Epstein implemented his belief that 'A l'écran il n'y a pas de nature morte. Les objets ont des attitudes. Les arbres gesticulent. Les mouvements signifient.'[19] Epstein illustrated Usher's anguish and grief for his dead wife by paying as much attention to billowing curtains and the log fire as to Usher, and it is the eventual contact of fire and curtains, together with doors flying open, that Alberti remembered in a section of 'El alma en pena'. In this passage he illustrated his awareness of his tormented soul and the presence of death by placing himself, as Epstein had situated Usher, in a context of frightening events and of a nature so tempestuous that it blows curtains horizontally against a fire:

* You alone ... Azure atmosphere. As they flowed past the waters looked sweetly at your eyes, blue as the sea.

Cerrojos, llaves, puertas
saltan a deshora
y cortinas heladas en la noche se alargan,
se estiran,
se incendian.*   [p. 274]

As I shall show more fully in Chapter 5, Alberti's emotions were
deeply engaged by the films he saw: in his memoirs he recalled
as the most striking feature of *Un chien andalou* and *L'Age d'or*
Buñuel's 'malaise' and 'violent protest', the same feelings Lorca
shared and explored when he wrote in New York his screenplay
Viaje a la luna.[20] The scenes of sadistic sexuality and vertiginous
motion which Lorca imagined make it clear that he was inspired
as much by the manner as by the matter of Buñuel's films, as
much by the 'rythme, *entre* les images' as—to continue Abel
Gance's apt phrase—'l'idée, derrière l'image'.[21]

It was the most sensitive Spanish poets who perceived the
idea behind the image, who responded to the attitudes and
beliefs that selected and disposed images on the screen, in
which they saw confirmation of their own attitudes towards, for
example, sex, religion, and authority. At one extreme of
authority are the despotic officers and murderous soldiers of
The Battleship Potemkin; at the other are the buffoonish policemen of American comic films. Both extremes converge in
Alberti's works, which offer us—in 'Harold Lloyd, estudiante'
—his obliquely reproving comment that the Police 'ignora el
suicidio de los triángulos isósceles' ('ignore the suicide of isosceles triangles') (p. 321) and—in a newspaper article—his
strident endorsement of *The Battleship Potemkin* as 'the exaltation of just violence and necessary vengeance'.[22] The scenes of
Viaje a la luna in which 'an invisible hand pulls off the covers' of
a bed or in which a harlequin boy bites a nude woman 'on the
neck and violently pulls her hair' suggests that Lorca shared
Buñuel's desire to transpose to the screen those deep, disturbing urges which led one man in *Un chien andalou* to caress a
woman's breasts and another in *L'Age d'or* to throw a live
archbishop through an upstairs window.[23]

Buñuel and many other gifted directors proved that anything

---

* Locks, keys, and doors leap suddenly and curtains which were frozen in the night
grow long, stretch out, burst into flames, move on and on.

is possible on the screen on which fantasies are authenticated by being played out before our eyes, on which reality and fantasy constantly overlap. When Keaton, in *Steamboat Bill Junior*, tries to escape during the hurricane by running at the backdrop on which a river is painted, he reminds us, as one critic has neatly put it, 'that we are indulging in a mere illusion, even though this illusion, by its very nature, has a closer connection to *felt* reality than most of our actual experiences'.[24] Fernando Vela had made the same point in 1925 when he stated, alluding to Don Quixote, that 'The cinema seat is our wooden wonder horse' and that in the cinema 'The marvellous is inserted inside reality itself.'[25] Films, particularly those of the most imaginative directors, invited poets to accept a series of illusions and fantasies defined with magisterial simplicity by William Carlos Williams in *The Desert Music*:

> Only the imagination
> is real! They have imagined it,
> therefore it is so.[26]

Films conditioned poets to expect the unexpected, to accept as normal the supernatural or the impossible, to witness the tempo of life capriciously changed, and to observe things or people in unusual contexts or couplings. The sight gags of comic films, whose laws ordained that in crashes and explosions no one got hurt, inspired the verbal pranks of Alberti's *Yo era un tonto*. Films could and did represent characters' dreams: those of Keaton in *Sherlock Junior*, of the imprisoned son in Pudovkin's *Mother*, of Chaplin in *The Gold Rush*. Images could be superimposed one on the other, as in *Mother*, where the blending of buildings, façades, steps, chimneys, and columns create a composite impression of the cold power of Tsarist Russia. The accelerated carriage in *Nosferatu* or the hearse shooting up a hill in *Entr'acte* subvert normal rhythms and challenge our minds as disconcertingly as two men's slow-motion leap into focus from either side of the camera in *Entr'acte*, which aroused in Francisco Ayala 'a soft, sad sensation like falling snow'.[27] When the camera swept along the floor in *La Chute de la Maison Usher*, or was fixed to the saddle of a horse in Gance's *Napoléon*, it was made to adopt two of those improbable angles and vantage-points which were matched by the strange perspectives imagined by Spanish poets, as when Lorca directed in *El paseo de Buster Keaton* that 'El paisaje se achica entre las ruedas de la máquina' ('The countryside shrinks between the wheels of his bicycle') (II, p. 234).

Film-makers strained probability even further when they placed people or animals or objects in bizarre places or absurd situations. Lorca's vision in New York of 'golondrinas con muletas' ('larks on crutches') or of 'el hombre vestido de blanco' ('the man clad in white')—Pope Pius XI—spitting 'carbón machacado' ('crushed coal') (I, pp. 482, 525–6) are as visually outlandish as the corpse lying on a ceiling in *L'Age d'or*, as a camel between the shafts of a hearse in *Entr'acte*, as a ballerina wearing a false beard, moustache, pince-nez in the same film, as Chaplin drilling holes in cheese in *Modern Times*. This cultivation of the incongruous was an essential feature of the liberation of fantasy achieved on the screen by film-makers, who in turn stimulated the imagination of Spanish poets.

There is of course nothing unique, or peculiarly Spanish, about the responsiveness to visual stimuli displayed by Spanish poets during the 1920s and 1930s. The sinners with whom Quevedo peopled his *Sueños* are as numerous and the punishments he devised for them as nauseatingly picturesque as those painted by Hieronymous Bosch, whose canvases he mentioned in *El alguacil endemoniado*.[28] John Keats was particularly fascinated by the visual arts, and his poetry is rich in references to sculptures and painters.[29] What was new in the 1920s and 1930s was that poets had the chance to view images that moved as well as to contemplate paintings that were static, as Alberti did in the early 1920s in his frequent visits to the Prado. In responding to a painting or to a film, the poet had to translate a visual stimulus into words; to use the excellent phrase of Sir Ernest Gombrich, his creation of a poem depended on his ability to 'code the message' he received.[30] That 'coding' will be the most original and sensitive in those poets already endowed with a strongly visual imagination, like Alberti and Lorca. It is in the way poets coded the fluid message of films that we can best gauge the intensity and consistency of their reactions to the cinema.

In the 1920s only the most ascetic—or acerbic—Spanish poets ignored the cinema, which inspired many poems devoted to its novelty, the speed of its images, and the charms of its

stars. With his dictum, expressed in 1962, that 'He who wishes
to be no longer who he is, he who wishes to obtain a soul on loan,
let him take refuge in the cinema',[31] Manuel Altolaguirre
explained his refusal to let the fantasy world of films deflect him
from his intense and constant scrutiny of his inner self. His
reluctance in his poetry to acknowledge the cinema's existence
does not, however, presuppose the contempt explicit in José
Moreno Villa's affirmation, in a poem of *Carambas* (1931), that
'los cines originan pasiones de oropel' ('cinemas arouse tinsel
passions').[32] Moreno Villa's blend of indignation and disdain
gave his references to the cinema a particularly hard edge in
Jacinta la pelirroja (1929), where he saw it and the handsome
hero John Gilbert as rivals for Jacinta's emotions, and certainly
more successful than him in mellowing and arousing her.
Whereas the sight of a jilted John Gilbert makes her grow pale,
the poet—her lover—elicits only a hard kiss:

> Por tu divina intención, un durísimo beso.
> Aunque luego te vea palidecer
> ante un drama sentimental
> donde Gilbert, John Gilbert,
> sufre la derrota de una estrella fotogénica.*[33]

Moreno Villa resented the cinema because it came between him
and Jacinta; his bitter allusion to 'kilometres, miles of boredom'
is a stern judgement on films and on the mind of a woman so
enraptured by the tidy solutions to artificial problems and so
entranced by a film's last, lingering kiss that she no longer
recognizes the dramatic circumstances of everyday life:

> No ve los dramas de la roca en la orilla,
> del pensamiento caminando sobre sí mismo,
> de la rosa en el fango.
> ¡Mundo resuelto,
> vida resuelta,
> final besucón de película!
> Sí... Pero...
> debajo de los muebles, detrás de las cortinas,

---

* Through your divine intention, I receive a hard, unfeeling kiss. Even though I then
see you grow pale before a sentimental drama in which Gilbert, John Gilbert, suffers
the defeat of a photogenic star.

en el fondo del baño, sobre el lino nupcial,
kilómetros, millas de aburrimiento.*[34]

Those miles of film which bored and embittered Moreno
Villa excited many others who had more reason to be thankful
than he to the cinema for opening up a new thematic range and
inspiring them to essay new techniques. Poets of slender fame
and of secure reputation banded in common devotion to the
cinema advertised by such modish titles as 'Cinemática' and
'Cinematógrafo'. Aleixandre's poem 'Cinemática', from *Ámbito*
(1924–7), displays its source and its theme as unambiguously
as J. Rivas Panedas's 'Poema cinemático. Ladrón' (1928).
And Pedro Salinas's 'Cinematógrafo', belonging to *Seguro
azar* (1924–8), identifies the place where that inspiration
was to be found as clearly as Pedro Garfias's poem of the same
title (1919) and as the section called 'Cinematógrafo' belonging
to Ildefonso Manuel Gil's book of poems *Borradores* (1931). Gil
used a series of semi-technical cinematic terms to recount
his allegorical dream of a 'Film de vanguardia' that would bare
people's souls:

> Un film trascendental cuyos protagonistas
> fuesen sombras de espejo
> movidas por los hilos invisibles
> de problemas nuevos.
> Un film cuyos primeros planos
> fuesen paisajes superpuestos.
>
> Un film que fuese reportaje
> de nuevas sensaciones
> y en el cual los objetos
> presentaran colores
> vírgenes de miradas.
> ¡Un film trascendental donde se viesen
> al desnudo las almas!†[35]

* She does not see the rock's dramas on the shore, or the mind retracing its steps, or
the dramatic plight of the rose in the mud. A resolved world, a resolved life, the last,
lingering kiss of a film! Yes ... But ... beneath the furniture, behind the curtains, at
the bottom of the bath, on the nuptial linen, kilometres, miles of boredom.

† A transcendental film whose protagonists would be shadows on a mirror moved by
the invisible strings of new problems. A film whose foreground shots would be
landscapes superimposed one on the other.
A film that would be a documentary of new sensations in which the objects would

The minor role played by the cinema in the poetry of Aleixandre and Salinas shows that it attracted and stimulated them without ever achieving the emotional depth and thematic significance it acquired in the works of Alberti, Cernuda, and Lorca. In the case of Buñuel and Dalí, their hotly disputed collaboration on *Un chien andalou* and *L'Age d'or*, and especially Buñuel's writings in *La Gaceta Literaria* and assistance to the Cineclub, give their poems a curiosity value, which invites us to seek some point of contact between their films and their verses. Dalí's poems disappoint us; the dead donkeys on the grand piano filmed in *Un chien andalou* were anticipated in the poem, written in 1927, in which Dalí imagined 'Un burro podrido zumbante de pequeñas minuteras representando el principio de la primavera' ('A rotting donkey buzzing with tiny street photographers representing the beginning of spring').[36] And they were recalled in the screenplay he wrote in 1932, *Babaouo*, in which he specified that 'Ce torrent entraîne toutes sortes de débris et des animaux morts (ânes, vaches, chevaux).'[37] Those who expect to find many more reminiscences of films in Dalí's poems will be disappointed, largely because he graded the cinema lowest in the art forms that express the 'fonctionnement réel de la pensée'; so much is clear from his provocative declaration in 1932:

Contrairement à l'opinion courante, le cinéma est infiniment plus pauvre et plus limité, pour l'expression du fonctionnement réel de la pensée, que l'écriture, la peinture, la sculpture et l'architecture.[38]

Buñuel did not share Dalí's views, and his verses offer a kind of counterpoint to his films. His allusions to Wagner complement and clarify the playing in *L'Age d'or* of the music from the death scene in *Tristan and Isolde*; the presence of a priest in an orchestra playing Wagner is thrown into relief by his poem 'Pájaro de angustia', written in 1929, which mentions 'el pecho aplastado por una música de recuerdos seculares' ('the heart crushed by a music of secular memories') as a symptom of the violent passion which dominates the poem from its opening lines:

---

offer colours that had never been gazed on before. A transcendental film in which souls would be seen in all their nakedness!

Un plesiosauro dormía entre mis ojos
mientras la música ardía en una lámpara
y el paisaje sentía una pasión de Tristán e Iseo.*[39]

In 1933 Buñuel again remembered that orchestra playing
Wagner when he composed 'Une girafe', his systematic and
astonishing exploration of what lies beneath a giraffe's spots,
which he had intended to include in a book entitled *El perro
andaluz*.[40] The title of this proposed book, which, according to
Buñuel, made him and Dalí 'wet themselves laughing' when
they thought of it, is part of a private game whose only moves
are from films to poems or from poems to films.[41] The reader of
Buñuel's eccentric writings is necessarily excluded from this
game unless he has also been a spectator of *Un chien andalou* and
L'Age d'or. The orchestra playing in *L'Age d'or* is still active in
'Une girafe', where Buñuel hears issuing through 'une petite
grille' under the fourth spot of the giraffe the sounds 'd'un
véritable *orchestre* de cent musiciens jouant l'ouverture des
Maîtres Chanteurs'. And the death's head moth which is filmed
in close-up in *Un chien andalou* is commemorated in Buñuel's
discovery under the ninth spot of 'un gros papillon nocturne
obscur, avec la tête de mort entre les ailes'.[42]

The title of a poem Buñuel planned to include in his book *El
perro andaluz*—'El arco iris y la cataplasma' (1927)—displays in
its conjunction of a rainbow and a poultice Buñuel's skill at
devising private, enigmatic titles and his refusal to make any
concession to the reader, who is the target of a series of gratuitously indecorous questions and nonchalant remarks:

> ¿Cuántos maristas caben en una pasarela?
> ¿Cuatro o cinco?
> ¿Cuántas corcheas tiene un tenorio?
> 1.230.424.
> Estas preguntas son fáciles.
> ¿Una tecla es un piojo?
> ¿Me constiparé en los muslos de mi amante?
> ¿Excomulgará el Papa a las embarazadas?
> ¿Sabe cantar un policía?
> ¿Los hipopótamos son felices?

* A plesiosaurus slept between my eyes whilst the music burnt in a lamp and the
landscape felt a passion as strong as that of Tristan and Isolde.

¿Los pederastas son marineros?
Y estas preguntas, ¿son también felices?

Dentro de unos instantes vendrán por la calle
dos salivas de la mano
conduciendo un colegio de niños sordomudos.

¿Sería descortés si yo les vomitara un piano
desde mi balcón?*[43]

However eccentric and offensive these questions may seem, they do let us see—in the persons of Marists, the Pope, a policeman, his mistress, and homosexuals—Buñuel's preoccupation with sex, religion, and authority which underpin his films. The first question he posed in his poem—'How many Marists fit on a bridge?'—exercised him sufficiently to warrant a visual reply in *L'Age d'or*, where he filmed four priests crossing a small bridge in the garden. And the scruples he feigns in his final question, in which the mention of discourtesy only intensifies the aggressive urge to vomit a piano, were stifled in *L'Age d'or*; the idea of throwing something from an upstairs window, which he proposed in his poem and which had already been put into effect by René Clair in *An Italian Straw Hat* (1928), was translated into action when his protagonist threw a live archbishop through an upstairs window.

With its private frame of references, 'El arco iris y la cataplasma' is a complement to rather than an offshoot of Buñuel's films, a restatement of basic themes and attitudes in terms as provocative and fanciful as the scenes that illustrate them. Ideally, our enjoyment of the many poems written in praise of stars or films should be enriched by setting the poem against the film or star that inspired it. The fame and availability of most of Buñuel's films enable us to recognize and evaluate these points of contact. On the other hand, the loss of many films and the

---

* How many Marists fit on a footbridge? Four or five? How many quavers has a ladykiller? 1,230,424. These questions are easy.

Is a piano key a louse? Will I catch cold between the thighs of my mistress? Will the Pope excommunicate pregnant women? Does a policeman know how to sing? Are hippopotami happy? Are homosexuals sailors? And these questions, are they happy ones as well?

In a few moments there will come hand in hand down the street two salivas leading a school of deaf-mute children.

Would it be impolite if I vomited a piano on them from my balcony?

obscurity of many actors who figured in them make it impossible for us to judge the inspiration of such poems as 'A Lulú
Alvarez. Naciente "estrella" de Hollywood', 'Mimí Jordán',
'Lilian Harvey', and 'Comentarios poéticos a un film. Chu Chin
Chow'.[44] The last poem demonstrates that a colourful spectacle
was no guarantee of a successful poem; it also showed the
cinema's capacity to bring out the worst as well as the best in
writers, to delude pedestrian versifiers into thinking that they
were gifted poets. Jaime Salas had neither the verbal flair nor
the acumen to communicate to us either the story or the spirit of
Chu Chin Chow, and he failed to capture his excitement with
lines as graceless and sing-song as:

> Camino del Bagdad de los sueños,
> una nube de flechas mortal
> cubre a Chu Chin Chow y los suyos,
> ¡Oh hazaña monstruosa de Hassán!*

Spain did not have a monopoly of fatuous poems about the
cinema, and Jaime Salas's verses are no worse and no more
ridiculous than the tribute one Ned Hungerford penned to
Theda Bara in 1919:

> You are but one of all the pagan glow-cups
> Holding out their wine before the careless breeze;
> You are but one
> Along the far, far hunted trail . . .
>
> Before your careless flame
> I leave my incense jar of worship-leaves.[45]

The primness and pretentious diction of these lines are thrown
into relief when they are set alongside a verse from Hart Crane's
'The Bridge', whose taut and highly personal phrasing captures
the cinema's hypnotic ability to entrance multiple audiences
with the same images:

> I think of cinemas, panoramic sleights
> With multitudes bent towards some flashing scene
> Never disclosed but hastened to again,
> Foretold to other eyes on the same screen.[46]

---

* On the road to the Baghdad of our dreams, a lethal cloud of arrows covers Chu Chin
Chow and his men, the monstrous deed of Hassan!

The Spanish poems inspired by the cinema in the 1920s and 1930s offer equally striking contrasts, but in greater number, spanning a range of talents, themes, manners, and attitudes. Many Spanish poets reacted with imagination and panache to the stimulus provided by the cinema, if only in one or two memorable poems. Francisco Ayala, author of some excellent stories devoted to the cinema, set his stylish tribute 'A Circe cinemática' (1929) in the traditional *lira* verse-form, which, together with his studiously deployed parentheses and the mythological figure around whom the poem revolves, takes the reader back in time; the modernity of the cinema and the excitement it generated are controlled by decorous phrases and cultured, Latinist constructions as Ayala represented the cinema as the new temptress:

> En sábana tendida
> de agua feliz dispuesta en un cuadrado
> —alerta, no dormida:
> el pulso acelerado—
> escucha Circe al viento enamorado
>
> que, en idas y venidas,
> desnudo de blancura y de recelos,
> al sujetar las bridas
> con juegos paralelos
> levanta por sus puntas los pañuelos.*[47]

In a series of poems published in *La Gaceta Literaria* in 1928, Rafael Laffón did not content himself with the simple square which framed Ayala's poised evocation of the cinema's magic, but interpreted the cinema and what he saw in it by means of a group of geometrical and arithmetical terms which had already appealed to him in his book of poems *Signo+* (1927). The first, brief poem of his 'Programa mínimo'—'(Ecrán)'—presents the problem or theorem: the distance between the cinema screen, which he visualized paradoxically as a moon, and the far-flung dreams it arouses:

---

* On a sheet of blissful water stretched tight and disposed within a square, Circe—alert, not asleep, her pulse racing—listens to the love-torn wind which, as it blows hither and thither, bereft of whiteness and of fear, ripples the sea like handkerchiefs lifted by their corners as it holds tight the bridles of Neptune's chariot as its wheels play on the sides.

Luna cuadrangular. (Y al fin y al cabo
provocas sueños duros
intercontinentales.)*[48]

In the second poem—'(Voz triangulada)'—Laffón focused
on the triangle of light which emerges from the projector and
associates the 'cone of joy' it creates with the illumination
brought by the Holy Spirit. That joy will spin on its axis, an
endlessly revolving sphere which Laffón defined as a 'bobbin of
joy', shedding light and joy as in an evangelical crusade:

Un vértice tercero
precisaba el triángulo
para engendrar su cono de alegría
—generación abstracta en alma y cubo—:
el Espíritu Santo
de la cámara obscura.

El cono entró en el ojo—bien salióse;
por eso el ojo fue (¿de la Providencia
bis?) tal que el ojo nutridor y oblicuo.
Y el verbo se hizo imagen
de luz civilizada.

Surgió así la alegría
que desarrolla un eje bien formado
—¡alegría montada sobre fuerza!—,
bobina de alegría
porque es continua y llega a todas partes:
alegría, sin duda.
—precisión, gran alcance, gran calibre—.†

Laffón's language is an uneasy blend of biblical echoes
and—in the last line—the smugly succinct hyperboles of arms
dealers. But the endlessly revolving circle is a constant of these
poems, and provides both the visual and emotional energy of
the last of the group, 'Mecánica celeste', which he dedicated 'A

* Quadrangular moon. (After all you provoke harsh intercontinental dreams.)
† A third vertex completed the triangle to procreate its cone of joy—an abstract
procreation in soul and cube—: the Holy Spirit of the camera obscura.
The cone passed through the eye—and forthwith emerged; for that reason the eye
was (also of Providence?) just like the oblique eye that nourished it. And the word
became an image of civilized light.
Thus was born the joy that is unfolded by a well formed axis—joy founded on
strength!—, a bobbin of joy because it is continuous and reaches everywhere: unambiguous joy—precision, long range, wide bore—.

Charlot en "El Circo"'. In it he created a tension between his own restless desire to fly and dance and a hypnotic series of circles starting with the 'plataforma giratoria' of the second line. The gyrations continue in Chaplin's 'retina', in the 'diámetro', and in the 'giro de tus pistas'. The poet's dancing feet and the gathering momentum of these gyrations make it inevitable that he be shot at a tangent into space. In concluding that he still does not know whether he is floating or treading the earth, Laffón paid simple but eloquent tribute to the balletic magic of Chaplin:

> Yo fui a mirarte y me encontré bailando
> sobre una plataforma giratoria,
> sin pensar que bailaba en tu retina.
> Y a la razón no le encontraba el cabo.
>
> Asirme, asirme. ¿Pero?
> ¿Y dónde hallar la idea fija entonces?
> (Al Gran Voltaje le pedí las alas
> —arcángel de nuevo modelo—:
> inútilmente mente.)
>
> Mis pies—el yo absoluto
> del ritmo personal e intransferible—,
> lucharon—¿duelo el vuelo?—,
> por liberarme de mi propio antípoda
> puesto allí al otro extremo del diámetro.
>
> Asirme, asirme. Pero
> no hallé cabellos a la ley de Newton.
>
> Y por fin este giro
> de tus pistas—gramófono sin tasa—,
> me lanzó en la tangente no medida
> con un disparo universal de alcance.
> (Yo aun no sé si he tocado tierra firme.)*

---

* I went to watch you and found myself dancing on a gyrating platform, without thinking that I was really dancing in your retina. And I could not find any reason for it.

Hold on. But how? And where then would I find the idée fixe? (I asked the Great Voltage for his wings—the latest model of archangel—with a mind that serves no purpose.)

My feet—the absolute ego of personal and non-transferable rhythm—strove—was the flight one of grief?—to free me from my own antipode placed at the other end of the diameter.

Hold on. But Newton's law could not sustain me.

And finally the gyrations of your tracks—a gramophone—launched me on the

Movement of a different kind—relentless advance—provides
the measure, the tempo, and the tension of a tribute to another
star, but unlike Laffón, who spins off into space, Emeterio
Gutiérrez Albelo is paralysed with fear, 'con los brazos en cruz',
as he watches Brigitte Helm moving in a cone of light bisecting
the darkness. In his 'Minuto a Brigitte Helm' (1932) Gutiérrez
Albelo revealed himself to be one of the poets who capitalized
on the fact censured by Moreno Villa in *Puentes que no acaban*
(1933): that

> todo es crimen en novelas, teatros,
> cines y gacetas . . . .*⁴⁹

With his refrain 'Avanzando, avanzando', the poet instils into
the reader a fearful anticipation, which is intensified visually by
such elements as a dagger, a blood-stained shadow, and a fateful
moon and structurally by clipped phrases and a nervous rhythm
suggestive of baited breath:

> Avanzando . . . avanzando . . .
> en un silencio de puñal tan hondo,
> tan sutil, tan helado.
>
> Avanzando, avanzando.
> Por un cono de luz, buida sombra,
> nocturna, ensangrentada.
>
> Avanzando . . . avanzando . . .
> ignorante de todo. Fatal. Fatalizada.
> Asesinando los robles más robustos
> con su fija mirada.
>
> Avanzando, avanzando.
> Con una veste de asfodelos y un collar de mandrágoras.
>
> Avanzando, avanzando, avanzando . . .
> con su aliento aquí—ya—
> onda negra.
> Salada.
>
> (Sin poder detenerla,
> yo, en la opuesta pantalla.

---

unmeasured tangent with a salvo of universal range. (And still I do not know if I have
touched terra firma.)
  * it is all crime in novels, theatres, cinemas and newspapers.

De manera tan fúnebre encalada.
Con los brazos en cruz.
Bajo la luna mala.)*[50]

When we reach the end of the poem, we realize that we have
learned nothing about the reasons for the actress's movement,
whose relentlessness is suggested in the assonance echoing from
'ensangrentada' in line 6 to 'mala' in the last line. Gutiérrez
Albelo's whole point and purpose was to present himself trans-
fixed before a sequence from *Metropolis*: the one in which
Maria, played by Brigitte Helm, is pursued through the cavern
by Rotwang, who frightens her with beams of light projected by
his torch. The poem operates by hint and understatement
rather than by explicit reference, and the reader is involved in
the poet's fear without really knowing why.

A different reaction is provoked by the following lines from
'Cinematógrafo', a poem Pedro Garfias wrote in 1919:

> Los volcheviques
> han cortado los cables eléctricos.
> La calle muere en el espejo.
> El avión,
> extraviado, se coló en la sala...†[51]

What prevents these lines from plummeting into melodrama is
the fantasy of an aeroplane landing in a living-room. Without
this strain of humour some of the poems devoted to the cinema
would be solemn, straight-laced tributes to melodrama, as
unmemorable as the films that inspired them. Crime is ostensibly the stimulus of the poem J. Rivas Panedas wrote in 1928
under the title 'Poema cinemático. Un ladrón'. Rivas Panedas
was faithful to the spirit and content of silent films by making

---

* Advancing . . . advancing . . . in a deep, subtle, frozen silence imposed by a dagger.
Advancing, advancing. A sharp-edged shadow, nocturnal and blood-stained, moving
through a cone of light.
Advancing . . . advancing . . . Oblivious to everything. Ill-fated. Doomed. Murder-
ing the strongest oaks with her staring eyes.
Advancing, advancing. With a gown of asphodels and a necklace of mandrakes.
Advancing, advancing, advancing . . . her breath ebbing and flowing like a black and
salty wave.
(And I powerless to stop her, on the facing screen, whitewashed in such a funereal
way. With my arms enfolded. Beneath the evil moon.)
† The Bolsheviks have cut the electric cables. The street dies in the mirror. The
plane, off its course, slipped into the living-room.

his two policemen firstly withdraw their feet rapidly from cold
water and then shake their fists in a gesture of impotent rage
hallowed by slapstick comedies. It is the thief who outwits the
police with all the cunning of Chaplin, whose acts of
ingenuity—such as overpowering the fearsome Eric Campbell
with a gas street lamp in *Easy Street* (1916)—suggested a
tactic of impudent athleticism which Rivas Panedas's thief was
to emulate. The fantasy of this piece is thrown into relief by
the precise, matter-of-fact prose in which the episode is
narrated:

> Dos guardias, con los sables desenvainados, trepan por la fachada
> de una casa persiguiendo a un ladrón. Este repele los sables con los
> pies y sube ligero con su botín. En unos segundos se halla en la azotea.
> Se despoja de la americana y se arroja a un tejado vecino. Una vez
> sumergido entre las tejas, comienza a nadar con actividad. Llega a una
> guardilla, levanta la capucha y asciende presuroso a su bordo. Con dos
> chimeneas planas, arrancadas al paso, hace bogar su embarcación.
>
> Los guardias, que ya están en la azotea, se despojan a su vez de las
> guerreras y prueban a sumergir un pie, que retiran con gesto de frío.
>
> Impotentes, pero presuntuosos, amenazan con la mano al
> fugitivo.*[52]

The thief's outsmarting of the police and his rooftop escape in
a boat, which is a fanciful superimposition of two commonplaces from adventure films, maintain the attitude of impudent
disrespect shown by comic films towards authority. When
Rufino Blanco-Fombona stated in his poem 'Cine'—also published in *La Gaceta Literaria* in 1928—that 'virtue triumphs
after an uneven fight', he directed his gentle mockery towards
those melodramatic films and serials with settings as varied as
docks, sordid doss-houses, and palaces and with labyrinthine,
heavy-handed plots in which goodness, beauty, and true love
are menaced constantly by evil, defined by the poet as 'Hatred,

---

* Two policemen, with their sabres drawn, clamber up the façade of a house in
pursuit of a thief. The thief repels the sabres with his feet and climbs nimbly with his
booty. In a few seconds he is on the roof. He strips off his jacket and jumps onto a
neighbouring roof. As soon as he is submerged amid the tiles, he begins to swim
vigorously. He reaches an attic, raises the cover and hauls himself rapidly on board.
With two flat chimneys torn off as he floated by, he makes his boat float.

The policemen, who are now on the first roof, follow his example and strip off the
jackets of their uniforms and gingerly immerse a foot in the water, which they withdraw
because of the cold registered on their faces.

Helpless, but presumptuous, they shake their fists at the fugitive.

lust, ambition'. Slowly illuminated in the closing lines of the poem is a beautiful woman whose beauty is a composite of cinematic clichés:

> De las dársenas, de las barcas pesqueras,
> de los tugurios sórdidos, salimos al palacio ducal;
> la angustia nos oprime el pecho;
> ¡qué anhelar, qué anhelar!
> Odios, lujurias, ambiciones,
> ascienden desde el arrabal;
> pero triunfa la virtud
> tras un combate desigual,
> y la niña de Whistler, rosa y blanca,
> encuentra al fin a su galán.
>
> Bombillas mofletudas
> soplan a su claridad:
> aparecen los brazos de la Venus de Milo,
> una boca de ajado coral;
> y sobre pecho ecuatoriano
> un rostro de aurora boreal.*[53]

The vices ultimately conquered by virtue are what appealed strongly to Guillermo de Torre, who expressed his ingenuous, childlike delight in mystery and melodrama in two telegraphically clipped lines belonging to his 'Poème dadaïste. Roues', written in 1920:

> dans l'écran cauchemar délicieux
> cinémas des sexes masquées[54]

The simple list of

> Persecuciones. Incendios.
> Tiros. Salvamentos†

he had inserted into his 'Friso ultraísta. Film', published in 1919, identified those 'delicious nightmares' as the stock

---

* From the docks, from the fishing boats, from the sordid doss-houses, we move to the ducal palace; anguish tightens around our chest; what anxiety we feel!

Hatreds, lusts, ambitions surge up from the dock area; but virtue triumphs after an unequal fight, and the Whistler girl, all pink and white, at last finds her gallant.

Round lights show up her brightness and there appear the arms of Venus de Milo, a mouth of faded coral, and above an Ecuadorian breast a mouth as bright as the aurora borealis.

† Chases. Fires. Gunshots. Rescues.

situations which he commemorated in two different modes of poetry, clearly labelled 'dadaïste' and 'ultraísta'.

Whatever the manner and however openly he advertised it, Torre was explicit about the source of the enthusiasm. The intimate connection he advocated in the essay he wrote in 1921 between American films and the 'new-shaped poem'was something he had already put into practice in his 'Friso ultraísta', where he had saluted American films with the cry: '¡HURRA POR EL FILM NORTEAMERICANO!'[55] This poem is an offspring of the union of those films and the 'new-shaped poem'; the *poemas fotogénicos* which comprise the eighth section of his *Hélices* are others. When Torre recalled in 1926 'that fever of image-making which consumes the young poets', he was of course quoting his own experience, for what characterized his own *poemas novimorfos* inspired by the cinema were precisely the fusion of 'lirismo y fotogenia' he urged on others.[56]

Torre was fascinated and excited by the nature and quality of visual, cinematic appeal; so much is apparent from the title 'Fotogenia' he gave to one of the poems of *Hélices*. By dedicating it to Jean Epstein, he divulged the origin of the word, which figures prominently in the epigraph he chose for this group of poems: Epstein's phrase 'Photogénie, photogénie pure, mobilité scandée ...' Torre did not realize the promise of his title, which leads us to expect a poetic evocation of a technical phenomenon he found exciting; the theme and purpose of the poem are summarized in two particularly lacklustre and pedestrian lines:

> Todos los elementos flotantes de la realidad
> adquieren categoría plástica.*[57]

In this poem Torre listed some of the elements of reality which fascinated him: facial expressions; and those machines and centres of transportation which proved irresistible to futurist and *ultraísta* poet alike:

> Una estación trepidante   vaivenes sincopadas
> Un puerto   balcón a lontananza
> Hangars   nidos de hélices.†

* All the floating elements of reality acquire plastic category.

† A shuddering station, syncopated comings and goings. A harbour, a distant balcony. Hangars, nests of propellers.

But Torre's habit of merely naming what he saw on the screen is unsatisfyingly superficial, for it tells us less about the nature of cinematic art than about the ingenuousness of the poet, as awe-struck before images of everyday life as those audiences who fled in terror before Lumière's film of an approaching train.

When Torre tried to interpret what he saw he resorted to a diction so strained and scientific that his verses fell into ostentatious obscurity. Impressive as it may sound, his definition 'Los cineactores son dinamómetros emocionales' ('Cinema actors are emotional dynamometers') is, once one has cut through the language, as obvious as his statement:

> El drama vibra en la celulosa
> Y la imantación retiniana
> volatiliza las sugestiones cinéticas.*

Far from persuading us to accept his unremarkable discovery that mechanical objects are photogenic, Torre's language obstructs the excitement he felt at watching films. He himself seemed to be aware of this, and it is his realization that explains the difference in verbal texture between two poems that set out to capture his thrill at being in a cinema: 'Friso ultraísta', and one he included in *Hélices*, 'En el cinema'. His retention in the second poem of a number of lines belonging to the first clarifies the thematic link between them. Firstly, the repetition of the metaphoric group

> Constelaciones de aviones.
> Sierpes de automóviles.
> Ramilletes de hélices†58

highlights the speed of modern life as a key factor in his emotions and a major element of the films he admired. And his dislike of sentimental subjects in favour of colourful heroics is displayed in his reiteration of the two lines

> y la incolora delicuescencia
> —besos trucos y claros de luna—‡

---

* The drama vibrates on the cellulose and the magnetism of the retina volatilizes the cinematic hints.

† Constellations of aeroplanes. Cars writhing like serpents. Clusters of propellers.

‡ and the colourless deliquescence—kisses tricks and moonlight.

Even though it contains such infelicitous phrases as 'potencial energético' and 'estímulo hipervitalista', 'En el cinema' is a much more convincing rendering of a felt experience than 'Friso ultraísta', in which the language is more important to Torre than his feelings, smothered by statements as self-defeating as

> Cabalgata de figuras adamitas,
> posesas del vértigo giróvago*

and as bewildering as

> El simultaneísmo accional
> multiplica las diplopias.†

Replacing pompous words and inelegant neologisms by bold metaphors, Torre created in the opening lines of 'En el cinema' a greater sense of impact, expectation, and involvement:

> Empaquetados de negro en la sala
> sentimos agujereadas nuestras carnes
> por la inyección vivificante de los films.‡

Although Torre had clearly made an advance on the earlier poem by defining his response and pruning his diction, 'En el cinema' still remains an uneven poem, unbalanced both in matter and in manner by the banal recounting of what he saw on the screen and by his enthusiastic attempt to capture the collective reaction of a cinema audience magnetized by the screen:

> Alto voltaje
> La sala del cinema
>   es una máquina electromagnética
> Foco de incitaciones
>   Acciones y reacciones
> Palpita el pulso de la vida
>   en las imágenes simultáneas de la pantalla
>   Todos nuestros sentidos ven únicamente
>   y abocan a la irradiación del haz angular
> El plural estremecimiento de los espectadores

---

* Cavalcade of Adamite figures, possessed by vagabond vertigo.

† Simultaneity of actions multiplies cases of diplopia.

‡ Enveloped in darkness in the cinema, we feel our flesh perforated by the vivifying injection of films.

se unifica en miles de miradas dardeantes
hacia la pantalla desbordada.*

When he turned his attention to stars or to their heroic actions,
his lines became more feeble and disjointed as he merely reeled
off names, or listed human motives—like 'El impulso la astucia
la celeridad' ('Impulse cunning speed')—or bold events like
'Cabalgadas disparos incendios' ('Cavalcades gunshots fires').
As they echo the melodramatic catalogue of

> Persecuciones. Incendios.
> Tiros. Salvamentos

found in 'Friso ultraísta', these parenthetic phrases show that
Torre may have revised his language but not his tastes. In
including himself among 'los cineastas' who comment archly
that 'La intriga es absurda' ('The plot is absurd'), he gave
himself a superiority that is unmerited, for his recognition of
the absurdity of some plots did not stop him in 'El 7°. episodio'
from commemorating serial films, highly popular entertainment woven out of far-fetched plots and cardboard characters.
Serials clearly appealed to Torre as much as they did to the
French surrealists, and his attitude to them was certainly more
reverential and affectionate than that of the wag who mused in
1921:

> If life were like the serial films, how fearsome it
> would be,
> There'd not be many of us left by 1923.
> Half of us would be very good, the others *very* bad,
> And they'd persecute the good ones, and want everything
> they had.
> We'd rush up precipices and we'd battle on the
> brink
> And throw each other in the sea tied up in sacks to sink;
> And burn each other's houses down and blow up rocks
> and trees;
> And have masked, mysterious helpers to confound our
> enemies.[59]

* High voltage. The cinema is an electro-magnetic machine, a focus of incitements,
actions, and reactions. The pulse of life throbs in the simultaneous images of the screen.
All our senses see and concentrate solely on the irradiation of the angular shaft of light.
The plural trembling of the spectators is unified in thousands of darting glances towards
the overflowing screen.

Those who seek a similarly burlesque evocation of serials in Torre's poem could seize on his allusion to the 'customary car' or to his asides, equivalent to stage directions: 'The lovers breathe in relief' and 'the spectators become less tense'.[60] They are, however, essential and factual elements in Torre's narrative, which is as mechanical, as devoid of motivation and ambiguity as the serials which it commemorates. The flat, casual manner he adopted deprives the episode of any tension, and we have to accept his word that the spectators breathe again with relief:

> El agua llega hasta sus cuellos
> Mary y William consternados
> preven su mueca última
> en el espejo horizontal donde sus enemigos les arrojan
> No hay un agujero de salvación
> —Pero aun estamos en el 7°. episodio—
> Súbito el botón secreto
> mueve la palanca de la invisible esclusa
> y se fulmina el rayo de huída
> De un brinco al auto típico
> que inyecta aire en los músculos del paisaje
> Los amantes respiran
> y sus sonrisas matizan el escollo tónico del episodio
> (La rueda de la aventura ha dado otra vuelta
> Y los espectadores aflojan la tensión)
> Mas en una sierpe de la carretera el film enlaza su
>   engranaje accional
> El rostro del ambiente arma sus resortes
>   Bajo un puente el odioso Tom
>   prende la mecha explosiva.*

The escapade which Torre recounted is an ideal subject for parody, but his careful, punctilious mention of a secret button,

---

* The water reaches their necks. Mary and William in consternation foresee their last grimace in the horizontal mirror where their enemies have cast them. There is no chink of salvation—But we are still in the seventh episode—Suddenly the secret button moves the lever of the invisible sluice and the lightning flash of flight explodes. With a single leap they reach the customary car which pumps air into the muscles of the landscape. The lovers breathe with relief and their smiles colour the dominant note of danger in the episode. (The wheel of adventure has given another turn and the spectators relax a little.) But on a bend of the road the film once more engages the gear of events. The landscape tautens its springs. Beneath a bridge the hateful Tom lights the fuse.

a sluice, a get-away car, a car-ride on a winding road, and the villain about to detonate an explosive charge under a bridge reveals his familiarity with the commonplaces of serial melodrama, and particularly with the threat of death by drowning. His poem is a homage to rather than a pastiche of those serials in which flooding is a menace, for example, *The Black Secret* (1919), whose fourth episode was entitled 'Below the Waterline'.[61]

In the remaining lines of the poem the victory of virtue is narrated as smoothly and as unfussily as the deeds of villainy. In celebrating the clear-cut triumph of good over evil as 'jubilosamente norteamericano', Torre revealed simple tastes, a candid delight in American initiative, and an attitude to right and wrong as unaffected and crystalline as his tributes to 'Color' and to Chaplin in the two remaining poems of the 'Poemas fotogénicos'. The new 'zodíaco fotogénico' ('photogenic zodiac') heralded in 'Color' needs a king, and that king is Chaplin, whom Torre sublimated in a series of hyperbolic definitions:

> Charlie Chaplin
> Rey de la Creación Fotogénica
> Signo de la nueva aurora cómica
> Dinamómetro del humor moderno.[*][62]

Torre was one of the first Spanish poets to recognize and exalt Chaplin's uniqueness, but the ingenuity and balletic grace of Chaplin's art are bogged down in the self-evident remark 'Charlot único igual a sí mismo' ('The one and only Chaplin comparable only to himself') and in the pretentious shorthand notes he penned as if he were preparing an entry for a reference work:

> Mímico y argumentista
> Creador integral de las farsas chaplinescas.[†]

Torre's eulogy of Chaplin, however sincere and well-meaning, is singularly graceless; to praise him as a 'Pulverizador de sonrisas intersticiales' ('Atomiser of interstitial smiles') was to let language garble rather than channel his devotion. The greatest tribute he could pay Chaplin was to apply to him three of his

---

[*] Charlie Chaplin, king of Photogenic Creation, star of the new dawn of comedy, dynamometer of modern humour.

[†] Mimic and writer of screenplays, the total creator of Chaplin's farces.

favourite words—*simultáneo, multiforme,* and *giróvago*—,which, allied with *girándula,* make the last four lines of his poem into a tribute so verbally stiff that many readers may perhaps fail to capture his meaning let alone sense and share his enthusiasm:

> Simultáneo y multiforme
> desde todas las pantallas y carteles
> su risa giróvaga
> acelera la girándula de las horas.*

The phrase 'Planos simultáneos' ('Simultaneous planes') which appears in the fifth line of Aleixandre's poem 'Cinemática', belonging to *Ámbito,* provides an obvious link between Torre and Aleixandre, who made it clear with his title, just as Torre did with his 'Fotogenia', that what he chose to commemorate was the rapid flow of images he saw on the cinema screen. Leopoldo de Luis has informed us that as a child Aleixandre went with his sister Conchita to the Cine Pascualini, in Madrid, 'a kind of hut where he saw the first comic films of Max Linder: *Les Débuts d'un patineur, Rencontre imprévue, Max aéronaute, Max fait du ski.*'[63] However, Linder's name appears nowhere in his poems, nor does that of any other actor or film. This lack of specific allusions to the cinema suggests that Aleixandre carefully controlled his interest in it, evident in his membership of the Cineclub, and recalled in his letter to me of 29 January 1972, where he could bring to mind only one poem—'Cinemática'—directly inspired by the cinema. With noticeable restraint he recalled:

I have been devoted to the cinema since I was a child, and have remained so all my life. And you are right: when I wrote *Ámbito* I tried in one poem to bring something of the technique of the cinema to poetry, and that can be seen in my poem 'Cinemática', in a movement of planes inspired by cinematographic projection. I do not think that there is any other poem close to the cinema or at least I was not conscious of it as I was in 'Cinemática'.

Aleixandre clearly did not resort to the cinema, as did Alberti, Cernuda, and Lorca, to seek in it themes, motifs, ideas, and an array of techniques; for him the cinema was no more than a challenge to accept, and as a visual inspiration was no

---

* Simultaneous and multiform, from every cinema screen and poster his vagabond laughter accelerates the girandole of time.

more important to him than the paintings of Ingres. He certainly never let films intrude on or neutralize the fertile powers of his own imagination, nurtured by his reading of Lautréamont, Rimbaud, and Desnos.[64] However, his studious control of the cinema as a mental stimulus does not mean that it did not leave its mark on his work. On a superficial level, some of the prose pieces he wrote in the late 1920s display a modish and self-conscious use of cinematic terminology. With his imaginative statement in 1929—'Filos te pasan sin agonía, pero te has hecho pura pantalla' ('Sharp edges penetrate you painlessly, but you have become purely and simply a cinema screen')—the metaphor of the *pantalla* allowed him to create a picture of spreadeagled passivity in the face of seemingly autonomous weapons. And the same sharpness characterizes the 'cinematic flow of trenchant realities' which in 1927 assailed him in a street at night:

Eché a andar por sus calles, y las vi desplomarse en sus moles, huecas de miradas, contra mis hombros helados, como rodándome por ellas, aunque no las sentía; oprimiéndome con sus volúmenes imperiosos, casi en cascada de cubos geométricos, cruces de calles, ángulos, sombras, esquinas; cinemática sucesión de realidades tajantes.*[65]

There are passages from the poems he wrote in the 1920s and 1930s which catch the eye not by their transparent use of such words as *pantalla* and *cinemático*, but by their content or technique. In the absence of any precise allusion, we can only speculate that such passages were conceived in the cinema; they certainly enrich our appreciation of his poetry and offer new insights into its sources. Aleixandre's obsession with sexual passion was nurtured visually by his delight in the sensual paintings of Ingres, whom he commemorated in *Ámbito* in the poem 'La fuente (Ingres)'. In his letter to me of 1972 Aleixandre acknowledged what his poetry suggests: that Buñuel's *Un chien andalou* 'interested me a great deal'. There is one scene in particular of Buñuel's film which, to judge from the fidelity of the poet's reminiscence, left its imprint on the poet's mind; it is

* I started walking through its streets, and I saw them collapse into its heaps, empty of human eyes, against my frozen shoulders, as if I were rolling through those streets, even if I could not feel them; oppressing me with their imperious shapes, almost a cascade of geometric cubes, street intersections, angles, shadows, corners; a cinematic flow of trenchant realities.

the one early in the film in which the male protagonist drools bloody saliva in lascivious desperation after cornering a plump heroine and pawing her breasts. The blood which dribbles from the corner of his mouth, the mouth which dominates the screen in an agonized close-up of the man's face, the cruel impulses implicit in his eyes and curl of the lips, are woven into two stanzas of 'El más bello amor', from *Espadas como labios*; they present the violent union of man and woman as a fearful blood-stained encounter menaced by weapons, corruption, and sadistic urges:

> Así, sin acabarse mudo ese acoplamiento sangriento,
> respirando sobre todo una tinta espesa,
> los besos son las manchas, las extensibles manchas
> que no me podrán arrancar las manos más delicadas.
>
> Una boca imponente como una fruta bestial,
> como un puñal que de la arena amenaza el amor,
> un mordisco que abarcase toda el agua o la noche ...*66

Intriguing as this reminiscence may be, it was the way in which images changed and succeeded one another, rather than what they actually represented, that fascinated Aleixandre. His most sustained tribute to the cinema—'Cinemática'—can be summarized in the phrase that captured his impression of a street at night: 'cinemática sucesión de realidades tajantes'. He chose the same nocturnal atmosphere for his poem, and the 'corners, shadows' which appear in both the prose piece and his ballad show that his attention was engaged by nothing more exciting or exceptional than streets at night; and it is night that he addresses and so dramatizes:

> Venías cerrada, hermética,
> a ramalazos de viento
> crudo, por calles tajadas
> a golpe de rachas, seco.
> Planos simultáneos—sombras:
> abierta, cerrada—. Suelos.
> De bocas de frío, el frío.
> Se arremolinaba el viento

---

* Thus, without that bloody coupling ending in silence, breathing a dense ink over everything, kisses are stains, extensible stains which delicate hands will not be able to snatch from me.

   An imposing mouth like a bestial fruit, like a dagger which menaces love from the sand, a bite which could take in all the water or night ...

en torno tuyo, ya a pique
de cercenarte fiel. Cuerpo
diestro. De negro. Ceñida
de cuchillas. Solo, escueto,
el perfil se defendía
rasado por los aceros.
    Tubo. Calle cuesta arriba.
Gris de plomo. La hora, el tiempo.
Ojos metidos, profundos,
bajo el arco firme, negro.
Veladores del camino
—ángulos, sombras—siniestros.
Te pasan ángulos—calle,
calle, calle, calle—. Tiemblos.
Asechanzas rasan filos
por ti. Dibujan tu cuerpo
sobre el fondo azul profundo
de ti misma, ya postrero.*[67]

Night moving through a windswept street is the subject of these lines, and Aleixandre attempted to create a sense of drama and menace by selecting such sinister elements as sharp edges, shadows, and raging wind and by pacing the poem in such a staccato way that our mind has to make a series of leaps between the multiple syntactic sections. The parentheses, enjambments, and elliptical phrases which the poet utilized sit uneasily within the confines of the Spanish ballad, and create a rhythm so jerky that as a tribute the poem is ambiguous. In his poem Aleixandre has captured none of the grace and innocence of the early cinema; whether he wanted to or not, he has evoked its technical immaturity, for his lines twist and turn, stop and start, splutter and hiccup like mechanical characters in an ancient film.

In 'Cinemática' Aleixandre set himself a specific task; but the

* You came sealed in, hermetic, driven along streets by the blows and lashes of a crude, dry wind. Simultaneous planes—shadows: opened, closed—. The ground. The cold emerging from mouths of cold. The wind spiralled around you, already on the point of amputating you. A deft body. In black. Encircled by blades. Alone, sparse, and stark, the silhouette struggled as the pavements strove to erase it.

A tube. A street sloping upwards. Leaden grey. The hour, the time. Deep-sunk eyes beneath the firm, black arch. Sinister keepers of the street—corners, shadows—. Corners pass you by—street, street, street, street—. Tremors. Ambushes sweep sharp edges through you. They outline your body, the last one left, on your own dark blue background.

result of his endeavour is so opaque in meaning, melodramatic in atmosphere, and disjointed in rhythm and composition that the poem must rank as a flawed experiment, which tells us little about the cinema and even less about the poet. The poem is altogether too studied and too laboriously mobile. However, when he relaxed and let the techniques of the cinema seep into him rather than strain to capture them in words, he did show himself capable of writing some imaginative passages. For example, the transformations that are so striking a feature of silent classics like *La Coquille et le Clergyman,* in which a woman's breasts change into shells, a crystal ball into a head, and a head into blackish liquid, are matched poetically in *Espadas como labios*, where he mused:

> Quién sabe si estas dos manos,
> dos montañas de pronto ...*[68]

And he showed in *La destrucción o el amor* that he could visualize an object and depict a scene from different angles. When René Clair, for example, filmed the wedding guests directly from above in *An Italian Straw Hat* to make them appear like ants, he adopted an aerial perspective which Aleixandre emulated in a series of precisely specified angles:

> Tu corazón redondo como naipe
> visto de perfil es un espejo,
> de frente acaso es nata
> y a vista de pájaro es un papel delgado.†[69]

The critic who uses 'Cinemática' as evidence of Aleixandre's interest in the cinema and seeks the repercussions of that interest elsewhere in his poetry runs the risk of seeing in its dense texture what he wants to see rather than what is actually there. Salinas's poetry offers no such pitfall; its pictorial range is so limited and its narrative situations so sparse in detail and perspective that a search for underlying cinematic motifs and techniques is both fruitless and unnecessary: Salinas's interest in the cinema lies clearly for all to see on the surface of his poetry. It advertises itself as candidly as the illuminated coloured sign for the 'Universum Cinema' in the poem 'Am-

---

* Who knows if these two hands, suddenly two mountains ...

† Your heart as round as a playing-card seen in profile is a mirror, from the front it is perhaps cream and from above it is a slender paper.

sterdam', from *Fábula y signo* (1931), or as openly, in *El contemplado* (1946), as his obligatory tribute to Chaplin's durability:

> Un hombre hay que se escapa, por milagro,
> de tantas agonías.
>
> No hace nada, no es nada, es Charlie Chaplin,
> es este que te mira.*[70]

To adduce two allusions separated by fifteen years is to suggest that Salinas's interest in the cinema was as fitful as the lights flashing outside a cinema, which he commemorated with naïve pleasure. The 'anuncios luminosos de la vida/en la noche' ('luminous announcements of life in the night') were as attractive to him as they were to Eugène Deslaw, who in 1929 summarized his film *La Nuit électrique* (1928), shown at the second session of the Cineclub in January 1929, in terms Salinas was to echo. In describing the film as 'A study of the brilliant patterns produced by photographing electric signs on rapid stock', some programme notes indicated how the film was made; Deslaw explained his reasons for making it when he evoked 'The lure of the advertisements, the luminous projection of the lights. The widespread, torrential blaze of a city. . . . A protest against the literary representation of night . . .'[71] No more subtle or profound is Salinas's allegorical narration of the invention of the cinema in biblical terms that echo the account in Genesis of the creation of the world. The poem 'Cinematógrafo', written in 1920 and included in *Seguro azar*, is based on two simple ideas, developed in two uneven sections: in the first, 'Luz', God projected life onto the blank screen; in the second, 'Oscuridad', the screen has become a 'tela maravillosa', a paradise of flowering valleys where souls may drift in bliss.

To equate the invention of the cinema with Genesis may strike some as naïve over-statement and others as tasteless travesty. What rescues the poem from hyperbole and bad taste is the level of deft humour which Salinas maintained, which enabled him to hymn in mock-heroic terms the reduction of chaos to order and the sentimental freedom induced by the 'marvellous canvas'. In the first section, the void is filled by

---

* There is a man who escapes by a miracle from so many afflictions.
He does nothing, he is nothing, he is Charlie Chaplin, it is he who is looking for you.

God; the solemn biblical start 'In the beginning there was nothing' is succeeded by the right hand of God turning the handle of the projector; and the event is recorded with a nonchalance, a lack of excitement, which suggests that the invention of the cinema was as inevitable as the creation of the world:

> Al principio nada fue.
> Solo la tela blanca
> y en la tela blanca, nada.
> Por todo el aire clamaba,
> muda, enorme,
> la ansiedad de la mirada.
> La diestra de Dios se movió
> y puso en marcha la palanca ...
> Saltó el mundo todo entero
> con su brinco primaveral.
> La tela rectangular
> le oprimió en normas severas,
> le organizó bruscamente
> con dos líneas verticales,
> con dos líneas horizontales.
> Y el caos tomó ante los ojos
> todas las formas familiares.*⁷²

Faithful to his exaltation of love and woman, which will sustain *La voz a ti debida* and *Razón de amor*, Salinas presented as an essential presence on the screen—as indispensable to man now as Eve was to Adam—woman and the feelings she inspires; it was she who, in the person of countless screen heroines, captured the heart of so many audiences, whose volatile feelings are played out on a metaphoric 'tela del sentimiento' which faces and matches the *tela* of the screen:

> Pero ya el instinto acechaba
> en los ojos de la mujer
> —la cabellera suelta al viento—
> y en el tejer y el destejer

---

* In the beginning there was nothing. Only the white screen and on the white screen nothing. Throughout the universe anxious eyes made their dumb and vast demands. The right hand of God moved and put the lever in motion ... With its vernal leap the whole world sprang into life. The rectangular screen compressed it into severe norms, it arranged it brusquely with two vertical lines, with two horizontal lines. And chaos assumed before those eyes all the familiar forms.

de la tela del sentimiento.
Y el primer día de la creación
se levantó de su rincón
y vino a asomarse a la tela:
la mano diestra llevaba
el primer corazón del hombre,
que era el último corazón.*

The 'Oscuridad' of the second section holds the audience in a
kind of religious awe, and sustains them until their next visit to
the cinema, which to Salinas is as pure as a temple:

Ya todas las almas sienten
su curso como de estrellas
que vivieron en valles floridos de la tierra
y besaron labios humanos.
Ahora, vueltas al espacio
extraterrenal,
siguen rodando hasta el día
que el destino astral las torne
a acercar al mundo puro,
la telā blanca.†

A woman's hair still flows in the wind in the poem 'Far West',
from *Seguro azar*, which is infused with the same sense of
child-like wonder as Salinas first stares hard at and then ponders deeply about the wind blowing through the woman's hair.
In the first part of the poem he was at pains to create an
impression of incredulity by following the hyperbolic exclamation of the opening line with a series of questions which direct
an unknown spectator's attention to the wind's activities:

¡Qué viento a ocho mil kilómetros!
¿No ves cómo vuela todo?
¿No ves los cabellos sueltos
de Mabel, la caballista
que entorna los ojos limpios

---

* But now instinct lay in wait in the woman's eyes—her hair blowing in the
wind—and in the weaving and unweaving of the fabric of emotion. And on the first day
of creation she arose from her corner and appeared on the screen: her right hand bore
the first heart of man, which was also the last.

† Now every soul feels its transit like that of stars who lived in earth's flowering
valleys and kissed human lips. Now, back once more in that extraterrestrial space, they
revolve in space until the day when their astral destiny takes them back to the pure
world, the white screen.

ella, viento, contra el viento?
¿No ves
la cortina estremecida,
ese papel revolado
y la soledad frustrada
entre ella y tú por el viento?*[73]

Salinas began the second part of his poem with a disturbing change of tone and a masterful change of direction as his incredulity gave way to the realization that what he saw on the screen was not the wind itself but 'the portrait of a wind that died'. With phrases such as 'on the other side' and 'a distant evening', he stressed the gulf between his status as a spectator and the wind that once blew in a remote place and now survives on celluloid:

Sí, lo veo.
Y nada más que lo veo.
Ese viento
está al otro lado, está
en una tarde distante
de tierras que no pisé.
Agitando está unos ramos
sin dónde,
está besando unos labios
sin quién.
No es ya el viento, es el retrato
de un viento que se murió
sin que yo le conociera,
y está enterrado en el ancho
cementerio de los aires
viejos, de los aires muertos.†

Salinas's coda, with its last line completing the circular pattern of the poem, is a tribute to the unique power of the

---

* What a wind blowing at five thousand miles per hour! Don't you see how everything is blown about? Don't you see the flying hair of Mabel, the horsewoman who half closes her limpid eyes as she races like the wind against the wind? Don't you see the shuddering curtain, that swirling paper and the solitude between you and her thwarted by the wind?

† Yes, I see it. Nothing more: I see it. That wind is on the other side, is in a distant evening of lands I never trod. It is shaking some placeless branches, it is kissing some faceless lips. It is no longer the wind, it is the portrait of a wind that died without my ever getting to know it, and it is buried in the vast cemetery of the old winds, of the dead winds.

cinema, which can immortalize something as transient and commonplace as the wind:

> Sí le veo, sin sentirle.
> Está allí, en al mundo suyo,
> viento de cine, ese viento.*

Intriguing as are the poems Torre, Aleixandre, and Salinas devoted to the cinema, they tell us little about the poets other than that they were fascinated by it and chose to evoke that fascination in poetry. Like the various poets whom I have considered in this chapter, they subscribed to a widespread literary fashion in Spanish poetry of the 1920s and 1930s. However, in Spanish poetry of that period the cinema acquired its full force and value as a theme and inspiration when through it a poet learned more about himself and projected himself through situations and characters he saw in films. That is why the cinema has a key role to play in our study of the three poets with whom I shall be concerned in the next two chapters of this book: Rafael Alberti in Chapter 5, and Luis Cernuda and Federico García Lorca in Chapter 6.

* Yes I see it, without sensing it. It is there, in its own world, that wind, that cinema wind.

V

RAFAEL ALBERTI

Yo nací—¡respetadme!—con el cine.*
Alberti, *Cal y canto* (1926–7)

WHEN he declared imperiously in *Cal y canto*: 'Yo nací—
¡respetadme!—con el cine' (p. 242), Alberti proclaimed both a
chronological and spiritual kinship with the cinema; his
passionate delight in it connects the open-air cinema he celebrated in *Marinero en tierra,* in the poem 'Verano', and the
Cinema Goya, Madrid, where on 4 May 1929 he recited during
the sixth session of the Cineclub his poems in homage to Chaplin, Lloyd, and Keaton.[1] Grouped under the self-deprecatory
title *Yo era un tonto y lo que he visto me ha hecho dos tontos* (1929),
these and kindred poems may delude the unwary into thinking
that his attitude to the comic heroes he called 'angels of flesh and
blood' was as zany and frivolous as the antics of those who
caught his imagination and aroused his affection.[2] However,
there is a deep vein of seriousness underlying the verbal buf-
foonery of his poems; their latent gravity reflects Alberti's
growing disillusion and aggressiveness as he found in films
more than the melodramatic amusement provided by 'Ban-
doleros de smoking' ('Bandits in dinner-jackets') aiming pistols
at him in 'Carta abierta' (p. 241): visual confirmation of his
increasing hostility to the Catholic church, the middle class,
and the aristocracy. His espousal of communism and his iden-
tification with the proletariat explains the profound impact left
on him by *The Battleship Potemkin* in Bruges in 1932 and his
endorsement in it of what he called 'just violence and necessary
vengeance'; a year earlier he had advocated that 'the poets of
today' should be 'cruel, violent, demoniac, frightening'.[3] And
in his *elegía cívica Con los zapatos puestos tengo que morir* (1930)
Alberti orchestrated into a monologue of seething indignation

* I was born—respect me!—with the cinema.

invective against priests and compassion for workers menaced by pistols:

> Ayer no se sabía aún el rencor que las tejas y las
>   cornisas guardan hacia las flores,
> hacia las cabezas peladas de los curas sifilíticos,
> hacia los obreros que desconocen ese lugar donde las
>   pistolas se hastían aguardando la presión
> repentina de unos dedos.* [p. 334]

Pistols and bullets are no longer counters in a cinematic game of bluff, which he celebrated playfully in the poem 'Estación del Sur. M.Z.A.', from *Cal y canto*, in the parenthetic stage-direction '(Un tiro. ¡Muerto un brazo!)' ('(A shot. An arm falls limp!)') (p. 212). The brutal deaths at point-blank range filmed in *The Battleship Potemkin* aroused in him not playful amusement but rage and the desperate urge to see blood spilt in Spain in a similar rebellious fight for liberty; his recollections of Eisenstein's film are dominated by thoughts of death, gunshots, and blood and set within the context of the militant unrest harrowing the cities, particularly Seville, and the countryside of Andalusia in the early 1930s:

The Battleship Potemkin in Bruges! In other words, rebellion, a protest against lethargy and sleep, against the monotony and anguish of wearisome routine and prison cells; the exaltation of just violence and necessary vengeance; confusion, tumult, death at point-blank range, hatred, anger, all this and more in the most backwater city on earth.... And I had to remember Spain, its authentic, irreplaceable blood, dreaming now more than ever of leaping freely from its veins...

In Andalusia, and especially in its present distressing situation, the showing of this film of Eisenstein would have caused shots and deaths in the cinema. Not so in Bruges.[4]

In that film Alberti witnessed one bloody revolt against tyranny and injustice through the eyes of Eisenstein, who, as Alberti's wife, María Teresa León, recalled in her memoirs, accompanied them during their visit to Russia in 1934.[5] Alberti

---

* Yesterday nothing was yet known about the grudge the tiles and cornices hold against flowers, against the bald heads of syphilitic priests, against the workers who are ignorant of that place where pistols get weary awaiting the sudden pressure of some fingers.

observed at first hand the hideous effects of social neglect when he and his wife accompanied Buñuel to Las Hurdes, a neglected backwater of Extremadura, during the shooting of his film. 'Do you see this wonderful valley?' Buñuel asked them: 'Well, this is where hell begins.'[6] Buñuel occupies a special place in Alberti's reminiscences of the social and political ferment of the late 1920s and early 1930s. Alberti's vague recollection in 1961 that 'le surréalisme correspondait parfaitement à cet état de protestation et de révolte qui était celui d'Espagne' was qualified and illustrated by his precise comment that 'Le "Chien Andalou" traduit notre état d'esprit à l'époque.'[7] 'Protest' is a recurrent word in Alberti's memories of films, and connects his responses to *The Battleship Potemkin* and *Un chien andalou*; it reappears in his graphic account of the impact which Buñuel's film caused on the Cineclub audience on 8 December 1929:

Into these days and into this field of battle, which was by now a real and not a literary one, Luis Buñuel entered like a comet. He arrived from Paris, his head shaven, his face even stronger in features, his eyes rounder and more prominent. He came to exhibit his first film, made in collaboration with Salvador Dalí. It was one of the unforgettable sessions of the Cineclub, which was directed by its founder: Giménez Caballero, who was by then already vitiated. The film made a strong impression and many were disconcerted by and everyone shuddered in his seat at that image of the moon, split in two by a cloud, which was succeeded immediately by the shocking scene of the eye cut by a razor. When the audience, alarmed, then asked Buñuel for a few words of explanation, I recall that he, getting to his feet for a few moments, spoke more or less the following words from his box: 'The film is simply a desperate, a passionate summons to crime'. Luis Buñuel also was living his malaise, his violent protest, 'expressing—as Georges Sadoul says—all that surrealist "mal de siècle" in *Un chien andalou*, the image of a young generation thrown confusedly into convulsions.' That film was a significant revelation as it coincided with a Madrid in the grip of fever, quite near to important political events. That immense wind which shook us was aimed directly at a breach, through which so many of us would emerge with our consciences clear, no longer darkened by the shadows from the deep pit of darkness in which we had fallen during those preceding years. Through that same breach, after *Un chien andalou* and *L'Age d'or*—the two masterpieces of the surrealist cinema—Luis Buñuel would emerge into *Tierra sin pan*, his magnificent documentary on the wretched life of Las Hurdes, in the region of Extremadura ...[8]

To Buñuel—and, in a smaller degree, to Dalí—Alberti gave the credit for sensing and reflecting the fevered political atmosphere of Spain in the late 1920s; his enthusiastic tributes to Buñuel's 'violent protest' and 'magnificent documentary' reveal an unstinting admiration, which will remain a constant in his writings. He made a point of insisting that it was Buñuel who organized and made possible the showing in the Residencia de Estudiantes, Madrid, of Clair's *Entr'acte*, Dulac's *La Coquille et le Clergyman*, Cavalcanti's *Rien que les Heures*, and Epstein's *La Chute de la Maison Usher*.[9] Other films which he could still recall some thirty years later are: Dreyer's *La Passion de Jeanne d'Arc*, Lang's *Metropolis*, Chaplin's *The Gold Rush*, Pudovkin's *Mother*, and, 'above all', *The Battleship Potemkin*.[10] In the same nostalgic vein and with *Yo era un tonto* in mind, he recalled affectionately in his memoirs 'the great and adorable comics: Buster Keaton, Harry Langdon, and the minor ones: Stan Laurel, Oliver Hardy, Louise Fazenda, Larry Semon, Bebe Daniels, Charles Bowers, etc., all of them heroes of my budding book . . .'[11]

There is a precise connection between what Alberti saw in the films of Clair, Dulac, Cavalcanti, and Epstein and what he proposed to achieve in the poems of *Cal y canto*. What he witnessed on the screen, he said, was 'a parade of surprising images, a montage of unexpected and absurd metaphors very much in keeping with European poetry and plastic arts of those days (Tzara, Aragon, Eluard, Desnos, Péret, Max Ernst, Tanguy, Masson, etc.).'[12] A similarly rapid sequence of images containing a new vision of life was his goal in *Cal y canto*, where, according to his eloquent account, his ambition was to pursue

like a madman linguistic beauty, the most vibrant rhythmic effects, creating images that at times, in a single poem, would succeed one another with cinematographic speed, because the cinema, of all the inventions of modern life, was the one that especially captivated me, as I felt that with the cinema there had been born something that brought a new vision, a new feeling which in the long run would set a farewell course for the old world order already crumbling amid the ruins of the First World War.[13]

The dense texture of many poems of *Cal y canto* is the direct consequence of that pursuit of verbal beauty and a new vision. In *Marinero en tierra*, in 'Verano', Alberti had placed the conflict between reality and cinematic illusion in a poem modelled on those traditional songs in which a dialogue between a mother and her son or daughter permitted the neat exposition of a simple emotional problem:

> —Del cinema al aire libre
> vengo, madre, de mirar
> una mar mentida y cierta,
> que no es la mar y es la mar.

> —Al cinema al aire libre,
> hijo, nunca has de volver,
> que la mar en el cinema
> no es la mar y la mar es.*   [pp. 60–1]

That prohibition fell on deaf ears; in 'Carta abierta', from *Cal y canto*, the poet once more mentioned the forbidden cinema as he narrated his confused memories of Anne Boleyn pursued by one of the ubiquitous policemen of American comic films:

> ... Y el cine al aire libre. Ana Bolena,
> no sé por qué, de azul, va por la playa.
> Si el mar no la descubre, un policía
> la disuelve en la flor de su linterna.†   [p. 241]

The fictional mother who speaks in 'Verano' is the voice of an older generation, which we have already heard in the strictures of Unamuno. If Alberti ignored her warnings, he could not help but find in the films he saw visual proof of his own increasing awareness of violence and death, which underpins and over-shadows the verbal antics he deployed in the poems of *Yo era un tonto*. In 'Fuego', for example, the cinema is not on the surface of the poem advertising itself as its theme; rather are films behind this poem of *Cal y canto* as the unnamed suppliers of illustrations. As we shall see in 'Cita triste de Charlot' and 'Wallace Beery, bombero ...', Alberti was familiar with the tradition of the comic fireman; but his reference in the first poem to the 'luna de hollín de los bomberos' ('the firemen's

---

* Mother, I come from the open-air cinema where I watched a sea both false and real, which is not the sea and is the sea.

My son, you must never return to the open-air cinema, for the sea in the cinema is not the sea and yet is the sea.

† And the open-air cinema. Anne Boleyn, I don't know why, walks along the beach, dressed in blue. If the sea does not find her, a policeman dissolves her in the flower of his torch.

moon of soot') (p. 319) and his mention in the second of 'esta
catástrofe' (p. 330) suggest that he was more concerned with the
havoc caused by fires rather than with the laughs they could
provide. What 'Fuego' offers is the frightening spectacle of a
raging fire; we feel its intense heat and its destructive ferocity in
the impacted images which melt one into the other as the fire
consumes the towers and belfries with the inexorable ferocity
Alberti had seen filmed masterfully by Epstein in *La Chute de la
Maison Usher*. By selecting the ballad form for his narrative,
Alberti gave his theme—destruction by fire—a consistency and
rhythmic unity as relentless as the fire itself:

> Truncos, llagados, caídos,
> nieblas de bulto, los barrios
> hambrientos de gas y voces,
> flama las sombras, quemados.
>
> Gubias de metal hirviendo,
> rojos formones y clavos,
> contra los yunques partidos
> de las piedras, martillando.
>
> Astillas clavan las nubes,
> de acero en los campanarios,
> tumbadas torres y agujas,
> antorcha ya los espacios.
>
> Mar de azufre se abalanza,
> sin corazón, todo salto,
> turbio remolino ciego
> de verdes lenguas y rayos.
>
> El oleaje del humo,
> bronco, se encarama al arco,
> pórtico de hollín y yesca,
> torcido, del cielo raso.
>
> Y una tromba de ceniza,
> sepulta, negra, los barrios,
> huecos los ojos y planas
> las sombras ya apagadas.* [p. 219]

---

* With the shadows in flame and the houses like blocks of mist, the districts hungered
for gas and voices, broken and scarred, fallen and charred.

Gouges of boiling metal, red chisels and nails, hammering against the split anvils of
the stones.

The compacted nouns and phrases, the graphic details and
bold colouring, the dynamic verbs perpetuating their movement in the present tense, all make 'Fuego' into a poetic newsreel, in which Alberti puts before our eyes—as if he were a
cameraman—expanding metal, shooting sparks, falling débris,
licking flames, spiralling smoke, and cloaking ashes. 'Fuego'
suggests that films did not merely furnish what Alberti termed
'a new vision', but encouraged him to take a fresh look at
commonplace events, to see things in a new light. Alberti thus
paid tribute to the cinema for increasing his and everyone else's
frame of visual references, for enriching the mind with new sets
of pictures and scenes as colourful and as varied as the paintings
he contemplated and copied in the Prado. His memory could
now flick through scenes and pictures, which are as neatly filed
and rectangular as images on a cinema screen; as the following
questions from 'Invierno postal', in *Cal y canto*, demonstrate,
Alberti represented his recollections as postcards he had seen in
a cinema or as line drawings he had seen in an album:

> ¿Dónde os vi yo, nostálgicas postales?
> ¿En qué cine playero al aire libre
> o en qué álbum de buques lineales?*   [p. 214]

In 'Carta abierta' Alberti repeated himself, as if he could not
believe what he was actually writing; his explanation—directed
more at himself than at anyone else—'Y es que el mundo es un
álbum de postales' ('It so happens that the world is an album of
postcards') (p. 242)—reveals his wonder at and delight in visual
stimuli, which, whether they were the paintings of the masters
in the Prado, the canvases of Maruja Mallo or scenes from a
film, make his poetry into as intensely pictorial an experience as
the albums he mentioned. We can identify and visualize every

Splinters nail the clouds, which are of steel, in the belfries, fallen towers and spires,
all space is now flaming torches.

A sulphur sea surges forward, heartless and turbulent, a turbid blind whirlwind of
lightning and green tongues.

The waves of smoke climb crudely up the arch, a twisted doorway of soot and tinder
to the flat heavens above.

And a spout of ashes buries the districts in black, the eyes all hollow and the stunted
shadows all extinguished.

* Where did I see you, nostalgic postcards? In which open-air sea-side cinema, or in
which album of drawings of boats?

element in the following scene of 'Expedición', from *Sobre los ángeles*, even though we can only guess at his reasons for devising it:

> La guitarra en la niebla sepultaba a una rosa.
> La herradura a una hoja seca.*   [p. 284]

Alberti stressed the interdependence of words and pictures when he stated in 1961:

Je suis un poète visuel, comme tous les poètes andalous, depuis Góngora jusqu'à García Lorca. Ma poésie est une poésie plastique. J'aime beaucoup préciser le contour des choses . . . Je crois que chez moi le poète est un prolongement du peintre, que le peintre aide le poète.[14]

This intimate collaboration of painter and poet was an ideal Alberti partially realized in 1929, when *La Gaceta Literaria* published some of the poems that were to be included in *Yo era un tonto* with drawings by Maruja Mallo. As Alberti did not realize his aim, announced in 1934, of publishing *Yo era un tonto* 'with drawings by María Mallo', we have to deem that liaison of poem and drawing as a trial marriage whose termination no doubt delighted Juan Ramón Jiménez.[15] Probably alluding to the drawings of Mallo that accompanied Alberti's poems to the comics, Jiménez censured Alberti in 1931 for being 'lamentably separated from his own beautiful natural being by the flabby green transfers of María Mallo and the brush of Salvador Dalí . . .'[16]

The conjunction of Alberti's poems and Mallo's drawings points to a common fount of enthusiasm and does nothing to illuminate for us the process by which the poet, alone and with a pen in his hand, strove to transpose the visual stimuli of films into words. His poetry indicates that he utilized the films he saw as an 'album of postcards', and it is an intriguing challenge to relate scenes depicted in a number of his poems to images or sequences he observed on the screen. In *Sobre los ángeles*, the curtains that are blown horizontal and catch fire in 'El alma en pena' record a tense, sinister scene from *La Chute de la Maison Usher*. The unnaturally large eyes which haunt and attack the poet in 'Los ángeles sonámbulos' are as menacing as the huge eyes which, arranged in a montage, look into the camera in

---

* In the mist the guitar buried a rose. The horseshoe buried a dry leaf.

Lang's *Metropolis*. In *Sermones y moradas* Alberti's hideous statement—'Sangran ojos de mulos cruzados de escalofríos' ('Mules' eyes bleed traversed by shudders') (p. 303)—puts us in mind of the suppurating eyes of the two dead donkeys Buñuel placed on a grand piano in *Un chien andalou*.

In *Sobre los ángeles* films also left their mark in other ways: in the use of technical terms in 'Los ángeles de las ruinas', where he declared: 'La cal viva es el fondo que mueve la proyección de los muertos' ('Quicklime is the backcloth moved by the projection of the dead') (p. 290); in the use of the flashback in 'Muerte y juicio', where the pretence of Alberti the child 'judging himself' generated a chronological flow of memories; in the panoramic sweep of 'Los ángeles muertos', in which Alberti ranged like Epstein's camera over scenes of decay and dereliction:

> Porque yo los he visto:
> en esos escombros momentáneos que aparecen en las
>   neblinas.
> Porque yo los he tocado:
> en el destierro de un ladrillo difunto,
> venido a la nada desde una torre o un carro.
> Nunca más allá de las chimeneas que se derrumban
> ni de esas hojas tenaces que se estampan en los
>   zapatos.*   [p. 291]

The 'mano enguantada' ('gloved hand') which he inserted into the last poem of *Sobre los ángeles*, 'El ángel superviviente', is an ostensibly melodramatic detail which, although now ominous in the context of his personal crises and disasters, harks back nostalgically to several poems of *Cal y canto*; it recalls wistfully and elegiacally those poems in which films of adventure and suspense left their memories of instantaneous and infantile shoot-outs in Alberti's mocking but unmalicious mentions of '(Un tiro. ¡Muerto un brazo!)' ('(A shot. An arm falls limp!)') (p. 212) and 'Sangre y tiros. / Sangre' ('Blood and gunshots. Blood') (p. 234). And when he affirmed in 'Telegrama' that 'Nick Carter understands nothing', he deflated the detective

---

* Because I have seen them: in those momentary ruins which appear in the mists. Because I have touched them: in the exile of a dead brick, fallen into the void from a tower or a cart. Never further than the collapsing chimneys or than those stubborn leaves which stick to one's shoes.

hero of millions of readers;[17] the successful sleuth is baffled by the nightmare world of New York, where triangles leave the blackboards recalled by Alberti in 'El ángel de los números' in order to assassinate bus conductors, who are made of tin:

> Nueva York.
> Un triángulo escaleno
> asesina a un cobrador.
>
> El cobrador, de hojalata.
> Y el triángulo, de prisa,
> otra vez a su pizarra.
>
> Nick Carter no entiende nada.
>
> ¡Oh!
> Nueva York.*   [p. 232]

New York was again in his mind in 'Carta abierta', where he undertook a simple analysis of a mind unfettered and bewildered at the same time by the restless geography of films, which in a kind of hallucination placed New York in Spain and situated Seville in three different countries:

> Nueva York está en Cádiz o en el Puerto.
> Sevilla está en París, Islandia o Persia.
> Un chino no es un chino. Un transeúnte
> puede ser blanco al par que verde y negro.†   [p. 241]

Although films appear to draw the world together, a cool, balanced mind such as Alberti's recognized that this geographic kaleidoscope is an illusion, that he has not moved from the cinema, that people are not what they appear to be. His avowal 'A Chinaman is not a Chinaman' reveals his awareness that the cinema, in fostering illusions, relies on a series of tricks and falsehoods; and those falsehoods were baldly announced by the bell-boy as products of the cinema when his lift stopped on the fourth floor of its ascent heavenwards in 'Venus en ascensor (Cielos: 1,2,3,4,5,6,7)':

* New York. A scalene triangle murders a bus conductor.
The conductor, made of tin. And the triangle leaps back to its blackboard.
Nick Carter understands nothing.
Oh! New York.

† New York is in Cadiz or in Puerto de Santa María. Seville is in Paris, Iceland or Persia. A Chinaman is not a Chinaman. A passer-by can just as well be white as green and black.

CUARTO: Cinema. Noticiario. Artificio. Mentira.*[p. 229]
And Alberti continued to illustrate that clash of reality and
illusion, apparent in the juxtaposition of newsreels and artifice,
by visualizing on the screen erected on the fourth floor Ceres, a
deity of the earth and fertile nature, pressing on Bacchus a
job-lot of tailor's dummies:

> En la pantalla anunciadora, Ceres
> instantánea, embustera,
> imprime a Baco un saldo de mujeres de alcanfor
> y de cera.†

These waxen women preserved in camphor are part of the
artifice Alberti saw—and poeticized—in the cinema; his vision
and his manner may be bizarre, but his recognition of trickery
was as honest and sensitive as his refusal to see nothing more
than horseplay in the films of Chaplin, Keaton, Langdon, and
Semon. In the poems of *Yo era un tonto* Alberti created his own
illusions: what appears to be verbal clowning overlays a gravity
of purpose and feeling which connects the work intimately with
Sobre los ángeles. The poems that he read during the sixth
session of the Cineclub on 4 May 1929 to Chaplin, Lloyd, and
Keaton demonstrate that the films of those comics, far from
acting on his mind as the 'brainsuckers' diagnosed by Giménez
Caballero, stimulated his imagination and sensibility to such a
degree that he succeeded in writing a genre of poems so challengingly novel that few works of Alberti have suffered as much
as *Yo era un tonto* the neglect of critics. However generous was
Juan Piqueras's admiration for the three poems that Alberti
read during what that critic called 'the first cinematographic
anthology of comedy', they none the less produced in his mind a
kind of shock which allowed him only to value 'firstly, an
extensive poetic sensibility, and secondly, a wonderful
individual capacity for interpretation, an exact and revealing
definition of which requires the invention of a new adjective'.[18]

The novelty of the poems of *Yo era un tonto* is undeniable, but
to exaggerate it brings the risk of understating themes and
emotions bridging *Sobre los ángeles* and *Yo era un tonto*, which, as
Alberti has reminded us, was 'also a product of the same malaise

---

* FOURTH FLOOR: Cinema. Newsreel. Artifice. Falsehoods.
† On the informative screen, a fleeting and mendacious Ceres presses on Bacchus a
job-lot of women made of camphor and wax.

and anarchy of that stage in my life'.[19] One critic—C. A. Pérez—has heeded Alberti's words, insisting rightly that 'the poems of *Yo era un tonto* occupy a coherent place in the poet's work' and affirming that in this work 'it is possible to see the anguish of the Alberti of *Sobre los ángeles*'.[20]Although comic films offered him a series of visual stimuli totally different from the preponderantly literary sustenance of *Sobre los ángeles*, Alberti could not but view and interpret them with the same sadness and disillusion. By remembering Chaplin's pathetic wait for Georgia on New Year's Eve in *The Gold Rush*, he expressed in the first poem of his collection, 'Cita triste de Charlot', the solitude and melancholy which he associated with his own childhood in 'Noticiario de un colegial melancólico', where his declension of 'snow' creates a sense of dreary routine which solemnifies such elegiac poems of *Sobre los ángeles* as 'El ángel de los números' and 'Los ángeles colegiales'. In *Yo era un tonto* death weighed as heavily on Alberti as in *Sobre los ángeles* and *Sermones y moradas*. The question he asked in 'En el día de su muerte a mano armada'—'¿Quién ha muerto?' ('Who has died?') (p. 324)—was answered by Larry Semon in his 'tele-gram' with the bleak—and accurate—report: 'También yo he muerto' ('I too have died') (p. 328).

In spite of being nurtured by comic films, *Yo era un tonto* is really 'A very sad book', as Juan-José Domenchina recognized in 1935, and if Alberti laughed in these poems, his laughter was hard, bitter, and sardonic.[21] He even turned his acrid humour against himself when, parodying newspaper headlines, he gave to one poem a bogusly objective title: 'A Rafael Alberti le preocupa mucho ese perro que casualmente hace su pequeña necesidad contra la luna'. Far from worrying about what the dog does, the poet was serenely unconcerned about its urinating against somewhere as romantically hackneyed as the moon. In Alberti's eyes, neither the moon nor flowers can remain fresh and intact; the ingenuous statement he attributed to Harry Langdon—

> no hay nada tan bonito como un ramo de flores
> cuando la cabra ha olvidado en él sus negras bolitas—*
>
> [p. 324]

---

* There is nothing as pretty as a bunch of flowers when the goat has left on it its little black droppings.

reveals his sober conviction, which he also expressed in 'Los ángeles feos', that the beautiful and the ugly, the fragrant and the foul-smelling, can no longer be easily separated or distinguished. In the juxtapositions of 'luna-pequeña necesidad' and 'flores-negras bolitas' he created a clash of tones and associations which he redoubled in 'Five o'clock tea' in his conjunction of 'merde-madame'. As a renegade bourgeois, Alberti condemned the middle class and the aristocracy to extinction with a truculence all the more mordant for being expressed in the French phrases with which they affectedly pepper their idle conversations:

> El aire está demasiado puro para mandaros a la merde.
> Y yo, madame, demasiado aburrido.
> > > Adieu.*

The duchesses and countesses whom Alberti satirized in 'Five o'clock tea' and 'Falso homenaje a Adolphe Menjou' demonstrate that if he saw comics on the cinema screen, he found even bigger fools in real life, and particularly in smart society. There are many buffoons in *Yo era un tonto*, and in order to extol those who were comics by genius and profession and to expose those who were fools by virtue of their pretensions and social status, the poet resorted to that vein of waggishness, of verbal clowning, which runs in his poetry from his first work, *Marinero en tierra*. Referring to the title that Alberti chose for his collection, José Bergamín observed aptly in 1929 that 'Out of this quotation from Calderón ... the poet Rafael Alberti has extracted a new form of jest, half lyrical and half comical, clearly poetic in appearance.'[22] In *Marinero en tierra*, *El alba del alhelí*, and *Cal y canto* Alberti had placed himself firmly in the tradition of literary games which encompasses the *letrillas* of Góngora, the *jácaras* of Quevedo and the *greguerías* of Gómez de la Serna; he thus gave a new dimension to humour in Spanish literature by translating into poetry the spirit as well as the substance and personalities of comic films.

Before writing the poems collected in *Yo era un tonto*, Alberti was mentally conditioned and poetically trained to formulate a rhetoric of absurdity; so much is clear from the incoherent sounds which compose *La pájara pinta* (1925), from the acceler-

---

* The air is too pure to commit you *à la merde*. And I, madam, am too bored. Adieu.

ated verbal games of 'Dondiego sin don', in *Marinero en tierra*, and from 'El Niño de la Palma', included in *El alba del alhelí*, where the alliterations, the rhymes, and the dancing rhythm capture the lithe grace and dexterity of the bullfighter:

> ¡Qué revuelo!
> ¡Aire, que al toro torillo
> le pica el pájaro pillo
> que no pone el pie en el suelo!
> ¡Qué revuelo!* [p. 178]

Even before he had chosen his abrasive, self-deprecatory title, Alberti had revealed his fondness for the word *tonto*, especially in *El alba del alhelí*, where the refrain '¡Qué tonto!' ('What a fool!') resounding in 'El pescador sin dinero', is reinforced by another refrain the poet turned against himself in 'El tonto de Rafael':

> ¿Quién aquél?
> ¡El tonto de Rafael!† [p. 180]

With this 'autorretrato burlesco' Alberti deflated the myth of the poet as a divine seer, as a heavenly being; those who seek in 'El tonto de Rafael' evidence to substantiate Rubén Darío's vision of the poet in *Cantos de vida y esperanza* as a 'celeste pararrayos' ('celestial lightning-conductor') will find only a series of graphic and melodious insults representing 'that fool Rafael' as penniless, hairless, and featherless:

> Tonto llovido del cielo,
> del limbo, sin un ochavo.
> Mal pollito colipavo,
> sin plumas, digo, sin pelo.‡ [p. 180]

Although he directed such jibes against himself, they could not fail to provoke some responses in his readers, one of whom took Alberti at his word. As Alberti openly called himself a fool, he could hardly have been surprised at the verbal joke played on him in 1928 by an anonymous versifier under the exact title '¡El tonto de Rafael!', or at the caustic endorsement of Juan Ramón

---

* What pirouettes, for the mischievous bird whose foot does not touch the ground pecks at the little bull. What pirouettes!

† Who is that fellow? That fool Rafael!

‡ A fool washed down from heaven, from limbo, without a cent. A naughty turkey-tailed chick, without a feather, I say, without a hair.

Jiménez, who took the trouble to write the following gratuitously offensive remarks to Alberti:

> For a year you have been telling us in *La Gaceta Literaria* that you
> are a fool. I thought that, as you were so pleased and proud of your
> discovery, you would enjoy my saying the same thing to you.
> In any case you write that you are a fool. I have the right to believe it
> and to repeat it. Don't you agree?[23]

Towards the end of the 1920s Alberti certainly went out of his
way to goad and offend people, and casualties of his shock
tactics were those members of the Lyceum Club Feminino who
were outraged by the lecture he gave there on 10 November
1929 under the title 'Paloma y galápago (¡No más artríticos!)'.
In February of the same year Ramón Gómez de la Serna had
delivered a lecture to the Cineclub dressed 'as a coon'.[24]
Alberti's garb was even more outrageous as he implemented his
watchword of 'merde-madame' in a haven of feminine elegance, where, according to a sardonic newspaper report, 'One
walks softly. One talks as if in church. Good tone. Elegant
women. Wafts of perfume.'[25] José Díaz Fernández was equally
ironic about the Lyceum Club Feminino in his novel *La Venus
mecánica* (1929), where he remarked pungently that 'The independence of those ladies consisted of reclining nonchalantly on
divans, smoking Egyptian cigarettes, and devising artistic
events which could be attended by members of the opposite
sex.'[26]

Alberti's lecture could hardly be classed as an 'artistic event'.
Had those 'elegant women' had any idea of what he was to say
and how he was to say it, it is more than likely that they would
not have opened the door to him. Unlike Ernestina de Cham-
pourcin, who retained 'the impression of a most lively and
entertaining hour in harmony with the mood of our time',
'Señora de X' unwittingly identified one of the models for
Alberti's behaviour when she branded him as 'a bullring Chaplin'.[27] 'Venus en ascensor', from *Cal y canto*, shows to what
extent incongruous garb and ridiculous appearances fascinated
Alberti; his Eros, with 'toga, monóculo y birrete' ('gown,
monocle and biretta') and his Narcissus, dressed in 'ligas verdes
y pechos de goma' ('green garters and rubber breasts'), offer
examples of grotesque refurbishing which he emulated in deed

when he appeared at the Lyceum Club, according to one reporter, 'stuffed into an enormous frock-coat, with trousers which
fell around his shoes like bellows, and a starched collar fit for a
circus clown'.[28]

Those ladies who, like 'Señora de X', were incensed by the
poet's garb, or were alarmed by the six revolver shots with
which he ended his talk, did not realize that both his rag-bag
uniform and his gun derived from comics and their films, and
that Alberti, by utilizing two of their features, was also repro-
ducing some of their spirit. Their indignation may have
mellowed had they recognized in Alberti's outfit the bowler hat
sported by Chaplin and Semon, the stiff collars worn by Laurel
and Hardy or the baggy trousers so proudly acquired by Langdon in *Long Pants*. It is hardly surprising that Alberti should
model himself on his favourite comics when he set out to
buttress the poems of *Yo era un tonto*, as he has reminded us,
'With elements from the films of Chaplin, Buster Keaton,
Harold Lloyd, and other minor comics'.[29] The reader does not
have to go beyond the title of his poem to Keaton to recognize in
the 'verdadera vaca' mentioned in it the cow—Brown Eyes
—with which Keaton fell in love in *Go West*, which was known
in Spain as *El rey de los cowboys* and, more pointedly, *Mi vaca y
yo*. And the Langdon who appears 'acatarrado' ('with a cold') in
one poem (p. 328) and with a cough in another[30] is the ailing,
snuffling comic whom Alberti had seen in *The Strong Man*,
where his attempt to pour a dose of cough mixture onto a spoon
in a moving bus led to his sneezing it over his neighbour.

As we saw in the previous chapter, most of the poems extolling cinema stars were written in Spain in the 1930s; few match
Alberti's psychological acuteness or imaginative vitality. To
perceive the originality of his poems, one has only to set them
alongside the banal but affected homage to Greta Garbo penned
in 1933 by one M.G.:

> Enigma espiritual
> el de tus ojos. Tu boca
> en pasión se vuelve loca
> de la locura carnal,
> y a lo que quiera que toca
> deja la lumbre infernal.
> Te miro en la proyección

y no llego a comprender
si es verdad o si es ficción
tu arte. A mi entender
eso lo puede saber
tan solo tu corazón.*[31]

In contrast with this bland acceptance of Garbo's 'enigma', Alberti's reactions to the comics and to those who—like Menjou—were not regarded as such were intensely personal and deeply felt. He was not content to see an actor from the outside, or merely to evoke in his poems films and episodes he found memorable. Boldly and imaginatively he faced the difficult task, after leaving the cinema, of finding a style, a verbal code, that would capture in words the tics, mannerisms, and personality of each comic. So sensitively and accurately did he accentuate the distinctiveness of each actor that *Yo era un tonto* can be read, in the words of an early critic of the cinema, as 'une sorte de plan psychologique, une série "d'états" et "de moments"'.[32] It was an inner compulsion as well as a gesture that Alberti recorded when he made Chaplin recite:

> Mi sombrero, mis puños,
> mis guantes, mis zapatos,†   [p. 320]

for in this ritual checking of his clothes we sense a fussy correctitude at odds with his ragged appearance. In *The Idle Class* (1921) Chaplin had exploited the comic potential of a similar contrast between gesture and dress when, acting as a rich, befuddled drunk, he made a deft two-handed check of his breast pockets—and left his hotel room without his trousers. Whereas Alberti used a technique as artless as enumeration to stress the fastidiousness of Chaplin, he resorted to another simple trick—the transposition of words—to capture the dynamic acrobatics of Larry Semon. Juggling three words to change 'Angelito constipado cielo' into 'Cielo constipado angelito' and then 'Angelito cielo constipado', Alberti invited us to visualize Semon darting impulsively from place to place like an uncoiling spring; his rapid hurdling of physical obstacles is neatly

---

* A spiritual enigma is that of your eyes. Your mouth when in the grip of passion becomes mad with carnal madness, and leaves its hellish light on whatever it touches. I watch you when you are projected on the screen and I do not discover whether your art is truth or fiction. In my view, that is something only your heart can know.

† My hat, my cuffs, my gloves, my shoes.

suggested in the almost total suppression of conjunctions and prepositions, which creates a staccato rhythm in harmony with Semon's jerky movements:

> Angelito constipado cielo.
> Pienso alas moscas horrorizado
> y en dolor tiernas orejitas alondras campos.*   [p. 328]

As a lover of films, Alberti detected and admired the individuality of each comic; as a poet, he respected it and tried to document it by enabling them to do in his poems what they could not do in the films in which they made their names: talk. Alberti's psychological insight into the actors whom he singled out was so profound that he convinces us that Chaplin, Lloyd, and Langdon would have talked in their films as they do in his poems. In the case of 'Charles Bower, inventor', the poem that confirms and illustrates his choice of Charley Bowers as 'one of my favourite comics' denies us the comforting experience of identifying in a series of words and images a comic we knew first through his actions and antics on the screen.[33] Alberti's inclusion of Bowers among his 'angels of flesh and blood' further advertises a familiarity with that comic baffling to those who wish to find some trace left by his films in Spain. Maruja Mallo's reticence about her liaison with Alberti makes it impossible to determine whether her drawing 'Charles Bower, inventor' was inspired by Alberti's poem or by films they saw together. Bowers's career as writer, actor, and director was so short and obscure that only scanty evidence allows us to conjecture why he appealed so strongly to Alberti. Summaries of his films lodged with the Library of Congress, Washington, enable us to interpret a number of lines of 'Charles Bower, inventor' as reminiscences of specific episodes. To start with, the title of the poem commemorates Bowers's role as inventor in *Egged on* (1926) and *A Wild Roomer* (1926); the 'Huevos irrompibles' ('unbreakable eggs') mentioned by the poet in line 26 mocks the comic's ambition in *Egged On* to invent a machine that would render eggs unbreakable. Bowers's compulsive tinkering with machines was also celebrated by Alberti when he listed three components of the comic's inventions and made a precise

---

* Little angel with a cold heaven. I think wings flies horrified and in pain tender little ears larks fields.

reference to the mechanical house-maid he devised in *A Wild Roomer*. The quaint allusion to 'dying at the hands of a sardine' evokes the rage evinced by Charley's uncle, who, having been dumped in the river by his nephew's contraption, returns to hit Charley with a fish:

> Aisladores,
> latones viejos y muelles rotos de las camas.
> Y tantísimos otros quebraderos científicos, Odette mía,
> para morir airadamente a manos de una sardina.*

However intriguing such detective work may be, it does not tell us who Odette is, and we have to turn to a press sheet promoting Bowers's film *There It Is* (1928) to find a possible explanation: that the comic's mother was a French countess. Nor does our sleuthing help the poem to come alive, or to transcend its sources, or to make it into anything other than a private, cryptic tribute to a comic whose inventiveness and technical ingenuity survive only in contemporary advertisements of 'The World Famous Bowers Process'.[34] Alberti's poem is as much an elegy as a tribute to Bowers, and in making the comic take his leave of us with the epitaph 'Difunto inventor' ('Defunct inventor'), Alberti mourned not the death of Bowers, which took place in 1946, but his professional demise: after 1928 he abruptly disappeared from all advertisements put out by Educational Films, which in January 1928 of that year had biled him as 'The "Wizard" Putting Mysterious Fun Tricks into *Bowers Comedies*'.[35] Although the elusiveness of Bowers's films deprives us of a visual point of reference and so condemns Alberti's poem to being a dated document rather than a self-contained poem, the poet's obvious compassion for a creator whose mechanical wizardry could not protect him from the vagaries of public demand reveals his melancholy suspicion that poet and film-maker will share a common fate. In making the comic say:

> Madame,
> voici la poésie:
> serrín,†

---

* Isolators, old tins and broken bed-springs. And so many more scientific puzzles, my dear Odette, to die angrily at the hands of a sardine.

† Madam, voici la poésie: sawdust.

Alberti suggested bitterly that the craft of poetry is no more authentic and no more durable than the tricks of Charley the Inventor, and that his poetry in particular will be victim of the neglect so abruptly suffered by Bowers after 1928.

However remote we may feel from the visual and emotional experiences that nurtured and shaped 'Charles Bower, inventor', a dramatic phrase such as 'voici la poésie' presupposes a gesture; and that sweep of the hand qualifies the poem for inclusion among the genre of *poemas representables* Alberti devised out of words he thought the comics would say vivified by gestures which they actually made. This hybrid genre continued to fascinate him; as he stated in 1962, he wrote his *Poemas escénicos* 'To be acted soberly, without a hint of declamation, either by an actor or actress'.[36] The poem of *Yo era un tonto* that could be dramatized most easily and most effectively is the one Alberti devoted to Buster Keaton. Taking as the starting-point of his poem the love which the lonely Keaton felt for the cow Brown Eyes, he composed a monologue in which the playful sound effects do not distract us from realizing that the comic does not find 'a su novia, que es una verdadera vaca' ('his sweetheart, who is a real cow'). It is Buster's puzzlement that dominates the opening lines of the poem, where we follow not only his finger as he counts four footprints, but the slow working of his mind as he ponders with child-like deliberateness—suggested by the earnest repetition and echoing assonance of 'cuatro-zapatos-zapatos-pato'—about who could have left those footprints:

> 1, 2, 3 y 4.
> En estas cuatro huellas no caben mis zapatos.
> Si en estas cuatro huellas no caben mis zapatos,
> ¿de quién son estas cuatro huellas?
> ¿De un tiburón,
>   de un elefante recién nacido o de un pato?
> ¿De una pulga o de una codorniz?*   [p. 322]

In the closing lines of the poem Buster acknowledges that these footprints belong to 'a sweet child' or to 'a real cow', as if there were no difference between them, and as he swings between the

---

* 1, 2, 3, and 4. My shoes do not fit in these footprints. If my shoes do not fit in these footprints, to whom do these footprints belong? To a shark, to a new-born elephant or a duck? To a flea or a quail?

two possibilities the poet accelerates the oscillating rhythm until they fuse in the comic's mind into what they were in the film *Go West*: a companion in his solitude. After all, we must remember that at the end of the film when the rancher, in gratitude for having his herd and livelihood saved, says to Buster: 'Everything I have is yours', Buster chooses Brown Eyes and not the rancher's daughter as his reward. It is these alternatives that the comic weighs in these vacillating lines:

¿Eres una dulce niña o eres una verdadera vaca?
Mi corazón siempre me dijo que eras una verdadera vaca.
Tu papá, que eras una dulce niña.
Mi corazón, que eras una verdadera vaca.
Una dulce niña.
Una verdadera vaca.
Una niña.
Una vaca.
¿Una niña o una vaca?
O ¿una niña y una vaca?
Yo nunca supe nada.*   [p. 323]

Although Alberti parodied hackneyed sentimental endings of boy marries girl by making Keaton seek happiness with a cow and not with a woman, Buster remains alone in Alberti's poem and ensures his solitude with a shot from a gun. '(¡Pum!)' is the most menacing sound heard in the poem. By accompanying the comic's words with the chirping of birds and the crowing of cocks, Alberti utilized such parenthetic effects as '(Pi, pi, pi, pi.)' and '(Cri, cri, cri, cri.)' to enliven his poem and give it the candour and phonic richness of children's stories. And he did not miss the chance of mocking with such parentheses the subtitles of silent films; the pathetic exclamation which Chaplin inserted as a subtitle in *The Gold Rush*—'Georgia! GEORGIA!! GEORGIA!!!'—is amplified and distorted in the desperate shouts uttered by Keaton, which increase in intensity from '¡Georginaaaaaaaa!' to '¡Georginaaaaaaaaaaaaaaaaaa!'

As a poet Alberti could transcend the limitations of a subtitle; he had the freedom to imagine what the comics could say if they

---

* Are you a sweet child or are you a real cow? My heart always told me that you were a real cow. Your daddy, that you were a sweet girl. My heart, that you were a real cow. A sweet child. A real cow. A child. A cow. A child and a cow? Or a child and a cow? I never got to know.

could express themselves with words instead of through mime. His skill as a 'painter-poet' enabled him to describe, when he chose to, the dominant physical trait of an actor, be it the simulated plainness of Louise Fazenda or the authentic ugliness of Ben Turpin. By describing the former as a 'marimacho' ('virago') in his 'Telegrama de Luisa Fazenda a Bebe Daniels y Harold Lloyd' (p. 325), the poet reminded us that Louise Fazenda, by the roles she chose and the clothes she wore, was consciously unfeminine; in *Tillie's Punctured Romance* (1928), for example, she appeared dressed as a soldier. By attributing to her the disturbing intention—'pienso parir burro delicado y feo niño' ('I intend to give birth to a delicate donkey and ugly child') (p. 326)—he evoked her frequent role as graceless farm-girl in such films as *Down on the Farm* (1920). In the same way, Alberti invited those who remember only the crossed eyes of Ben Turpin to also bring to mind his pursed lips with the slightly coarse question he posed in 'Carta de Maruja Mallo a Ben Turpin':

> ¿Alguna vez el culito de un pollo te besó, como
> sin querer, la boca?*

These strokes of a caricaturist do summarize the dominant feature of an actor's appearance. However, Alberti brought a more searching gift to his poetic tributes: the ability to do with each comic what he did with himself in *Sobre los ángeles*: penetrate his personality, analyse it, and translate it into poetry. Alberti realized what the comics themselves came to recognize in the 1920s: that they needed a distinctive manner, an instantly identifiable personality. As the screen personalities and styles of Langdon, Lloyd, and Laurel and Hardy are totally different, different will be the poems Alberti devoted to them. In 'Harry Langdon hace por primera vez el amor a una niña', the poet stressed the innocence and mental slowness of Langdon, which were expressed visually and physically in his films by his rapid blinking of his wide eyes, his blank gaze, his hesitant waves of his hand, and, above all, by his white and stony face, which Luis Gómez Mesa described graphically in 1932 as a 'motionless face—the face of a simpleton, of a ninny, of a clock without hands'.[37] Apart from making him confess that 'soy un niño muy desgraciado' ('I am a very unfortunate child'), who rips his

---

* Was your mouth once kissed, as if unintentionally, by a chicken's bum?

trousers as carelessly as a small boy, Alberti made him reason like a child whose vision of the world, limited by his simplemindedness, is deformed by the effects of love. So ponderous is the working of his puny brain, and so insecure does he feel, that, after convincing himself of a truth, he lets himself be assailed immediately by doubts:

> Verdaderamente
> no hay nada tan bonito como un ramo de flores
> cuando la cabra ha olvidado en él sus negras bolitas.
> ¿Me habré dado yo cuenta de que no hay nada tan
>   bonito como un ramo de flores
> y sobre todo si la cabra ha olvidado en él una
>   o más bolitas?*

[p. 324]

By using in 'bolitas de cabra' a diminutive as infantile as the 'angelitos' and 'pajaritos' the poet also put into his mouth, Langdon not only talks like a child who hears his mother say 'caquita', but reveals in his ingenuous linking of flowers and excrement his inability to distinguish between beautiful and ugly, good and bad, secure and dangerous. As Vicente Huidobro perceptively pointed out in 1928, Langdon 'strolls through danger as if through a field of flowers'.[38] Alberti realized that Langdon, with the blindness of innocence, did not seek or see dangers. With equal acumen he knew that Laurel and Hardy caused disasters and mayhem by stupidity and gaucheness. The minimal intelligence of this pair did not allow them to achieve anything they set out to do, whether it was selling Christmas trees in *Big Business* (1929) or waiting patiently in a traffic jam in *Two Tars* (1928). From the banana skin which sets in motion the frantic salvoes of cream tarts in *The Battle of the Century* (1927) to the line of ravaged automobiles in *Two Tars*, there is always in their films a gulf between cause and effect whose poles are recorded by Alberti in the discursive title he chose for his poem: 'Stan Laurel y Oliver Hardy rompen sin ganas 75 o 76 automóviles y luego afirman que de todo tuvo la culpa una cáscara de plátano'.

Oliver Hardy recalled in 1954 that 'These two fellows we created, they are nice, very nice people. They never get anywhere because they are both so very dumb but they don't *know*

---

* Truly there is nothing as pretty as a bunch of flowers when the goat has left on it its little black droppings. Have I really understood that there is nothing as pretty as a bunch of flowers and especially if the goat has left on it its little black droppings?

that they're dumb.'[39] What Alberti saw was that the peculiar stupidity of the one exacerbated and complemented the distinctive doltishness of the other. The arrogant, old-world gentility of Ollie appears in all its hollowness beside the weak-kneed and tearful cowardice of Stan. Alberti respected the inseparability of the two comics in his poem, whose rhythm and texture capture faithfully the mannerisms of a twosome who, according to a Spanish critic, were 'two robots who unconsciously move when one of them wills it'.[40] They interlock in the poem as inextricably as they do in their films; as the poem is a duet, the reader has to decipher their parts in order to decide which of the two is speaking, that is, when the poet let one of them speak alone. By exaggerating at the same time the presumptuousness of Ollie and the sentimentality of Stan, Alberti composed in the central section of his poem a duet which dramatizes, as it duplicates the oscillating rhythm of 'vaca-niña', the oafishness so successfully and convincingly simulated by Laurel and Hardy:

Me parece que voy a tener que llorar.

....

NOS PARECE QUE VAMOS A TENER QUE LLORAR

....

Me parece que se nos han pasado las ganas de merendar,
de llorar,
de merendar,
de llorar y merendar
o de merendar y llorar.
NOS PARECE QUE YA NO VAMOS A TENER NUNCA GANAS DE
LLORAR NI DE MERENDAR.*   [p. 329]

Alberti's skill at devising a technique and selecting material to express the personality of each comic led him to penetrate the comic mask of Harold Lloyd, composed of 'his perennial dentifrice smile', according to the picturesque phrase of Rosa Chacel, and by his tortoise-shell spectacles, which another critic has categorized no less tartly as 'the starting point of Lloyd's success and style' and 'also the ending point—the limit to his imagination'.[41] Alberti's poem is animated by the single-minded

* I think I am going to have to cry. We think we are going to have to cry. I think that we no longer feel like eating, crying, eating, crying and eating or eating and crying. We think that we shall never again feel like crying and eating.

ambition which propelled Lloyd through the films he made after abandoning the roles of Willie Work and Lonesome Luke in order to adopt that of the bespectacled go-getter: the overweening ambition to be accepted and admired. Alberti interpreted this urge to show off in 'Harold Lloyd, estudiante', in which the comic, taking very seriously the role of student he played in *The Freshman* (1925), strives to display his eagerness to learn and his irrepressible desire to recite what he thinks he has learned. The classroom and the echoes from it reverberating in a student's mind establish an intimate relationship between Lloyd the comic and Alberti the poet, both of whom belong to the *ángeles colegiales* whose jumbled recollections of data partially absorbed and imperfectly recited censure obliquely the educational methods that put the recitation of facts before the understanding of them. It is Alberti's own sadness that suffused his recollection in 'Los ángeles colegiales' that 'Ninguno comprendíamos el secreto nocturno de las pizarras . . .' ('Not one of us understood the nocturnal secret of the blackboards . . .') (p. 284). With masterful control he simulated Lloyd's ostentatiousness as he put into his mouth a medley of disconnected echoes of his classes, from mathematical terms to a sentence by Cicero. His quoting of 'Quosque tandem abutere Catilina patientia nostra?' loses its initial impact when we bear in mind a fact something Alberti carefully utilized: that it is the first line of a text as well-known and well-thumbed in schools as Cicero's first discourse against Catilina. Similarly, Alberti deflated the comic's allusion to John Napier (1550–1617)—the English mathematician who published in 1614 the first logarithm tables, entitled *Mirifici logarithmorum canonis descriptio*—by placing it in an absurd context and following it with a burlesque deformation of 'unusquisque' in order to signify an odd, if not ugly, face:

> La primavera llueve sobre Los Angeles
> en esa triste hora en que la Policía
> ignora el suicidio de los triángulos isósceles
> más la melancolía de un logaritmo neperiano
> y el unibusquibusque facial.*   [p. 321]

* Spring rains down on Los Angeles in that sad hour in which the Police ignore the suicide of isosceles triangles plus the melancholy of a Napierian logarithm, and the facial *unibusquibusque*.

Alberti attributed equally eccentric statements to other comics, such as Chaplin, who declares solemnly that 'La mariposa
ignora la muerte de los sastres' ('The butterfly ignores the
tailors' death') (p. 319). In Lloyd's case the incongruousness of
what he says is justified by Alberti's presentation of him as a
buoyant but muddleheaded student. In 'Harold Lloyd,
estudiante' the comic knows a little about many subjects, from
prosody to geometry, from Latin to French. With his ludi-
crously encyclopaedic poem Alberti constructed a verbal equivalent to Lloyd's films, which, in the words of one critic, 'seemed
to be coming from a bottomless reservoir of gags, in which
sometimes potentially brilliant gags were thrown in, and
wasted, just to keep everything moving at top gear'.[42] If Alberti
imagined Lloyd asking in schoolboy French: 'Avez-vous le
parapluie?' it was because that question, so beloved by out-
moded phrase-books, represents exactly—with its mistaken
gender—the calibre and level of the comic's linguistic skill.
However, in 'Five o'clock tea' and 'Falso homenaje a Adolphe
Menjou' the French quoted by Alberti is not that of an innocent
schoolboy but that of a polished man of the world who asks:
'Votre mari est un petit cocu?'[43] The facile love affairs of the idle
classes were one of Alberti's targets in 'Five o'clock tea', where
he declaimed in affected wonder: 'Comtesse: Votre cœur es un
pájaro.' The French words with which he encrusted his poem
are a simple but acid criticism of a snobbish verbal fashion
which was reflected in the early 1920s in song titles such as
'Fleurs d'été', 'C'est ça', 'Betsy, Betsy, va t'en au Lycée', and 'Je
garde une fleur'. The phrases which Lloyd rehearses and trans-
lates into French are so elementary that, however accurate his
rendering, he appears more as a parrot than as a polyglot:

> ¿Tiene usted el paraguas?
> Avez-vous le parapluie?
>
> No, señor, no tengo el paraguas.
> Non, monsieur, je n'ai pas le parapluie.   [p. 320]

Lloyd discloses the reason why that umbrella preoccupied
him in two other questions, which he poses to 'Alicia': '¿Fuiste
tú la que tuvo la culpa de la lluvia?' ('Was it you who was guilty
of bringing rain?') and '¿por qué me amas con ese aire tan triste

de cocodrilo ...?' ('why do you love me with that sad crocodile air ...?') (pp. 320, 321). So bewitched was Lloyd by the adventures of *Alice in Wonderland* that its heroine came to exist in his mind as a real person, particularly when he recalled her escapades in the second chapter, 'The Pool of Tears', in which Alice, before singing 'How doth the little crocodile ...', shed 'gallons of tears, until there was a large pool all round her, about four inches deep and reaching half down the hall'.

This precise echo of *Alice in Wonderland*, which was published in 1927 in the Spanish translation of J. Gutiérrez Gili, clarifies a fact fundamental for the understanding of *Yo era un tonto*: that the sources of the poem were not, and could not be, exclusively cinematic. To act the fool in his poems and to commemorate the antics of screen comics, Alberti could not dispense with the written word; his mind was open and resourceful enough to utilize any verbal expression, conscious or unwitting, of the absurd, from the staccato shorthand of telegrams to the occasionally bizarre headlines of newspapers, from childhood songs and stories to the sophisticated essays of Ortega y Gasset.[44] Although he included in *Cal y canto* a poem entitled 'Telegrama', its preponderantly octosyllabic lines and three cases of rhyme suggest that he had not yet realized that the rhythm and text of a telegram lent themselves to comic effects. Alberti achieved those comic effects in sections of 'A Rafael Alberti le preocupa ...', in 'Larry Semon explica ...', in 'Charles Bower, inventor' and especially in 'Telegrama de Luisa Fazenda a Bebe Daniels y Harold Lloyd'. In this last poem Alberti displayed the sexual frivolity of Louise Fazenda as it was seen in Spain in 1926 in the film *La terrible coqueta*—which may have been the Spanish title of *Footloose Widows* (1926), *Ladies at Play* (1926) or *The Lady of the Harem* (1926)—firstly by a brazen use of French, and then by a string of words, mostly nouns, whose staccato tempo captures the comedienne's vivacity and coquettishness:

> Decidida mostrar le cul et les jambes aux soldats
> acepto empleo fino marimacho
> imprudente viento me confundió ayer cabra
> río*   [p. 325]

* Resolved to show le cul et les jambes aux soldats I accept job as refined virago unwise wind confused me yesterday with goat I laugh.

With his juxtaposition in the same poem of 'laughter-navel' and 'donkey-delicate', Alberti strained the humorous possibilities of the telegram, subjecting it to the same burlesque process he applied in other poems to newspaper headlines. In 'Carta de Maruja Mallo a Ben Turpin' his impassive declaration that 'En un hotel de Londres ha aparecido violado el cadáver de un ángel' ('In a London hotel the corpse of an angel has been found raped') exaggerates the horror of those headlines that began with a location in order to summarize some event as violent as the one Alberti could have read in the *Heraldo de Madrid* on 11 June 1927: 'In a Paris hotel/A Mexican kills his three children with a hammer and commits suicide'. There is a strong vein of horror in *Yo era un tonto*; in 'Cita triste de Charlot' Alberti narrated grimly that 'En la farmacia se evapora un cadáver desnudo' ('In the pharmacy a naked corpse evaporates') (p. 320); in 'A Rafael Alberti le preocupa ese perro ...' he harmonized actual and apocryphal memories to represent his childhood as an ugly, physically repugnant, experience. His mentions of 'a tender worried calf', 'cows', 'school', and 'an uncle of mine' sketch out lightly but deftly his truant escapades in which he fought like an aspiring bullfighter the pregnant cows of his uncle José Luis de la Cueva.[45] And he elaborated around his memories of that actual event a series of categoric statements and incredulous questions which the embittered adult projected backwards in time onto his childhood:

> Sé que en aquellos tiempos habitan mis cejas las
>   cucarachas y todo un campamento de húngaros
>   mis orejas.
> ¿He olvidado que mis axilas eran un pozo de hormigas
> y que en mi ombligo solía dormir una cabra?*   [p. 327]

It is worth emphasizing that it was Alberti who chose to include such a grimly personal piece in a collection of poems ostensibly devoted to the comics of the silent screen. The films he saw clearly aroused in Alberti a wide range of emotions which went beyond the exclusive appreciation of a comic's art and embraced spiritual autobiography and social criticism. His

---

* I know that in those times cockroaches inhabit my eyebrows and a whole encampment of Hungarians live in my ears. Have I forgotten that my armpits were a pit of ants and that a goat would sleep in my navel?

references to adultery in 'Falso homenaje a Adophe Menjou' point to a web of sordid sexual manoeuvres which throw into relief 'aquel corazón tan hermoso' ('that beautiful heart') of 'Madame la marquise', who, according to the poet, devoted herself along with others of her class to sailing around the world, taking tea, and playing bridge. Alberti obviously shared José Díaz Fernández's conviction, expressed in *La Venus mecánica*, that 'An aristocrat is good for nothing.'[46] By making the marchioness sigh 'Amor, divino suceso' ('Love, a divine event') after asking 'Votre mari est un petit cocu?', Alberti turned her affectations against a class whose hypocrisy and immorality he attacked in a homage he announced openly as 'false': false because he felt no respect for that class, and false because it was represented on the screen by an actor who in his films was not a man of flesh and blood but an elegant puppet, a robot-like man of the world. When he made Menjou affirm that 'mi chaleco entiende de cuernos' ('my waistcoat knows about the cuckold's horns'), he linked sartorial elegance and cuckoldry in a succinct categorization of Menjou's roles as seducer and man of the world in films like *A Woman of Paris* (1923) and *The Marriage Circle* (1924). Alberti concentrated his contempt for the aristocracy on Menjou because the latter perpetrated a double deceit: he mocked an audience's credibility by acting out stereotyped roles as dandy and seducer; and he represented a social stratum so false—in Alberti's eyes—that it paid more attention to a 'dulce bigote apasionado' ('sweet passionate moustache') like Menjou's than to the pain and distress which could be caused by seduction and chicanery.

In 1929 Alberti saw nothing amusing in Menjou's moustache, or in seduction, or in the golfing trousers he mentioned in 'Five o'clock tea'. *Yo era un tonto* indicates what he was to acknowledge half a century later: that 'I am deeply moved by things that happen ... by current events.'[47] These poems demonstrate that Alberti contemplated the cinema screen lovingly and attentively; they also show that he focused on the world outside the cinema, on its absurdities—like American Prohibition, commemorated in his poem to Laurel and Hardy in his mention of 'la ley seca' (p. 328)—and its crimes—like the armed robberies which, subject to military law following a decree in 1924, the poet recalled in 'En el día de su muerte a mano armada'.[48] Although the comics and the films in which they starred provided the theme and the inspiration of most of the poems of *Yo era un tonto*, it was the poet's attitudes and states of mind that shaped and modulated them and harmonized tributes to individual comics with other poems as patently subjective as 'Noticiario de un colegial melancólico'. What makes the latter poem into a litany of sadness is not the simple fact that Latin declensions still resound in his ears, but his replacement of the ubiquitous *mensa* with *nieve*, which symbolizes the passage of time in his elegiac memory of his irretrievable past:

> Y estos pronombres personales extraviados por el río
> y esta conjugación tristísima perdida entre los árboles.*
>
> [p. 326]

His thoughts of snow and loss advertise a kinship between him and Chaplin, who in 'Cita triste de Charlot' senses the loneliness of an 'árbol perdido' ('lost tree') and laments the loss of his walking-stick, an essential element of his screen persona:

> Se me ha extraviado el bastón.
> Es muy triste pensarlo solo por el mundo.†   [p. 320]

Chaplin's melodious dirge—

> Es que nieva, que nieva,
> y mi cuerpo se vuelve choza de madera,‡   [p. 319]

and Alberti's sorrow in 'En el día de su muerte a mano armada' on realizing

> . . . lo desgraciada
> que suele ser en el invierno la suela de un zapato.§ [p. 324]

derived from the same episode of *The Gold Rush*—the one in which Chaplin eats his boot in the log cabin—and from the same state of mind: the mind that detected loss all around him, be it that of a queen's crown or that of faith in life itself.

---

* And these personal pronouns lost by the river and this sad conjugation lost amid the trees.

† I have mislaid my stick. It is very sad to think of it alone in the world.

‡ It snows, it snows, and my body turns into a log cabin.

§ how miserable is the sole of a shoe in winter.

When he imagined in 'El ángel avaro' that people remarked of him:

> Ese hombre está muerto
>   y no lo sabe,*   [p. 276]

he provided one answer to the question he posed in 'En el día de su muerte a mano armada': '¿Quién ha muerto?' ('Who has died?'). By imagining himself as dead, Alberti associated himself with Larry Semon, whose melancholy epitaph—'También yo he muerto' ('I too have died')—marks his death in October 1928 exhausted and forgotten after his fleeting success and his bankruptcy. Having once enjoyed fame, Semon is now laid low: the awareness of his own degradation which Alberti imputed to him gives the poem a deeply pathetic quality as well as documentary authenticity as the comic associated himself with spittle and cigarette ends:

> Preguntad por mí a saliva desconsolada suelo
> y a triste y solitaria colilla.†   [p. 328]

In his poem to Wallace Beery—'Wallace Beery, bombero, es destituído de su cargo por no dar con la debida urgencia la voz de alarma'—Alberti was concerned with the disgrace befalling the negligent fireman and not with the antics of Beery and his companion Raymond Hatton in a film—*Fireman, Save My Child* (1928)—that perpetuated the tradition of the comic fireman started by Chaplin in *The Fireman* (1916) and by the Keystone Fire Department in *Bath Tub Perils* (1916). A critic who went to see Beery's film in Spain, where it was released as *Reclutas Bomberos*, reported that the audience of which he was a part 'laughed uproariously throughout the film'.[49] Alberti was unable or unwilling to react in the same way and saw in that film what he wanted to find and not what was actually in it. If Beery's bumbling incompetence amused many, it saddened Alberti, who insinuated that Beery the actor has his mind more on love than on duty when he made him exclaim: '¡Y toda esta catástrofe por tu culpa, amor mío!' ('And this whole catastrophe through your fault, my love!') (p. 330).

The question Alberti put into the comic's mouth at the end of

* That man is dead and does not know it.

† If you want to know where I am ask the disconsolate saliva on the ground and the sad and lonely cigarette end.

the poem—'¿Qué van a pensar de mí los periódicos de mañana?' ('What will tomorrow's newspapers think of me?') (p. 330)—is one that both comic and poet had good cause to ask, to judge from headlines in the *New York Times* and the *Heraldo de Madrid* in 1928 and 1929. The headline 'Girl to Renew Wallace Beery Suit', which referred to a million-dollar suit 'charging assault, filed two years ago by Juanita Montanya, a screen actress', gave Beery the unwelcome publicity which Alberti attracted, for different reasons, in the headline 'Las musas de vanguardia se rebelan contra su poeta. Una conferencia de Rafael Alberti, una paloma, un galápago, una zapatilla y unos insultos'.[50] In Alberti's poem Beery is aware of his ignominy and of his guilt, and Alberti associated himself with them in the same way as he identified himself with the melancholy solitude of Chaplin, the decline of Semon, and the bewilderment of Langdon. The poems of *Yo era un tonto* register profound changes in the personality and emotional fibre of Alberti, and it was his use of comics and actors to mirror those changes that gave his poems a human warmth, a value much greater than that of being reminiscences of certain films and tributes to certain actors. Alberti was of course playing, but his game was a serious one. The reader who wants to see how earnest it was will make the effort to bridge the ever widening gap between the poems and the films that inspired them, a gap that in some cases threatens to imprison the poems in the years in which they were written. The poems of *Yo era un tonto* are documents of an age and of the enthusiasm aroused in it by the silent cinema. They also constitute something important and lasting in Alberti's work; that imaginative and idiosyncratic chronicling of his love for the cinema, which he defined in 'Harold Lloyd, estudiante' as 'este puro amor mío tan delicadamente idiota' ('this pure love of mine that is so delicately idiotic') (p. 321), broadened the range of his poetic art and added a new chapter to his spiritual and poetic autobiography.

VI

LUIS CERNUDA AND FEDERICO GARCÍA LORCA

¡El cine siempre!*
Cernuda (1929)

¿Por qué hemos de ir siempre
al teatro para ver lo que pasa
y no lo que nos pasa?†
García Lorca, *Comedia sin título*

(A) LUIS CERNUDA

WHEN he read 'Forever in the cinema!' in the letter Cernuda wrote to him from Toulouse on 19 January 1929, Higinio Capote could not have failed to sense in the impassioned brevity of that phrase a passion for the cinema that bordered on addiction.[1] A letter to a friend thus enabled Cernuda to drop his guard and put aside the restraint he had shown in 1926, when in a series of 'Anotaciones' he adopted the pose of the sage to aver—without wit or profundity—that 'Shadow is to cinema as silence is to music' and that 'Chaplin says: I am the cinema'.[2] The composure with which he publicly referred to the cinema was something he took to his poetry, where his enthusiasm for it must be sought in contrasts, hints, and allusions woven with almost perverse caution into the texture of his poems, particularly those of *Un río, un amor* (1929) and *Los placeres prohibidos* (1931). As if exulting in having outsmarted his readers, in 1959 he divulged information about two poems, 'Sombras blancas' and 'Nevada', which he had written thirty years earlier and had included in *Un río, un amor*. Concerning the first poem he recalled: 'In Paris I had seen the first talking picture, whose

---

* Forever in the cinema!
† Why must we always go to the theatre to see what happens on stage and not what happens inside us?

title, *White Shadows in the Southern Seas*, suggested to me the third poem of the collection.' And he threw light on the genesis of 'Nevada' with this reminiscence:

One of the posters of a silent film I saw in Toulose presented me with this curious phrase: 'in (I cannot remember the name of the place mentioned) the railroads have names of birds', and I used the phrase, as if in a collage, in my little poem 'Nevada'.[3]

Cernuda could also have added that *Nevada* was the title of a 1927 film starring Gary Cooper, which was shown in Spain.[4]

There is a tension between the titles and the substance of these two poems, and any mental picture they may conjure up of light and space and adventures in distant lands are immediately dispelled by the nature of those shadows and the symbolic geography of 'Nevada': the white shadows are illusions which tease and thwart the poet, while Nevada and its railroads represent the chill transit of time into a bleak and infinitely repetitive future devoid of hope or relief. When he chose those titles, he established in his mind a deliberate strain between what they heralded in two films and what they suggested to him. This tension between film titles and personal feelings was one feature of that conflict which preoccupied him from his earliest writings between a life he found odious and dreams he found unrealizable. The title he gave to the successive editions of his poetry, *La realidad y el deseo*, acquires a new depth and dimension when we set alongside it his passion for the cinema. From his first poems in *Perfil del aire* (1927) Cernuda presented himself as a compulsive hermit whose natural habitat is a sealed room and whose sole companions are a divan and a dim light. He began one *décima* of *Perfil del aire* with the lines:

> La soledad. No se siente
> el mundo; sus hojas sella.*[5]

When he re-wrote these lines in the misnamed *Primeras poesías* as:

> En soledad. No se siente
> El mundo, que un muro sella,†   [p. 23]

* Solitude. The world cannot be sensed; it seals its leaves.
† In solitude. A wall seals off the world, which cannot be sensed.

he maintained his stubborn exclusion of the world with
renewed vigour and sterner resolve reflected in the more clearly
drawn verbal picture of a wall. That wall is the common
denominator of private room and public cinema; the sealed,
ill-lit chamber and the darkened cinema were retreats into
which he withdrew; and the cinema screen was as much a
mirror for Cernuda as the water in which his 'Narciso
enamorado' ('enamoured Narcissus') contemplated himself in a
poem of *Perfil del aire*.[6] Solitude was thus a theme, a state of
mind, and a refuge, for Cernuda did more than poeticize his
loneliness: he recorded those dreams he dreamed in solitude:
his dreams of escape and adventure, nurtured by such bucc-
aneering actors as Douglas Fairbanks, and his visions of a
disintegrating society, sustained by surrealist literature. It was
the cinema that fed some of those dreams through the films he
saw and through the magazines he read; the twenty-one numbers of *La Pantalla* and the forty-five issues of *El Cine* contained
in his library suggest that Cernuda found something worth
reading in the often superficial literature generated by the
cinema.[7]

In the privacy of his room, which constituted a self-imposed
exile, Cernuda enjoyed the mental liberty inspired by films, and
the inseparability in his mind of the cinema and the hermit's
retreat is demonstrated by a prose poem he published in 1926
under the title 'El indolente'. Firstly, he related how he closed
the door of his room, 'dejando fuera el invierno' ('leaving winter
outside'). Then, justifying the psychological compulsion to
escape into dreams with the epigram 'To voyage is a necessity', he
transported himself rapidly through time, space, and a range of
experiences with a quick nod in the direction of *The Gold Rush*,
Western films, and the bullfighting beloved by the Spanish film
industry. In his transport he witnessed a robbery with such
intense concentration and attention to detail that he became
involved in the escape and in the ritual pursuit hallowed by
comic films:

Navegar es necesario. Yo seré buscador de oro en Alaska, cowboy en
Australia, torero en Sevilla ... Inútil sería para mí que a la puerta
aguardase un automóvil embridada su velocidad, porque no habría de
conducirme al campo de los modernos héroes: la pantalla. (Veo un
hombre que, procurando adaptar bien a su figura el aspecto de

malhechor, maniobra: manos en los bolsillos, gorra calada hacia los ojos, movimientos bruscos. Sobre un mueble está el collar codiciado. Sin embargo para conservar las buenas costumbres tradicionales es necesario fracturar la cerradura. Se apodera del collar; desordena un poco los muebles; deja caer unas sillas; encendiendo todas las luces procura marchar oculto entre las sombras. Pero a la puerta, hermoso Júpiter, aparece la heroína—fieltro negro, skung.—presta a lanzar treinta balas como aquél rayos. El ladrón devuelve las perlas. En automóvil huimos perseguidos por la velocidad y por los disparos de los cómplices.) Los muros que me ciñen recobran su estabilidad.*[8]

Cernuda's waggish tone, which was to echo in 1928 in Rivas Panedas's 'Poema cinemático. Un ladrón', and his placid acceptance—in the thirty bullets to be fired by the spirited heroine—of the melodramatic overstatements endemic to adventure films, reveal his awareness of and his delight in the larger-than-life fantasies enacted on the cinema screen. And his return to the slower tempo of a routine existence is marked by his focusing once more on the walls around him. His dreams of being gold-hunter, cowboy, and bullfighter and his visions of attempted robbery and escape were a parenthesis as finite and as ultimately futile as his visits to the cinema. 'Forever in the cinema!' summarizes Cernuda's persistent attempts to fuel and sustain *el deseo; la realidad* was the world which lay in ambush for him every time he left the cinema.

What 'El indolente' makes clear is that films, their heroes, and their escapades enabled Cernuda to convert his lonely room into a dream factory in which his mind could participate in adventures and dynamic actions while his body remained motionless on that dream-inducing divan. The situations he saw in films also allowed him scope to utilize and refine the

---

* To voyage is a necessity. I shall be a gold-hunter in Alaska, a cowboy in Australia, a bullfighter in Seville ... It would be useless to have a fast car ticking over at my door waiting for me, because it would not have to take me to the land of the heroes of our time: the cinema screen. (I see a man who, trying to assume the manner and features of a wrongdoer, manoeuvres; hands in pockets, cap pulled over his eyes, sudden movements. The coveted necklace lies on a piece of furniture. However, to maintain traditional good manners he must break the lock. He grabs the necklace; pulls the furniture out of place; tips over a few chairs; and lighting all the lights tries to slip away hidden among the shadows. But at the door appears the heroine, a beautiful Jupiter—clad in black felt and skunk—ready to fire thirty bullets which would move, like him, with the speed of lightning. The thief returns the pearls. We flee in a car pursued by the speed and by the gunshots of his accomplices.) The walls which contain me recover their stability.

technique he himself described as 'projecting my emotional experience onto a dramatic, historical or legendary situation'.[9] In a scene from *The Cabinet of Dr. Caligari* the somnambulist Cesare appears engrossed in a flower which he holds in his hand. In 'Esperaba solo', from *Los placeres prohibidos*, Cernuda made a flower into the focal point of his poem as it is first held in the narrator's hand and then transformed into a mountain by one of those magical metamorphoses which can take place only in the mind of a poet or film director, who can photograph the impossible through the technical trickery of dissolves:

> Esperaba algo, no sabía qué. Esperaba al anochecer, los sábados. Unos me daban limosna, otros me miraban, otros pasaban de largo sin verme.
>
> Tenía en la mano una flor; no recuerdo qué flor era. Pasó un adolescente que, sin mirar, la rozó con su sombra. Yo tenía la mano tendida.
>
> Al caer, la flor se convirtió en un monte. Detrás se ponía un sol; no recuerdo si era negro.
>
> Mi mano quedó vacía. En su palma apareció una gota de sangre.*
>
> [p. 74]

The still figure of the narrator provides the backbone of the poem, which moves calmly but deliberately from the vague 'something' of the first phrase to the precise and graphic 'drop of blood' in the last. The people who pass him by, the flower which is brushed out of his hand, and the sun which sets behind a mountain constitute the essential scenic and human elements of a situation which acquires visual impact and symbolic dimensions only when the apparently purposeful passivity of the inert narrator is succeeded by dramatic changes in nature. The final image of the empty, outstretched hand now spotted with blood is as perplexing as the image of the hand covered with ants in *Un chien andalou*; it is also tantalizingly inconclusive, as it points outside the poem to causes and consequences at which the reader can only guess.

---

* I was waiting for something, I knew not what. I would wait at nightfall, on Saturdays. Some gave me alms, others stared at me, others passed by without even noticing me.

In my hand was a flower; I cannot recall what flower it was. An adolescent passed by who, without looking, brushed against it with his shadow. My hand was outstretched.

As it fell, the flower was transformed into a mountain. Behind it a sun was setting; I cannot recall if it was black.

My hand remained empty. In its palm appeared a drop of blood.

As it sets the narrator's immobility against the movement of people and things, this poem encapsulates one of the most poignant features of Cernuda's passion for the cinema: while he sat and sought abstraction in dreams, others moved and enacted his dreams. The films and actors he mentioned in his letters reveal lowbrow tastes surprising in a writer whose reading was vast and whose critical standards were idiosyncratically harsh. While Alberti enthused about *The Battleship Potemkin* and Lorca exalted Cocteau's *Le Sang d'un poète*, Cernuda enjoyed *The Merry Widow, Monsieur Beaucaire, The Black Pirate, The Thief of Baghdad*, and *The Big Parade*. The 'delightful moments' he told Higinio Capote in 1926 he found in *The Merry Widow* and *Monsieur Beaucaire* could only have been visible to a man sympathetic by nature to stylish costumed fantasies.[10] He named no actresses in his letters; it was actors whom he singled out for praise. The heroine who appeared in his vision in 'El indolente' looked and behaved more like a man than a woman, and in exalting her as a 'beautiful Jupiter' retaliating with a gun Cernuda was measuring her looks and her nature against masculine standards. The actors who starred in the films he listed—Douglas Fairbanks, John Gilbert, and Rudolph Valentino, together with George O'Brien, whom he also admired[11]—were models of the manhood sublimated by Hollywood; athletic, heroic, virile, charming, and irresistible to women, they were unambiguously masculine. Cernuda's admiration for these 'modern heroes' mentioned in 'El indolente' is all the more significant when we remember that he himself was by nature stern, easily offended, introspective, aggressively reserved—and homosexual. Whereas he was preoccupied by *placeres prohibidos* (forbidden pleasures), his heroes pursued permitted pleasures with that virile orthodoxy exalted by Hollywood—and demanded by the American League of Decency.

On the screen those men were everything that Cernuda was not; they enabled him to fantasize about roles and identities he could never assume in real life. His dreams in 'El indolente' of being a bullfighter or cowboy were enacted by Valentino as the bullfighter El Gallardo in *Blood and Sand* (1922) and by George O'Brien as a cowboy in *The Iron Horse* (1924) and *Sunrise* (1927). As they lived out his dreams, they widened the gulf between illusion and reality and accentuated the difference in his mind between vigorous manhood and his own nature and temperament. Cernuda's hero-worship placed him among 'the majority of spectators' for whom, according to one critic, 'the stars are not so much actors as *alter egos*, or at least close personal friends . . .'[12] They embodied those manly characteristics he himself did not possess but would have liked to possess; he admired in them the man he would have liked to be. They do not appear in his poems; only Fairbanks as the Black Pirate has a poetic counterpart in the Romantic figure of the Corsair whom Cernuda addressed in *Los placeres prohibidos* in the poem 'Adónde fueron despeñadas'. In Cernuda's eyes the Corsair conformed to the Romantic stereotype, represented by Zorrilla's pirate: the passionate adventurer whose self-appointed mission is to generate sensual pleasures and to incite sexual contact. It is the sexually experienced Corsair who can answer the question posed by the poet as he rephrases Villon's 'Où sont les neiges d'antan?' To his question

> ¿Adónde fueron despeñadas aquellas cataratas,
> Tantos besos de amantes . . .?*

the poet replies accusingly:

> Tú lo sabes, Corsario;
> Corsario que se goza en tibios arrecifes,
> Cuerpos gritando bajo el cuerpo que les visita,
> Y sólo piensan en la caricia,
> Sólo piensan en el deseo,
> Como bloque de vida
> Derretido lentamente por el frío de la muerte.† [pp. 69–70]

Although Cernuda delighted in the elegant, dandified Valentino as Monsieur Beaucaire, he peopled his poems with such spectral figures as a grey man—in 'Remordimiento en traje de noche'—and as a headless horseman—in 'La canción del oeste'—, two of the identities he adopted as he viewed himself in *Un río, un amor* and *Los placeres prohibidos* as in a mirror and from different angles. Valentino embodied desire and inspired dreams; Cernuda's regard for him only throws into relief his

---

* Where were those cataracts and lovers' kisses flung?

† You know the answer, Corsair; a pirate wallowing in warm reefs, bodies shrieking beneath the body that visits them and thinking only of the caress, thinking only of desire, like a block of life melted slowly by the cold of death.

projection of himself in 'Destierro', from *Un río, un amor*—as a cold outcast whose only companion is a shadow:

> Fatiga de estar vivo, de estar muerto,
> Con frío en vez de sangre,
> Con frío que sonríe insinuando
> Por las aceras apagadas.
>
> Le abandona la noche y la aurora lo encuentra,
> Tras sus huellas la sombra tenazmente.*   [p. 44]

If Valentino and other actors briefly took Cernuda out of himself, the realization that he was after all so totally different from them plunged him more deeply into bitter introspection. He may have enjoyed watching the muscular vigour of George O'Brien, who was a boxer in *Is Zat So?* (1927). He may equally have revelled in the devil-may-care acrobatics of Fairbanks in *The Thief of Baghdad* and *The Black Pirate*, where he checked his slide down the sail of a galleon by rending it with his sword. But Cernuda did not wish to fight or cavort; instead of visualizing himself as a dashing hero, he likened himself in 'Estoy cansado', from *Un río, un amor*, to a parrot wearily squawking a few words. Instead of adopting the cinematic fantasy of direct and virile action in order to right wrongs, he embraced the poetic illusion of withdrawal into a truculent pacifism contemptuous of fists, steel, and glory. In 'Déjame esta voz', included in *Los placeres prohibidos*, his plea to be left in peace rebounds against what society expects of him:

> Déjame vivir como acero mohoso
> Sin puño, tirado en las nubes;
> No quiero saber de la gloria envidiosa
> Con rabo y cuernos de ceniza.†   [p. 77]

'Glory' was a word which Cernuda used with particular venom. In '¿Son todos felices?', a poem introduced by a question that mocks the forced gaiety of circus and music-hall, his calculated repetition of 'honour' and 'homeland' exposes the futility of sacrificing one's life for one's country. Cernuda had

---

* Weariness of being alive, of being dead, with cold instead of blood, with cold which smiles as it glides along the extinguished pavements.

Night abandons him and dawn finds him, the shadow tenaciously at his heels.

† Let me live like rusty steel without a hilt, prostrate in the clouds; I wish to know nothing of envious glory with its tail and horns of ash.

seen in King Vidor's *The Big Parade* the violent death of valiant
men in the cause of ideals and values he found increasingly
hollow. '¿Son todos felices?' is his reply to *The Big Parade*, and
in contending through images of savagery that the hope and
heroism represented by John Gilbert were doomed to failure,
Cernuda lent his voice to the international chorus that during
the 1920s and 1930s denounced militarism and the horrific
wastefulness of war:

> El honor de vivir con honor gloriosamente,
> El patriotismo hacia la patria sin nombre,
> El sacrificio, el deber de labios amarillos,
> No valen un hierro devorando
> Poco a poco algún cuerpo triste a causa de ellos
> mismos.*   [p. 61]

Unlike John Gilbert, who perpetuated the Hollywood tradition of returning to his faithful sweetheart, Cernuda rejected
the solace of a woman's arms. Although he shared many of the
attitudes of the French surrealists, he did not exalt as they did
sexual passion and a woman's body. The amorous exploits of
Fairbanks and Valentino, however carefully filtered through
the contemporary codes of decency, stand in ironic counterpoint to the repugnance he expressed in 'La gloria del poeta',
from *Invocaciones* (1934–5), for marriage and the engendering
of offspring 'en la densa tiniebla conyugal' ('in the dense con-
jugal darkness') (p. 116). Such films as *The Merry Widow* and
Monsieur Beaucaire romanticized and exhibited as both normal
and desirable the physical attractiveness of man to woman and
woman to man. The many essays on the 'science of kissing'
make it clear that the only embraces Cernuda could have witnessed on the screen were those between a male and a female;
his poem 'Qué ruido tan triste', from *Los placeres prohibidos*,
thus serves as a sour and scornful commentary on the emotional
and sexual premise postulated by the films he mentioned—and
enjoyed:

> Qué ruido tan triste el que hacen dos cuerpos cuando
> se aman,
> Parece como el viento que se mece en otoño

* The honour of living gloriously with honour, patriotism towards a nameless
homeland, duty with yellow lips, these are not worth a branding iron slowly devouring
some body which they themselves have made sad.

Sobre adolescentes mutilados,
Mientras las manos llueven,
Manos ligeras, manos egoístas, manos obscenas,
Cataratas de manos que fueron un día
Flores en el jardín de un diminuto bolsillo.*   [pp. 70–1]

The considerable time which Cernuda confessed to have spent in cinemas enabled him to abstract himself sporadically from a Spain he sensed to be 'decomposing' under the dictatorship of Primo de Rivera and from a world he indicted in *Invocaciones* as 'Esta sucia tierra donde el poeta se ahoga' ('This filthy earth where the poet chokes') (p. 117).[13] But his bitter realization on emerging from the cinema that what after all he had contemplated with such ardour was a series of dreams and fantasies cast him more deeply into himself, into a private courtroom where he judged even more harshly the values of life and affirmed even more stringently the principles of his own existence. Films thus helped Cernuda to know himself.

(B) FEDERICO GARCÍA LORCA

Lorca advertised his interest in the cinema as openly as Alberti: in his lecture 'La imagen poética de Don Luis de Góngora' he quoted Jean Epstein; and the 'interminable *film* de brisa' ('endless film of a breeze') (I, p. 1153) he inserted as a fashionable metaphor into his article 'Historia de este gallo' (1928) gave way in 1936 to his direct announcement that the three acts of *La casa de Bernarda Alba* 'tienen la intención de un documental fotográfico' ('are intended as a photographic documentary'). His recital of two poems—'Oda a Salvador Dalí' and 'Romance de Thamar y Amnón'—during the 'Intermedio oral' of the fifth session of the Cineclub in April 1929 illustrates once more the Cineclub's magnetic ability to foster in writers an enthusiasm for the cinema. And Lorca's readiness to strengthen the alliance of cinema and literature was demonstrated simply by the report that, after reciting his poems and receiving a prolonged ovation, he 'set off that night for Bilbao, invited by our fraternal Cineclub and Ateneo of Vizcaya'.[14]

---

* What a sad noise two bodies make when they make love, it is like the wind which sways in autumn over mutilated adolescents, whilst hands fall like rain, nimble hands, selfish hands, obscene hands, floods of hands which once were flowers in the gardens of a minute pocket.

We can only wonder why Lorca did not read to the members of the Cineclub a piece directly related to and inspired by the cinema; *El paseo de Buster Keaton* would have been a more appropriate choice than the two poems he selected, which lead our minds towards modern art and the Old Testament. As I shall show later in this chapter, Lorca used Keaton as a mask for his own fears and anxieties, and the reading of that piece would have constituted a public confession, however obliquely or enigmatically expressed, of his innermost feelings. Any inhibitions he may have felt in 1929 about exhibiting his emotional commitment to the cinema were overcome by 1935; when asked 'What is it that interests you at the present time?', he outlined a project which he never realized:

—To make a film out of everything related to the art of bullfighting. Not the fight itself, definitely not. The atmosphere: folk-songs, dances, legends . . .   [II, pp. 1061–2]

In August of the same year he contributed to an inquiry about censorship conducted by the magazine *Nuestro Cinema*. During the 1930s the Spanish government had banned a number of films made in Soviet Russia. In opposing censorship, Lorca advocated freedom for the Soviet cinema and for what he called 'the foreign cinema', extolling the 'excellence' of the former and deriding the 'vulgarities and absurdities' of the latter as pungently as those vocal opponents of the American film industry. In a vigorously worded statement Lorca claimed that Soviet films were best understood by Spaniards because of their 'harshness of expression, their rural passion and their rhythm':

The great pre-revolutionary Russian literature has influenced and largely shaped the soul of my generation. This did not happen in France, but exclusively in Spain. Therefore, the cinema of Soviet Russia, with even more cause than the pre-revolutionary literature of Dostoievsky, Gogol, Tolstoy, and Pushkin, is best understood by Spaniards through its harshness of expression, its rural passion and its rhythm. For that reason I regard the Soviet cinema as a factor to consider in the development of the culture of our people.[15]

Lorca's choice in 1928 of Buster Keaton to embody his preoccupations and his defence in 1935 of the techniques and social content of Soviet films thus illustrate both his catholic tastes and his sensitivity to the diverse moods and subjects of films. After seeing *L'Age d'or* in 1931, he declared that it contained 'magnificent things'; after seeing Cocteau's *Le Sang d'un poète* and R. Livet's *La Mort d'un ruisseau* in 1932 he remarked to his friend Carlos Morla Lynch that films such as those defy explanation; their greatness lies, he claimed, in the freedom we all enjoy to interpret them as we will:

—If you have them explained to you ... you understand even less than before. And that is the great thing about these films. They accept no responsibility for being good or bad, beautiful or horrendous, logical or absurd ... It makes no difference ... The director is quite happy for each of us to interpret them as we will. Hang those who do not understand a thing about them. It's their loss![16]

Lorca advocated the need for imaginative sensitivity to the visual arts in the lecture he gave in 1928 on contemporary painting, in which he affirmed that in the canvases of Dalí, Ernst, and Miró

The inexpressible begins to be expressed. The sea fits inside an orange ... Art has to advance as science advances day by day, in the incredible region which is believable and in the absurd which is then transformed into a pure edge of truth.[17]

Like Alberti, Lorca was responsive to visual stimuli. His play *Amor de Don Perlimplín con Belisa en su jardín* (1931) was suggested to him by a nineteenth-century *aleluya*, a kind of strip cartoon with a verse commentary.[18] The exhibition of his drawings in the Galeries Dalmau, Barcelona, in 1927 publicized his desire to be taken seriously as an artist, and his drawings illustrate his absorption of the incredible and the absurd as exemplified in paintings and films. In one of his drawings, to which he added the title or explanation 'Only mystery makes us live, only mystery', a twig sprouts out of a man's eye; it does so because Joan Miró made it possible in his painting *Head of a Man Smoking*.[19] Another drawing represents a rigid, black-clad figure connected by cables to a pump and to pyramids; he is as inert, as dependent on those cables as the robot wired to a generator in Rotwang's laboratory in Lang's film *Metropolis*.

Fascinating as these drawings are, it is Lorca's writings that reveal the range of his responses to films: to scenes, techniques, actors, and modes of acting. His plays and poems contain characters modelled on stylized figures he saw in films. For example, the two characters he introduced into his play *Así que pasen cinco años* (1931)—the ones he specified as 'dos figuras vestidas de negro, con las caras blancas de yeso' ('two figures dressed in black, with their faces plaster-white') (II, p. 424) are as visually striking as the heavily made-up actors in *The Cabinet of Dr. Caligari*, who display the same stark contrast between black garb and white faces. In his ballad 'Reyerta', belonging to *Romancero gitano*, in which two men fight with knives, he appeared to be unmoved by the brutal waste of human life and more fascinated by the visual and dramatic possibilities of the encounter. Unlike the detailed reports of gypsy brawls current in the press of his day,[20] his poem shows us none of the fight; rather does it concentrate on the flashing blades and scenic effects of horses rearing, sunshine glinting on steel, and old women dressed in black who await the bloody climax like vultures in a tree. And when one of the combatants falls, he 'rueda muerto la pendiente': he rolls down the slope in the standard manner prescribed by many a Western film. A similarly derivative reaction occurs in *La zapatera prodigiosa*; the three suitors spurned by the shoemaker's wife enact what Lorca called 'casi una escena de cine' ('almost a scene from the cinema') when he made them bewail in rapid succession '¡Ay! ¡Ay! ¡Ay!' ('Woe! Woe! Woe!') (II, pp. 284–5). The same exaggerated, sentimental posturing was in his mind when he talked about *Doña Rosita la soltera* (1935), if not when he wrote it. In 1935, in his conversation with Silvio d'Amico, he associated Rosita with the Italian film actress Francesca Bertini, who at the start of her long career showed her fondness for melodramatic and historical subjects with such films as *La dea del mare* (1904), *Il Trovatore* (1909), *Re Lear* (1910), *L'Ernani* (1910), *Lucrezia Borgia* (1910), *La rosa di Tebe* (1912), and *Lagrime e sorrisi* (1912). His play, Lorca told d'Amico,

is the comic story of a dilettante and sentimental spinster of the kind seen in the pre-war cinema: someone like Francesca Bertini. A member of the *petite bourgeoisie*, without a penny to her name, who acts the *femme fatale* and talks in French.   [II, p. 1052]

Although a series of newspaper reports furnished him with the theme and substance of his tragedy *Bodas de sangre*, he derived his title from the Italian historical film, *Bodas sangrientas*, which, shown in Barcelona and Madrid in 1927, was based on the novel *Beatrice Cenci* by Luciano Doria.

Some of Lorca's stage directions demonstrate that he was also intrigued by cinematic techniques, particularly by the various movements and tempi which a film-maker could create with technical trickery. In *La doncella, el marinero y el estudiante* (1928) it is not a normal, workaday canoe that he imagined crossing the bay, but a motorized one whose propeller leaves a wake in the water; he could well be narrating an antic from a comic film when he specified that 'Una canoa automóvil llena de banderas cruza la bahía dejando atrás su canto tartamudo' ('A motorized canoe full of flags crosses the bay leaving behind it its stuttering song') (II, p. 239). In *El público* he directed that a bed spin on its axis and then imagined the light on stage assuming the 'tinte plateado de pantalla cinematográfica' ('the silvery hue of a cinema screen') (II, p. 521). In a poem written in 1935, 'Tierra y luna', he activated the moon, endowing it with the mobility which Epstein and Gance gave to their cameras as he imagined that 'la luna subía y bajaba las escaleras' ('the moon went up and down the stairs') (I, p. 809). The fantasies of a bed spinning on its axis and a moon going up and down stairs show that films expanded the range of Lorca's imagination, which was enabled to visualize movements that, however rapid or strange, were inspired or authenticated by what he had observed on the screen. He came to realize that the effects he imagined for a play or for a film could express his anxieties and tensions as eloquently as the images he coined for a poem. In *Así que pasen cinco años* he directed that the image of an ace of hearts be projected onto a shelf of a bookcase. In the second scene of *Luces de bohemia* Valle-Inclán directed that Zaratustra play a beam of light along shelves of books; in *Así que pasen cinco años* Lorca wove his projected image into the fabric of his play and made it represent an emotion when one of the characters draws a pistol, shoots the ace of hearts with an arrow, and puts a hand to his heart.

In *Poeta en Nueva York* Lorca fired many shots and arrows—and had his hand to his heart the whole time. One of his companions in New York, Herschel Brickell, has recalled that 'it was easy to perceive that the spectacle of New York, especially of Harlem, had troubled his soul very deeply'.²¹ The months he spent in that city were both a stimulus and a jolt to his poetic sensibility and emotional balance. The poems of *Poeta en Nueva York* are the concrete product of that stimulus and the expression of his sense of outrage in a city that acquired for him all the features of a hell on earth. Lorca's New York is as cold and soulless as Lang's Metropolis. There is a strong similarity of urban landscaping between Lang's sets, with their emphasis on heights, angles, and windows, and Lorca's images of 'mountains of cement', 'ledges', and 'swarms of windows' which 'acribillaban el muslo de la noche' ('riddled with holes the night's thigh') (I, p. 471). There is also a precise parallel between the visions which the director and the poet expressed of men dehumanized by and enslaved to soulless toil. The aseptic modern buildings and elevated railways of Metropolis are maintained by an army of robot-like workers condemned to perpetual toil in subterranean gloom. The inhabitants of New York, according to Lorca, are no freer than Lang's slaves as they shuffle insensibly to their labours; in 'La aurora' those who emerge into the streets through which light barely filters either stagger like insomniacs or know through the ache of their bodies that what they are about to do serves a science that shows no thought for the mind or body of the individual. The 'fruitless sweat' to which they are doomed had bathed the son of the Master of Metropolis, who learned by his toil and by his exhaustion what Lorca put into words in the last two stanzas of 'La aurora':

> Los primeros que salen comprenden con sus huesos
> que no habrá paraíso ni amores deshojados;
> saben que van al cieno de números y leyes,
> a los juegos sin arte, a sudores sin fruto.
>
> La luz es sepultada por cadenas y ruidos
> en impúdico reto de ciencia sin raíces.
> Por los barrios hay gentes que vacilan insomnes
> como recién salidas de un naufragio de sangre.*   [II, p. 485]

* The first ones who emerge realize with their bones that there will be no paradise or leafless love; they know that they go to the slime of numbers and laws, to games without art, to sweat without fruit.

The light is buried by chains and noises in a shameless challenge of rootless science. Through the districts there are people who stagger like insomniacs as if they had just survived a shipwreck of blood.

In Lorca's vision, as in Lang's, humanity divided itself into two categories: the oppressed, such as workers, negroes, and abandoned children, and the oppressors, such as millionaires. Both categories intermingle to create a strident and barbaric world of nightmare as laden with figures and incidents as the canvases of Hieronymus Bosch. In New York Lorca also felt the need to give visual expression to his anger and to his anguish; he did a series of drawings, one of which he called 'Urban perspective with self-portrait', where he presented himself as a blob, a deformed shape menaced by weird animals and dwarfed by skyscrapers whose windows are numbers and letters. He also wrote a screenplay in which he gave free rein to his imagination under a title as reminiscent of Jules Verne and Lumière as *Viaje a la luna*. The film which inspired the writing of its seventy-eight scenes was *Un chien andalou*, for he composed them after discussing Buñuel's film with a Mexican friend, Emilio Amero.[22] Lorca had already advertised his friendship with Buñuel in *Canciones* (1921–4), where the section entitled 'Juegos' carries the playful—and misspelt—dedication: 'Dedicados a la cabeza de Luis Buñuel. En grand plain' (I, p. 327). As a homage, *Viaje a la luna* has a totally different tone and complexion. Although the events specified and narrated in it are in themselves disturbing, the techniques Lorca chose to connect and represent them show how much he respected and duplicated Buñuel's refusal to impose on his scenes an easily apprehended narrative and a chronological order. His desire to compose a mentally disconcerting montage of images is seen in the techniques to which he resorted; a mind conditioned to sense and sequence will find it difficult to plot a course through seventy-eight scenes which contain thirteen cases of double exposure, eighteen fades, two dissolves, and one spectacular shot, reminiscent of Lumière's pioneering film of an express train racing towards the audience, of a 'triple double exposure of fast trains' (scene 52).

Although the 'sky with a moon' which he specified in scene 18 recalls the opening sequence of *Un chien andalou*, Lorca turned to his own poems for much of the action and many of the incidents he included in his screenplay. He was after all first and foremost a poet, and although *Viaje a la luna* is as valuable as the work of a poet as the 'cinéma-drame' *La Bréhatine* which

Apollinaire wrote between 1912 and 1914, his fame rests firmly on his poems and plays. Buñuel's obsession with sexuality clearly fascinated Lorca; however, it was the latter's tensions and preoccupations that underpinned *Viaje a la luna* and related it in theme and in spirit to the poems he wrote during the same agonizing period. As one critic has aptly pointed out, '*Trip to the Moon* reveals a storehouse of images associated with the poems composed during Lorca's New York phase.'[23] The bird whose neck is twisted in scene 49 is victim of the wanton cruelty which in 'Panorama ciego de Nueva York' caused some pitiful casualties: larks hobbling on crutches (I, p. 482). By presenting in three separate scenes 'a little boy who is crying' (scene 11), the same boy beaten by a woman (scene 12), and a boy caught by the neck by a man who 'stops up his mouth with the harlequin suit' (scene 26), Lorca focused on individual cases of child-abuse documented in *Poeta en Nueva York* by such collective phrases as the 'abandonados niños' ('abandoned children') inserted in 'La aurora'.

In the same way, Lorca separated into a series of close-ups and single shots the vomiting crowd which he situated, according to the subtitle of 'Paisaje de la multitud que vomita', in an '(Anochecer de Coney Island)'. The reports in the *New York Times* of the Annual Orphans' Day Outing make it clear that for many children Coney Island represented a brief interlude in their lives of misery and deprivation.[24] Lorca's poem demonstrates that he felt isolated amid and revolted by a carnival atmosphere as noisy, brash, and frenetic as the Coney Island Mardi Gras of 9–15 September 1929, which has been described as 'a spectacular occasion with carnivals, baby and beauty contests, parades of floats, brass bands, merrymakers in bizarre costumes and showers of confetti and streamers'.[25] He could not share the supercharged, hysterical gaiety of Coney Island, for it was there that in his mind and in his memory vomit acquired an autonomous existence with its own hideous music as it drove him into his private refuge of disgust:

> Llegaban los rumores de la selva del vómito
> con las mujeres vacías, con niños de cera caliente,
> con árboles fermentados y camareros incansables
> que sirven platos de sal bajo las arpas de la saliva.
> Sin remedio, hijo mío, ¡vomita! No hay remedio.

El vómito agitaba delicadamente sus tambores
entre algunas niñas de sangre
que pedían protección a la luna.
¡Ay de mí! ¡Ay de mí! ¡Ay de mí!   [I, pp. 473–4]

In *Viaje a la luna* it is not an anonymous crowd that is vomiting, but a series of individuals, as Lorca literally faced up to and wanted his audience to confront a series of close-ups of 'a head that vomits' (scene 19), 'a woman's head that vomits' (scene 35), 'a head that vomits' (scene 59), and 'a little Negro boy' who 'is also vomiting' (scene 61).

Apart from the repulsive sight and sound of people vomiting, there is another link between 'Paisaje de la multitud que vomita' and Lorca's screenplay: the setting of Coney Island. Coney Island offers an insight into Lorca's attitudes, emotions, and techniques in *Viaje a la luna* and reveals the debt his screenplay owed to New York and to his experiences in it. By devoting a poem to Coney Island, Lorca showed how much it horrified and fascinated him at the same time; the disgust and antagonism it aroused in him suffuse two lines which he expunged from his first draft of 'Oda a Walt Whitman':

Blooklin [*sic*] se llenaba de puñales,
y Coney Island de falos ...†[26]

The line with which he closed his poem—'la ciudad entera se agolpó en las barandillas del embarcadero' ('the whole city pressed against the railings on the pier') (I, p. 474)—derived from direct observation, for the crowded pier combines a hint of possible vomiting during the return journey to the city with a factual allusion to the ferry linking New York and Coney Island. His visit to Coney Island and his retention of what he saw there also provided him with the title of his screenplay. Luna Park, which was burned down in 1949, was, according to one writer, 'a magic fairyland of spires and minarets and towers'; it included amongst its attractions A Trip to the Moon, a cyclorama which enjoyed enormous success at the Buffalo

* The sounds came from the forest of vomit with the barren women, with children of hot wax, with fermented trees and tireless waiters serving plates of salt beneath the harps of saliva. There is no hope, my son, vomit! There is no hope.
The vomit delicately shook its drums among some little girls of blood who were asking the moon for protection. Woe is me! Woe is me! Woe is me!

† Brooklyn filled with daggers, and Coney Island with phalli.

Exposition in 1901 and which enthralled many thousands of visitors to Luna Park with the spectacular illusion of a lunar exploration 'in the world famous air ship "Luna"'.[27] As another writer has carefully recounted,

visitors entered a spaceship in the middle of a large building for an imaginary ride to the moon. Peering out of the portholes, they beheld a series of shifting images that gave the illusion of a flight into space, a sense reinforced by the rocking of the ship itself. After supposedly landing on the moon, passengers left the spaceship to explore its caverns and grottoes, where they met giants and midgets in moon-men costumes, the Man in the Moon upon his throne, and dancing moon maidens, who pressed bits of green cheese upon them as souvenirs of the lunar voyage.[28]

The designer of A Trip to the Moon clearly had a vivid imagination; Frederick W. Thompson must therefore be included among those who, like Góngora and Joan Miró, engaged and stimulated Lorca's fantasy.

We can only conjecture whether Lorca visited A Trip to the Moon or merely commemorated its fame and its title, which appears as a 'legend' between scenes 30 and 31. However, Coney Island and its amusement parks did leave their imprint on his mind and on his techniques: the ascents and descents of a switchback railway, found in such Steeplechase Park attractions as The Barrel of Love and The Earthquake Stairway, offer a pattern and a velocity which are duplicated in scenes 39 and 40:

39 The camera, with an accelerated pace, descends the stairs and, with a double exposure, ascends them.
40 A triple exposure of the ascent and descent of the stairs.

Similarly, the speed with which fanciful tableaux succeed one another in a funfair ride is matched by the rapid change of setting and object imagined by the poet:

6 A long, narrow passage with a window at the far end, surveyed by the camera.
7 View of an avenue (Broadway) by night, with flashing signs.
8 Which all fades into the preceding scene.
9 Two legs oscillate rapidly.
10 The legs fade into a group of trembling hands.

27 Everything fades out on a double exposure of snakes, this into
crabs, and this into other fish, all rhythmically.

And the tricks of lighting and colourful, mercurial spectacles
which constitute the appeal of many funfair rides are suggested
by two scenes in which fish leap in agony within the mouth of a
fish:

29 Within the fish's mouth appears a large design on which two fish
leap in agony.
30 These are converted into a kaleidoscope in which a hundred fish
leap and palpitate in agony.

Whether Lorca was inspired directly by a ride on A Trip to
the Moon or merely by an account of it, it is clear that he utilized
the idea of an excursion into fantasy—like Lumière in *Le
Voyage dans la lune* (1902)—in order to plot his own journey,
which is sinister, menacing, and dangerous to the mind as well
as to the body. The value of Lorca's screenplay lies in the fact
that it was written by a complex man and a sensitive poet
preoccupied by human relationships and sexual impulses, as
the opening sequence illustrates:

1 A white bed against a grey-walled background. Over the bedcovers
appears a dance of numbers, 13 and 22.
2 An invisible hand pulls off the covers.
3 Big feet run rapidly, wearing exaggerated, long stockings of white
and black.
4 A frightened head looks towards a point and fades into a head made
of wire with a background of water.
5 Letters saying HELP! HELP! and moving downwards with a double
exposure of a woman's sexual parts.

Lorca again associated sex with pain and fear in a later scene,
in which the phallic symbolism of a bird having its neck twisted
is reinforced and explained by the frank, explicit image of a
penis and a screaming mouth:

49 ... Another figure looks at the moon and the head of a bird appears
in full flight. He twists its neck until it dies in front of the lens. The
third [figure] looks at the moon; on the screen a moon appears,
outlined on a white background that fades into a male sex organ
and then into a screaming mouth.

As he focused in other scenes on feet (scene 3), on legs (scene 9), on hands (scenes 10, 53), and on women's breasts and hands (scene 32), Lorca suggested through his visions of these disconnected, isolated parts of the body the lack of physical and emotional harmony in himself and in others. It was his own sense of bewilderment and revulsion that he conveyed in the disturbingly inconclusive image of 'a woman's outlined head that vomits, rapidly nodding positively and negatively, negatively and positively' (scene 35). In Lorca's *Viaje a la luna* nothing is simple, straightforward or harmonious; when towards the end of the screenplay a man and a woman actually meet in the elevator beloved by American films, the passion of their encounter is quickly punctuated by sadistic urges:

62 The harlequin boy and the nude woman ascend in the elevator.
63 They embrace.
64 A view of the sensual kiss.
65 The boy bites the girl on the neck and violently pulls her hair.
66 A guitar appears and a hand quickly cuts its strings with a pair of scissors.
67 The girl defends herself from the boy, who with great fury gives her another profound kiss and places his thumbs over her eyes as if to plunge them into their sockets.
68 The girl screams . . .

The last two people to appear in the screenplay—'A fellow in a white dressing gown and rubber gloves, and a girl dressed in black'—kiss after an act of irreverent, almost necrophiliac, mockery reminiscent of Duchamp's painting of a moustache on the Mona Lisa in his *LHOOQ*: 'They paint a moustache on the dead man's head and kiss each other amid bursts of laughter' (scene 75). In imagining that they indulge in 'a cinematic kiss . . . over a tomb' (scenes 76–7), Lorca firstly established a visual link between love and death and then derided that kiss as an act of facile sentimentality by setting it against a landscape as cinematically hackneyed as a 'landscape of a moon with trees swaying in the wind' (scene 78). In Lorca's screenplay a kiss is either violent, irreverent or melodramatic; it is never a simple, spontaneous demonstration of love. In 'La casada infiel', from *Romancero gitano*—the poem that was dramatized in an eleven-minute film of homage, *A Federico García Lorca*, made in 1937 by Ediciones Antifascistas[29]—the boastful gypsy who relates the erotic escapade had stressed his own virility and his beautiful partner's submissiveness by describing her unglamorously as 'Sucia de besos y arena' ('Dirty from sand and kisses') (I, p. 407). In *Viaje a la luna* Lorca accentuated the distance between impulse and action, between desire and deed, when he devised a scene in a bar; elegantly dressed men want to drink but are prevented from doing so:

54 These [piano keys and hands playing] fade into a bar occupied by several fellows dressed in dinner jackets. The waiter sets glasses of wine before them but the glasses are so heavy they are unable to raise them to their lips. An almost nude girl enters, and a harlequin: they dance. The others try to drink but cannot. The waiter pours the wine until the glass overflows.

The waiter, the men in dinner jackets, the harlequin, and the almost nude girl belong to the richly varied cast of *Viaje a la luna*, which is as extensive as that of *Poeta en Nueva York*. The 'bandaged head' appearing in scene 57 is a graphic sign of a climate of cruelty and terror in which a woman beats a child (scene 12), a man stuffs a harlequin suit into a boy's mouth (scene 26), another man twists a bird's neck (scene 49), and another squeezes a frog (scene 56). And the man who lies 'dead upon discarded newspapers and herrings' (scene 73) shows that if Lorca saw little charity or tranquillity in life, he visualized no dignified release in death. Through the cumulative horror of such scenes Lorca aimed to shock his potential audience with the aggressiveness displayed by Buñuel in *Un chien andalou*. We can only picture in our minds this screenplay transposed to the screen; when reading it we are never allowed time or mental respite in order to seek sense or narrative sequence in images which flow with the speed of a roller-coaster and change with disconcerting ease. Lorca's intention was one he shared with the designer of A Trip to the Moon in Luna Park: to numb our senses, to detach us from the normal tempo, laws, and spectacles of life so that our minds may be conditioned to accept without shock or nausea a series of visions such as these:

15 Through a window passes the rapid fall of a double exposure of letters in blue, HELP! HELP!

16 Each HELP! HELP! sign fades into a footprint,
17 And each footprint into silkworms upon a leaf on a white background.
18 From the silkworms emerges a large skull and from the skull a sky with a moon.
19 The moon divides and there appears a sketch of a head that vomits and opens and closes its eyes and which dissolves into:
20 Two little boys who are walking along singing with their eyes closed.

Many similar sequences of images in *Poeta en Nueva York* demonstrate the intimate connection in Lorca between the poet and the potential film-maker. In poems and in screenplay the effect and intention of such images coincide: to transport us to a plane of fantasy where physical laws are no longer valid, where things are not what they appear to be, where people are not what their uniform makes them seem. The harlequin figure who moves through *Viaje a la luna*—and who reappears in *El público*—is more at home in the canvases of Picasso than in this city of violence, and Lorca denied the harlequin suit the remotest chance of provoking amusement when he imagined it thrust into a boy's mouth. In order to stress that people are not what they appear to be, he dressed his characters in strange garbs and disguises; a boy is clad 'in a bathingsuit dotted with large black spots and white spots' (scene 24); the harlequin boy who tries to gouge out the girl's eyes in the elevator turns his back and 'takes off his jacket and a wig' (scene 68); and when that harlequin boy dances with an almost nude woman, bites her on the neck, and pulls her hair, we realize that the clown has been transformed in Lorca's mind into a sensualist and a sadist. The harlequin is clearly not what we think he ought to be. Nor is Buster Keaton, whom Lorca transformed into a murderer in *El paseo de Buster Keaton*.

The first character who appears in this brief piece is The Cock; its crowing is the cue for the entry of four children with their father, Buster Keaton, who takes out a wooden dagger and kills them with the unbelievably ingenuous words 'Pobres hijitos míos' ('My poor little children'). After painstakingly counting them in a display of elementary arithmetic copied by Alberti's Keaton—'Uno, dos, tres y cuatro' ('One, two, three, and four')—he moves off on a bicycle which is conveniently to

hand. Despite these murders, Lorca's Keaton remains an innocent whose candour was contained for the poet in his eyes,
which are best and most often remembered in a celebrated still
from *Go West*. Those eyes so bewitched and moved Lorca that
his tribute to them is a blend of lyrical tributes and uncom-
plimentary impressions whose common denominator is
Keaton's melancholy dreaminess:

Sus ojos, infinitos y tristes, como los de una bestia recién nacida,
sueñan lirios, ángeles y cinturones de seda. Sus ojos, que son de culo
de vaso. Sus ojos de niño tonto. Que son feísimos. Que son bellísimos.
Sus ojos de avestruz. Sus ojos humanos en el equilibrio seguro de la
melancolía.*   [II, p. 234]

The sadness he sensed in Keaton suffuses the sight of a negro
eating a straw hat, whom Lorca situated with his degrading
symbol of minstrel or coon amid an urban mess of old tyres and
petrol cans. The physical and spiritual debasement of the negroes he imagined in *El paseo de Buster Keaton* was something he
was to see with his own eyes in 1929–30 and condemn in *Poeta
en Nueva York*.

Even though Lorca refused to make fun of the negro, the
latter—like the cock that heralded the Pathé newsreels—belonged to the cinema, where he was frequently and
tastelessly ridiculed in such Keystone films as *Rastus and the
Game Cock* (1913) and in Keaton's own *The Blacksmith* (1922)
and *Seven Chances* (1925). The bicycle ride which set Keaton
exploring life and garnering experience derived from an early
scene of *The General* (1926)—the one in which Keaton, as
Johnnie Gray the engineer, begins his pursuit of his loco-
motive, stolen by Union troops—, and Lorca's choice of a bicycle
for the comic's journey reveals not only his acquaintance with a
particular film but his affection for an evergreen piece of comic
apparatus. The stunts on a bicycle with which Harry Langdon
tried to impress a woman in *Long Pants* were emulated
some forty years later by Paul Newman in *Butch Cassidy and
the Sundance Kid* (1969). Comic films contained many
chase sequences which justify Lorca's narrative statement,

* His eyes, sad and infinite like the eyes of a newly born beast of burden, dream of
lilies, angels, and silk sashes. His eyes, which are like the base of a glass. His eyes of an
idiot child. Ugly eyes. Beautiful eyes. His ostrich eyes. Human eyes in the precise
balance of melancholy.

resembling a stage direction, in his story 'Nadadora sumergida': 'Los policías suben y bajan las dunas montados en bicicleta' ('The police go up and down the dunes mounted on bicycles') (I, p. 994). Lorca also introduced into *El paseo de Buster Keaton* as constant a target of comics' mockery and disrespect as the police: Keaton's bicycle, like that of such acrobatic comics as Harold Lloyd, is no ordinary machine; it is, said Lorca, 'una bicicleta como todas, pero la única empapada de inocencia' ('a bicycle like any other, but the only one drenched in innocence') (II, p. 234). When Alberti made Lloyd exclaim: 'Sígueme por el aire en bicicleta' ('Follow me through the air on a bicycle') (p. 321), he celebrated the apparently magical gift of flight with which Keaton's machine is also endowed as it makes off on its own in pursuit of two butterflies:

BUSTER KEATON cae al suelo. La bicicleta se le escapa. Corre detrás de dos grandes mariposas grises. Va como loco, a medio milímetro del suelo.* [II, p. 234]

Although Lorca's piece was thus nurtured by the cinema, his stage directions constitute a lyrical narrative which could be filmed only partially as they blend precise detail and personal commentary in the manner explored by Valle-Inclán, who specified in the third act of *El embrujado*, for example:

DON PEDRO BOLANO hállase atento a los rumores de la noche, vencido, amedrentado, caviloso, sintiendo en el oscuro enlace de todas las cosas lo irreparable y lo adverso del Destino.†[30]

A director, however talented, would find it difficult to film many of Lorca's instructions, which particularize more of his musings than the events he imagines, as the following passage demonstrates:

A lo lejos se ve Filadelfia. Los habitantes de esta urbe ya saben que el viejo de la máquina Singer puede circular entre las grandes rosas de los invernaderos, aunque no podrán comprender nunca qué sutilísima diferencia poética existe entre una taza de té caliente y otra taza de té frío. A lo lejos brilla Filadelfia.‡ [II, pp. 234–5]

---

* Buster Keaton falls to the ground. The bicycle runs away from him. It runs after two large grey butterflies. It races like a maniac, a half-millimetre off the ground.

† Don Pedro Bolano listens attentively to the sounds of the night, vanquished, fearful, hesitant, feeling in the obscure intertwining of all things the irreparable and adverse nature of Destiny.

‡ In the distance Philadelphia can be seen. The inhabitants of this city already know that the old man of the Singer sewing-machine can circulate amid the great roses of the

Directions and asides such as this comprise approximately seventy-five per cent of *El paseo de Buster Keaton*, and the dialogue is consequently as subordinate to them as the subtitles of silent films are to the filmed action. Keaton's words are particularly childlike, and glide easily and without psychological motivation between basic feelings. His sorrow at the death by his own hand of his four children, expressed in the candid words 'Pobres hijitos míos' ('My poor little children'), is abruptly and astonishingly succeeded by delight as he looks away from his victims and exclaims: '¡Qué hermosa tarde!' ('What a beautiful evening!') (II, p. 233). His reactions to the thinly veiled sexual questions of An American Woman, who represents the frank, uninhibited modern female whom Alberti satirized in such poems as 'Falso homenaje a Adolphe Menjou', are those of a puppet. When she asks him: '¿Tiene usted una espada adornada con hojas de mirto?' ('Do you have a sword adorned with myrtle leaves?') he shrugs his shoulders and lifts his right foot. When she inquires: '¿Tiene usted un anillo con la piedra envenenada?' ('Do you have a ring with a poisoned stone?') he slowly closes his eyes and raises his left foot. The answer he gives parries her curiosity about his sexual identity, and expresses only a hope, a dream:

Quisiera ser un cisne. Pero no puedo aunque quisiera. Porque¿dónde dejaría mi sombrero? ¿Dónde mi cuello de pajarita y mi corbata de moaré? ¡Qué desgracia!* [II, pp. 235–6]

In Lorca's eyes Keaton is thus the captive of his own image, reputation, and uniform. When a young girl appears and asks him who he is, she faints at the sound of his name. Earlier in the piece a voice had typecast him as a *tonto*—a fool, a comic—in the same way as critics were during the same years calling Lorca a gypsy-poet and others, like the painter Gregorio Prieto, were depicting him as a romantic visionary. In several of the letters he wrote in 1927 and 1928 Lorca protested indignantly against

conservatories, although they will never be able to understand what subtle poetic difference exists between a cup of hot tea and a cup of cold tea. In the distance Philadelphia glows.

* I should love to be a swan. But I cannot even though I should like to be. Because where would I leave my hat? Where would I leave my fly-away collar and my silk tie? What a misfortune!

such false and facile categorizations, which denied him the complexity he detected in himself and found in others beneath their labels, uniforms, and masks.[31] In 'El rey de Harlem' Lorca showed us the negro king in 'un traje de conserje' ('a janitor's outfit') (I, p. 460); the negro was expected to serve, Keaton was expected to amuse—and the 'gypsy-poet' was expected to enchant. Ironically, Lorca set Keaton's longing to be a swan, his desire for personal and artistic freedom, in Philadelphia; but the longing for freedom which moved him in the city where the Declaration of Independence was signed is menaced at the end of the piece by the lights of the police flashing on the horizon.

By imagining that '(En el horizonte de Filadelfia luce la estrella rutilante de los policías)' ('(On the horizon of Philadelphia there shines the flashing star of the police)') (II, p. 236), Lorca simply but subtly questioned the American dream of liberty, and the harsh strictures on American society he was to pronounce in his New York poems are here foreshadowed in *El paseo de Buster Keaton* by the gramophone which usurps the place of nightingales; instead of letting them trill their own song, the gramophone relays 'en mil espectáculos a la vez' ('simultaneously in a thousand cinemas') a message the audience is expected to believe unhesitatingly: 'En América hay ruiseñores' ('In America there are nightingales') (II, p. 236). The threats to their songs and to their existence will become explicit in *Poeta en Nueva York*, where the cancer consuming 'El niño Stanton' longs to claim nightingales as well (I, p. 495). However, *El paseo de Buster Keaton* is more than an indictment of features of American life: it is a comment on the strains of living, of being oneself, and on the conflicting demands made on a sensitive mind by poetic modes and poetic material. It is a visually variegated work which mentions a cock, a parrot, an owl, Adam and Eve, a bicycle, a Singer sewing-machine, a rose, the moon, a gramophone, the police. Keaton's brief journey acquires point and purpose as an exploration of the uneasy overlap of the old and the new and as a dramatization of the difficulty of harmonizing two worlds, two sets of stimuli. The cock and the owl of childhood stories have to coexist with a silent cinema comic and a provocative American woman. A young girl who, with her wasp waist and beehive coiffure, belongs to historical films spans the centuries as she rides on a bicycle and falls off it when she learns that she is addressing Buster Keaton. Without wanting to, merely by being himself, Keaton causes a woman to faint, and the only way in which he can revive her is to act a part alien to him, that of Prince Charming who breathes life into Sleeping Beauty with a kiss. At the end of his journey Keaton is the captive of a cinematic cliché, in the same way as Lorca saw himself as the victim of glib characterizations.

El paseo de Buster Keaton has a density and a profundity out of all proportion to its size. Despite its comic inspiration, there is nothing to laugh at in it, for Lorca's compassion for and under-standing of Keaton not only tell us a great deal about his feelings towards poetry, but anticipate his sensitive concern for people's problems which was to inform *Poeta en Nueva York* and his three tragedies. Keaton's wish to be a swan points to a yearning for the impossible which will be echoed by Yerma's desire for a child and Adela's longing to 'salir' ('go out') and so escape the tyranny of her mother Bernarda Alba. Keaton did not enable Lorca to forget himself; rather than using him as a release, he saw in him another victim. In his unfinished play known as *Comedia sin título*, the Author asks: '¿Por qué hemos de ir siempre al teatro para ver lo que pasa y no lo que nos pasa?' ('Why must we always go to the theatre to see what happens on stage and not what happens inside us?')[32] His presentation of Keaton on the one hand and the emotional and sexual complex-ities he dramatized in *Viaje a la luna* on the other are challenging answers to that question and demonstrate that what he saw on the cinema screen enabled him to analyse and know himself.

VII

SPANISH NOVELISTS

Para el futuro debe la pantalla
influir en la novela, y no la
novela sobre la pantalla.*
Rafael Marquina (1928)

In Benjamín Jarnés's novel *Viviana y Merlín* (1930) the sorceress Vivien uses a piece of twentieth-century magic firstly to enchant the Knights of the Round Table with her 'cajita milagrosa' ('miraculous little box') and then to enrage them with a film of Don Quixote and Sancho Panza.[1] The story 'Charlot en Zalamea', which Jarnés included under the label 'film' in his *Escenas junto a la muerte* (1931), also spans the centuries as he incorporated Chaplin's screen personality into the play *El alcalde de Zalamea* by the seventeenth-century dramatist Pedro Calderón de la Barca. These two examples of fictional fantasy illustrate Jarnés's rhapsodic claim that the cinema 'is a splendid gift of the gods'.[2] How that gift encouraged Spanish writers of prose fiction to explore new themes and devise new techniques is something that may be gauged with particular clarity from the stories of Francisco Ayala and from the novels of Jarnés, Rosa Chacel, and José Díaz Fernández.

Little critical acumen is needed to perceive that since the early days of film-making novels and short stories have been for the cinema industry not a divine gift but its daily bread. The phrases 'the film of the book' and 'based on a story by' which appear so often in screen credits reveal the cinema's insatiable appetite for literary sustenance as varied as *The Canterbury Tales* and Ian Fleming's James Bond novels. And the cross-fertilization of literature and film has continued and increased in the 1970s with the new trend of novelization of filmscripts, a fashion one American reporter has called 'the

---

* In the future the cinema must influence the novel, and not the other way around.

hasty and often not very artful metamorphosis of script into book'.[3]

The indebtedness of films to literature is seen not just in the *novelas cinemáticas* serialized in Spanish magazines of the 1920s and 1930s and the 'telenovels' of the 1970s, but in the way in which some directors have woven literature—in the form of a book, or memoirs, or a diary—into a film's texture. A book is thus visually a theme of a film and the mainspring, usually in flashback illustrations, of what we see in it. In the 1920s F. W. Murnau used a diary as the starting point and as the unifying image of his *Nosferatu* (1922), and in *La Passion de Jeanne d'Arc* (1928) Carl Dreyer filmed a hand turning over a manuscript in the Bibliothèque Nationale, Paris. Almost half a century later two French directors so refined this technique that what is being written in the film itself is inseparable from the scenes that are filmed as a consequence of what has been written; in Alain Robbe-Grillet's *Trans-Europe Express* (1966) Jean, who is played by Robbe-Grillet, is writing a filmscript, and the scenes he devises are translated immediately into a film in which he is the protagonist acting out his own fantasies. In Eric Rohmer's *Le Genou de Clair* (1970) the central character, who is a novelist, enacts situations which he had planned and pondered in his diary.

Literature, and particularly novels and short stories, has sustained the cinema. My purpose in this chapter is to consider to what extent the cinema nourished Spanish writers of fiction in the 1920s and 1930s. The presence of films and film stars is inescapable in some works of Francisco Ayala, Rosa Chacel, José Díaz Fernández, and Benjamín Jarnés, all of whom would undoubtedly endorse Gabriel García Márquez's assertion that 'my experience in the cinema ... has broadened my perspectives as a novelist.'[4] Their writings evince a response to the cinema at once deeper and more imaginative than Blasco Ibáñez's use of the adjective 'cinematographic' in his novel *Entre naranjos* (1900); however superficial it may seem to us now, the mention of 'Aquel viaje, rápido como una visión cinematográfica' ('That journey, rapid like a cinematic vision') contains a simile that was bold in the year in which it was coined.[5] In the novels and stories of Ayala, Chacel, Díaz Fernández, and Jarnés characters go to the cinema, react emotionally and psychologically to films, model themselves on cinema stars, and use 'film' as a modish metaphor. Rosa Chacel's self-conscious reflections about the cinema in her novel *Estación, ida y vuelta* (1930), where she assured her reader that 'Mi drama será cinematizable a lo Harold Lloyd' ('My personal drama can be filmed only in the manner of Harold Lloyd') and concluded that 'Tampoco en el cine hay espacio para el complejo proceso de mi protagonista') ('Not even in the cinema is there room for the complex proceedings of my protagonist'), make it clear that not only did films fascinate and inspire her, but that the nature of that fascination and inspiration constitute a theme to be treated in her novel.[6]

The nervous response of Spanish novelists to the cinema is apparent in the compulsion some felt to justify it as a theme and a stimulus. And those who utilized the cinema most imaginatively—Jarnés and Ayala—were the ones who were most concerned to examine the relationship between films and novels. In 1929 Ayala enthused about the writer's chance to create 'a beautiful mosaic' and illustrated the inexhaustible permutations of images on the screen by visualizing 'a dawn alongside a twilight; a snatch of music next to a woman's arm; the image of a bottle next to the sensation of a perfume'.[7] In 1933 Jarnés used more sober language to advocate the cinema's 'inescapable social duty'; when he asked: 'What good film could not be recounted in great detail? What good novel could not be made into a film?', he revealed the common sense displayed by the French critic André Levinson, who declared in 1927: 'Film et roman sont au même point des formes d'art cinématiques.'[8]

If the ways in which films influenced Spanish novels and stories during the 1920s and 1930s is a matter of critical judgement, the places where the films were shown present no such problem of recognition or evaluation. Together with cars, dance halls, hotels, and cabarets, cinemas were part of the feverish social climate which Alberti satirized in his poem 'Five o'clock tea' and which one critic has categorized as the 'strident cosmopolitanism' of Spanish novels of that period.[9] The protagonist who goes calling in Antonio Espina's story 'Pájaro pinto' (1927) is told by the maid that her masters 'Se han ido al cine' ('have gone to the cinema'); they had joined the enthusiastic procession of cinema-goers who file through other stories and novels.[10] In 1929, in Díaz Fernández's *La Venus mecánica*, Elvira urges her companion Víctor: 'Vámonos a un cine, a un café, a cualquier sitio. No quiero ponerme triste' ('Let's go to a cinema, to a café, to any place. I don't want to get sad').[11] In the same year, in Jarnés's *Paula y Paulita*, the narrator promises: 'Nos sumergiremos en esa tina de purificación. Vamos al cine' ('We shall submerge ourselves in that purifying bath. Let's go to the cinema').[12] And in 1931, in *Escenas junto a la muerte*, Jarnés's first-person narrator proposes forcefully: 'Entraremos en un café, en un cine. Me gustaría ver *Charlot en Zalamea*' ('We shall enter a café, then a cinema. I would like to see *Chaplin in Zalamea*').[13]

The character who urges a visit to the cinema or to 'any place' in *La Venus mecánica* seeks not an uplifting aesthetic or spiritual experience but an escape from the social and political unrest afflicting Spain towards the end of Primo de Rivera's dictatorship. The characters who hold together this restless, anxious novel are Víctor, who like his creator was arrested by the police for his political activities, and Obdulia, whose career as a model, sandwiched between her employment in a night club and her abortion, leads her to describe herself bitterly as a 'Venus mecánica, maniquí humano' ('mechanical Venus, a human puppet').[14] As they pass from the '"cabaret" del Alkázar' to bars, from the streets to the Club Femenino—transparently the Lyceum Club Femenino which Alberti startled in December 1929—Víctor and Obdulia encounter and ridicule types inimical to their author: the actress who rises 'de tabernera a duquesa' ('from barmaid to duchess'); Mary Sol, 'el tipo acabado de *flapper*, de jovencita pervertida' ('the epitome of the flapper, of the perverted young woman'); Maruja Montes, the painter, doubtless modelled on Maruja Mallo, Alberti's companion before he met María Teresa León.[15] Díaz Fernández was so concerned with the sickness of Spanish society under Primo de Rivera, and particularly with the police charges against strikers, that he advocated not a facile, illusory escape in the cinema but an actual way out through 'vengeance' and 'the great revolution'.[16] So dismayed was he by what he felt to be the degeneracy and demoralization of Spain that his anger encompassed the aristocracy at one extreme and the cinema at the other. Mocking the desire for a vigorous and independent Spanish film industry, Díaz Fernández introduced into his novel *Esperanza Brul*, whose ambition—expressed in the simple words 'Hay que hacer la película española' ('We must make purely Spanish films')—is immediately deflated by the type of film she wants to make: *¡Viva Sevilla!* Its title and its subject were, as I pointed out in Chapter 3, a frequent target of cartoonists and satirists, and Díaz Fernández swelled their ranks when he made Esperanza prattle excitedly about a 'Cosa de toreros, ¿sabe usted? Juergas, amoríos. ¡Precioso!' ('A film about bullfighters, you know. Celebrations and love affairs. Delightful!').[17]

Díaz Fernández dealt only a glancing blow at the Spanish cinema, for he was more concerned to deride the melodramatic straitjacket constraining it than to explore the repercussions of watching films on people's behaviour and personalities. For a fictional account of the effects films have on people's minds, we have to turn to the stories Francisco Ayala wrote in 1929 and 1930, where he developed what Antonio Espina had only hinted at in his story 'Pájaro pinto', in which a Poeta de Cabaret asks:

—¿No adviertes cómo vas fundiendo y confusionando tu vida, en la frágil pantalla de la cinegrafía? Desvitalizándote ... Perdiéndote, como un fantasma.*[18]

In 1929, in his essay 'El Cine. Arte y espectáculo', Ayala tried to define sensitively the turmoil of ideas and sensations aroused in the mind of a creator by the images he sees on a screen:

The creator moves, guided only by his aesthetic intuition, in a universe of things, of sensations, of ideas which appear jumbled and disorganized to his imagination. In his mind he will have to choose the pieces necessary to construct his machines—perfectly useless and without equivalents in the natural order of the world—.[19]

Both the experience and the psychological consequences of sitting before 'a universe of things, of sensations, of ideas' constitute the theme of the autobiographic tale 'Hora muerta' (1929). Phrases found in other stories show that films inspired Ayala to visualize and narrate episodes in cinematic terms. In

* —Don't you see how you are melting and blurring your life, on the fragile cinema screen? Draining yourself of life ... Evaporating, like a phantom.

'Cazador en el alba' (1929) his perception of the world around him is split, as if by double vision, into a montage of foreground and background, in which 'el presente se componía de dos planos cinematográficos: un gran plano con el rostro de Aurora y, a través de él, todo un paisaje en movimiento.'*[20] And in 'Erika ante el invierno' (1930) he illustrated his statement 'De pronto, todo quedó inmóvil, parado' ('Suddenly everything became frozen, motionless') with an explanatory allusion to technical hitches: '(Un *film* que se corta.)' '(A film which snaps.)'; no less derisive is his reference in the same story to 'este desenlace de *film* en que la pugna de dos hermanos gladiadores de armas distintas, se resuelve con el triunfo de la bondad sobre la perfidia'.†[21]

'Hora muerta' explores the effects of watching films on a person's mind, and it is Ayala's own fevered reactions that give the story its purpose, its coherence, and its disturbing restlessness. The narrator's recollection—'Y salí del cine con fiebre. Con violencia interior' ('And I left the cinema in a fever. With violence inside me')—is the key both to his emotional disquiet during and after his visit to the cinema and to the ways in which the author-narrator tried to capture that disquiet in prose.[22] In the cinema Ayala was as bewildered and bemused as Alberti by the profusion of faces and figures defiant of time and space; Alberti's juxtaposition in 'Carta abierta' (from *Cal y canto*) of Anne Boleyn, a policeman, and bandits in dinner jackets telescopes time with a waggish fantasy which Ayala developed in greater detail. As it echoes Valle-Inclán's credo—expressed in *Luces de bohemia*—that 'Las imágenes más bellas en un espejo cóncavo son absurdas' ('The most beautiful images are absurd in a concave mirror'),[23] Ayala's belief that 'el cine—al fin y al cabo—es una concavidad' ('the cinema, after all, is a concavity') so distorted his sense of time and space that Charlemagne, Chaplin, and Hamlet interchange roles as they form a trio even more fantastic than Alberti's:

Carlomagno—barba florida—había olvidado su espada en la bastonera, junto al bastoncillo de Chaplin.

* the present was composed of two cinematographic planes: a foreground with the face of Aurora and, beyond it, a whole landscape in movement.
† this cinematic ending in which the struggle of two brother gladiators differently armed is resolved in the triumph of good over treachery.

Y Chaplin—Hamlet—atravesaba la cortina con la espada del Emperador. Sin encontrar—por supuesto—el cuerpo de Polonio.

La confusión era espantosa. El reloj hacía horas extraordinarias. (Reclamaba el Sindicato...)*[24]

The narrator's drifting asleep in the cinema only disconcerts him further as he wakes up to face new images so perplexing that they compel him to leave:

Mi cabeza se había inclinado como si hubieran aflojado la cuerda. Oscilaba tristemente, arrastrando por el suelo miradas turbias.

De pronto, un tirón violentísimo. La cabeza, erguida. Las miradas de repercusión—fusil de repercusión—a la pantalla.

... Y la dama de aquella hora perdida había desaparecido. Totalmente. Sin dejar ni el sitio.

La pantalla estaba ocupada ahora por un puente de hierro. Muy estremecido. Muy transitado.

La sugestión del tránsito me empujó a la calle. En busca de la calle. No hubiera podido permanecer más. Y salí del cine con fiebre. Con violencia interior.†[25]

However, his emergence into the street only transfers to real life the bewilderment caused in him by the images on the screen, and an anguished ejaculation of words captures the dismay of being bombarded by multiple and disconnected sounds and sights which he noticed fitfully rather than absorbed calmly as part of a common, daily experience:

Codazos. Empujones. Brechas. Huecos de perplejidad. Momentos atónitos, imaginativos.

---

* Charlemagne—with a flowing beard—had left his sword in the cane stand, next to Chaplin's cane.

And Chaplin—Hamlet—pierced the curtain with the Emperor's sword. Without finding, it goes without saying, Polonius's body.

The confusion was dreadful. The clock showed the most extraordinary times. (The Union registered complaints...)

† My head had sunk to one side as if someone had loosened the string. It rolled sadly, trailing troubled glances along the floor.

Suddenly, a violent jolt. My head, bolt upright. My eyes recoiling—like a recoil rifle—to the screen.

... And the heroine of that lost hour had disappeared. Completely. Without even leaving the place.

The screen was now occupied by an iron bridge. Trembling with traffic. Crisscrossed by traffic.

The very sight of traffic pushed me towards the street. In search of the street. I could not have stayed there any longer. And I emerged from the cinema in a fever. With violence inside me.

(Jonás persiguiendo al tranvía, que se niega a tragarle. Un timbrazo aplastado que cae en un charco y se sumerge rápidamente.

Nada.)*[26]

When the narrator arrives home he is still prey to disquiet, and an equally jerky, staccato style records a series of impulsive, irrational acts. First of all, he narrates, 'Una ansiedad inexplicable me llevó a la alcoba' ('An inexplicable anxiety led me to the bedroom'); then, he recalls, 'me quedé—allí, en medio de la habitación—parado' ('I stood stock still right there, in the centre of the room'); then it occurred to him to 'sofaldar la cama' ('lift up the covers of the bed'); then, he relates, 'Me pasé la mano por la frente' ('I passed my hand over my brow'); and, finally, to complete these pointless actions, he was led to 'probar el interruptor de la luz' ('try the light switch').[27]

What makes 'Hora muerta' into a striking example of a story inspired by and devoted to the cinema is the imaginative way in which Ayala harmonized the effects exercised on his mind and on his style by the experience of watching films. The images he saw on a screen he imagined to be 'concave' inspired a manner of writing that constitutes an intuitive analysis of an excitable, impressionable mind. Emulating the technique of the panning, panoramic shot, he picked out the salient physical features of the city as it spun like a globe before his bewildered gaze:

La ciudad, gran plataforma giratoria.
Estación, Pista. Fábrica. Velódromo. Universidad. Circo.
Gimnasio.
Y cine.†[28]

A visit to the cinema dominates the second section of the story 'Polar estrella' (1928), in which Ayala narrated poignantly a man's infatuation with the star Polar, who is as seductive as Pola Negri and as inaccessible as the polar star, which provides

---

* Elbows. Shoves. Gaps opening up in the crowd. Spaces full of perplexity. Moments of astonishment, of fantasy.
(Jonah pursuing the tram, which refuses to swallow him up. The ring of a bell which plunges into a puddle and is quickly submerged.
Then nothing.)
† The city, a great gyrating platform.
Railway station. Racetrack. Factory. Cycle track. University. Circus.
Gymnasium.
And cinema.

the pun in her name and in the title. Ayala's Polar is unques-
tionably Greta Garbo, whom César M. Arconada exalted in
1928 and whom Ayala eulogized a year later as 'a soul as ardent
as the snow', as a 'nordic Circe', and—in an allusion to Garbo's
Flesh and the Devil (1927)—as '*the devil of flesh*, the spirit of
flesh'.[29] Arconada's fantasy—the 'Posesión lírica de Greta
Garbo'—also entrances Ayala's protagonist, whose adoration of
Polar as a 'siren on the mirror's shore' echoes Arconada's tribute
to Garbo as a 'Siren amidst the foam of light'.[30]

Using Polar's anonymous admirer to give his tale unity and
purpose, Ayala wrote a beautifully paced and constructed story
in which the pivotal visit to the cinema in the second section
ends the suspense and anticipation his character felt in the first
and motivates the disenchantment he will feel in the third. The
story thus literally revolves around the cinema in the same way
as the protagonist's life gyrates around Polar. Ayala suspended
his hero, whom he labelled simply 'the lover', in an endless wait
for the evening showing of Polar's new film. With acute insight
into the effects of waiting on an impatient, fanatical person,
Ayala made him perform acts symptomatic of his nervous state:
he removes his cinema ticket from his wallet and puts it back; he
caresses a piece of film, raises it to the light to study 'el rostro de
Polar en gran plano' ('Polar's face in close-up'), which is as
dominant as Aurora's face in 'Cazador en el alba'.[31] In the
second section Ayala's infatuated hero chooses to prolong and
savour the sense of anticipation; he takes a roundabout route to
the cinema, studies the posters and the flashing neon signs, and
waits until the lights are out before taking his seat. Ayala's
idealistic view of newsreels as 'a unifying instrument, which
confronts and synthesizes nations' makes his protagonist's indifference to them all the more symptomatic of his obsession
with Polar.[32] The distant warfare intimated by a newsreel of
embarking troops could not claim his attention or divert his
thoughts from one long awaited moment: the appearance of
Polar in her new film. So intensely had he awaited her appearance on the screen that to see her suddenly before him paralyses
his breath in his body as his mind confirms once more her
inaccessibility. In two paragraphs remarkable for their detailed
and sustained description of a worshipper's physical and mental
reaction before the object of his reverence, Ayala made his hero

strain to follow Polar's gaze across the screen so that when their eyes seem to meet a current of excitement courses through him and accelerates his pulse-rate:

Cuando, amanecida la ventana del *écran*, irrumpió la estrella con fresco vestido de luz, el amante se sintió conmovido por un cataclismo visceral: el diafragma le redujo el tórax, mientras brotaba en su ánimo la evidencia difícil de lo astral, de lo inasible.

¡Polar, estrella de cine! ¡Belleza imposible, lejana y múltiple! En las salas de todo el mundo su canción muda atraía hacia el borde de la pantalla el oleaje admirativo, reiterado, del jazz. Y el reflejo azul de sus ojos hipnotizaba—bola de rotación suave—el alma enamorada. El se desvivía por forzar aún los más agudos ángulos de su gran mirada, y cuando recibía el disparo ineludible, una corriente le anegaba de ausencia.

La cinta pasaba como pauta apretada de emociones, que su pulso iba llenando.*[33]

Ayala did not leave his story on this rapturous level, and the ambiguity of his attitude towards the cinema and towards his besotted lover emerged when he made human malice or technical clumsiness interrupt his hero's adoration. Through 'Una irregularidad de la máquina, o una perfidia del cameraman' ('A fault in the machine, or the projectionist's malevolence'), the film slips in the projector to display a Polar dismembered and misshapen by a mechanical fluke:

El accidente había quebrado el ritmo de la cinta y la cintura de la estrella. La mitad superior de su cuerpo, abajo. Los pies, en un segundo piso del *écran*. Era una terrible pesadilla su cuerpo disociado: su bella cabeza, sonriente y encendida, por los suelos.†[34]

---

* When the star burst upon the screen, illuminated like a window at daybreak, clad in her bright new tunic of light, the lover felt himself shaken by an abdominal cataclysm: his breathing was suspended as his diaphragm pressed on his chest, whilst there grew in his mind the painful demonstration of the astrally remote, of the inaccessible.

Polar, star of the cinema! A beauty that was impossible, distant, and multiple! In cinemas throughout the world her silent song attracted to the edge of the screen the endlessly echoing waves of jazz tributes. And the blue reflection of her eyes—like a gently revolving crystal ball—hypnotized our lover. He strained to bisect the most acute angles of her imperious gaze, and whenever her eyes fell unavoidably on him, he lost all sense of time and place.

The film flickered on like a rhythmic sequence of emotions, which his pulse kept moving.

† The accident had broken the film's rhythm and the star's waist. The upper half of her body, at the bottom. Her feet, on the upper level of the screen. Her disconnected

The trembling which possesses the *amante* during his contemplation of the accidentally deformed Polar reveals a nervous agitation intensified at the end of the section, where he feels 'turbado' ('troubled') as the star prepares for her bath and 'resentido y nervioso' ('resentful and edgy') when he cannot see her take it; Ayala's sensuous description of her back, upraised arms, and legs, which he imagined as 'serpientes lívidas' ('white serpents'), serves only to exacerbate his protagonist's frustration as she disappears from view 'en la inhibición absoluta de un cambio de escenario' ('in the total inhibition of a change of scenery').[35]

Although Polar's worshipper is clearly tense and disturbed after watching her film, we are not prepared for his neurotic reactions in the final section or for Ayala's seemingly cavalier, lighthearted narration of the surprise dénouement: the lover's suicide. Realizing the hopelessness of his passion, he first burns clips of her films—his 'colección de recuerdos' ('collection of memories')—and then decides to kill himself. The cinema stage-manages his death in the same way as it had warped his life; and by recounting in cinematic terms his climb and his leap to his death, the author Ayala leaves the reader to judge whether he is mocking or passing judgement on his hero. There is certainly no compassion in his account, equivalent to a stage direction, that as his hero goes towards the bridge his eyes could not see the city as it really was but as a montage of scenic clichés, 'paisajes de cine en planos superpuestos' ('cinematic landscapes superimposed one on the other').[36] And the derision hinted at in the final words of the story is confirmed by Ayala's conviction that slow motion 'applied to any movement, however solemn, highlights it and exaggerates it to the point of casting it to the depths of the ridiculous'; the 'comic effect' he himself saw in slow motion underlies the way he related his protagonist's answer to his frustrations:

se arrojó al espacio.

Pero en seguida se sintió flotando en sorpresa. El aire le había recogido en su seno. El dios del cinema tenía dispuesta su caída *au ralenti*.*[37]

---

body was a terrible nightmare: her beautiful head, smiling and radiant, lay on the ground.

* he threw himself into space.

Critic and story-teller go hand in hand in inviting the reader to see something absurd in the lover's suicide and, by extension, in his hopeless passion. The god of the cinema—a deity who by technical trickery can make the impossible appear possible —could arrange the illusion of his graceful floating to earth, but he could not prevent the lethal impact of the lover's body against the ground below.

The theme of the cinematically stylized suicide also appealed to Rosa Chacel in *Estación, ida y vuelta*, in which she made fun of herself as much as of the cinema by comparing her acrobatic nonchalance with that of Harold Lloyd:

Yo podría plagiándole, invitar a la muchedumbre a mi suicidio, y arrojarme sobre los congregados desde lo alto del rascacielos, dejarme caer sencilla y distraídamente, entreteniéndome por el camino en contar los pisos a la inversa . . . Además, como todo buen *film*, terminaría en el abrazo de la novia.*38

The first-person narrative used by Chacel enabled her thoughts to follow the rambling circuit suggested by the title. If she imagined that in her fall to earth she could count 'in reverse order' the storeys she passes, then films achieved no more than to loosen her grip on reality and to enfold her in fantasy. The self-examination proposed by the first-person narrator is undertaken in a series of monologues and musings, in which the cinema operates not as the stimulus to fictional situations, as it did for Ayala, but as a gallery of illustrations of her feelings and attitudes. She corroborated the amusement some people derive from the discomfiture of others by reference to a stock comic situation exemplified in *The Cure* (1916), in which Chaplin treads on Eric Campbell's bandaged foot:

Sensaciones de este género han llegado a ser trucos cómicos del *cine*. Todos, en cuanto vemos aparecer en la pantalla al hombre del pie malo, con su pata estirada atravesando la escena, amerengada de

---

But to his surprise he immediately found himself floating. The air had taken him to its bosom. The god of the cinema had arranged for his fall in slow motion.

* I could plagiarize him by inviting the crowd to my suicide and throwing myself on the assembled throng from the top of the skyscraper, letting myself fall simply and absent-mindedly, amusing myself on the way down by counting the storeys in reverse order . . . Moreover, like every good film, it would end in the embrace of the sweetheart.

algodones llamativamente blancos, sabemos que es para que se la pisen. Y no querríamos; si pudiésemos, acaso lo evitásemos; . . . y, al mismo tiempo, ¡qué risa!, ¡qué risa más indomable, sobre todo si es el boxeador el que le pisa! ¡Y no digamos si es el alpinista, con sus botas de clavos!*[39]

In incorporating her thoughts about the cinema into her purportedly autobiographic novel, Rosa Chacel showed a lack of adventure and creative thrust. Instead of using the films she saw as a member of the Cineclub as the inspiration for stories, situations, and narrative techniques, she used what is ostensibly a novel to set down—in a long section of hypothesis—what she would do in a film. When she pondered whether to give her heroine 'un par de lágrimas, pendientes de sus pestañas' ('a pair of tears, dangling from her eyelashes') and wondered whether anything went through her mind before stepping onto a tram, she was clearly refusing to take seriously her heroine, the banal circumstances in which she placed her—or herself as the writer of a screenplay.[40] By leavening this and other episodes with mockery, Rosa Chacel exposed her unease and self-consciousness as a writer, her ambivalent attitudes to films as a stimulus, and her reluctance—or inability—to let them suggest fictional situations which her imagination could elaborate.

No such lack of confidence had inhibited the Chilean poet Vicente Huidobro from writing in 1921–2 *Cagliostro*, which he defined in the preface he penned in 1931 as 'a visual novel, with a technique influenced by the cinematograph'.[41] Certainly, the images conjured up in a fish bowl derive as directly from cinematic tricks as his account that Lorenza's face 'se torna fluídico y la carta toma el sitio de su frente' ('dissolves and in the place of the brow appears the letter').[42] And Huidobro's belief that in the novel influenced by the cinema 'Events have to move rapidly, otherwise the public is bored' explains the many scenic changes in his novel, in which his characters do not think but

* Feelings of this kind have become comic tricks of the cinema. All of us, as soon as we see appear on the screen a man with an ailing foot, with his outstretched leg traversing the scene, swathed in flamboyantly white bandages, know that he is there only to have his leg trodden on. And we would prefer it not to happen; if we could, perhaps we would prevent it; . . . and yet, what laughter! What uncontrollable laughter, especially if it is a boxer who steps on him! And even more uncontrollable it will be if the culprit is the mountain climber, with his nailed boots!

move like robots, devoid of motive or credibility.[43] So concerned was he to activate his characters that he denied them depth and dimension; when we read that 'Albios monta a caballo sobre el borde de la ventana y penetra en la habitación' ('Albios sits astride the open window and clambers into the room'), we think of Douglas Fairbanks; and the darting movements and cat-and-mouse pursuits of comic films come to mind when we read that 'Cada vez que Cagliostro aprieta el paso para alcanzarla, Marcival levanta la mano y Lorenza acelera también su marcha' ('Every time that Cagliostro quickens his pace to overtake her, Marcival raises his hand and Lorenza also quickens her pace').[44]

In writing *Cagliostro*, Huidobro calculated that

the public of today, which has acquired the cinema habit, may be interested in a novel in which the author has deliberately chosen words of a visual character and events that are best suited to comprehension through the eyes.[45]

But the fluttering bats, the coach 'Dejando tras ella una enorme nube de polvo' ('Leaving in its wake a great cloud of dust'), the dark laboratory with a furnace and secret levers, suggest that Huidobro was writing down to the level of his public and pandering to its tastes with the melodramatic scenes and elements it had come to expect in adventure serials.[46] More disturbing are the lapses in his consistency and concentration. His choice of 'words of a visual character' is strikingly illustrated by his statement 'los floretes de sus miradas al chocarse en el aire hacen saltar todas las chispas del odio' ('as the swords of their glances crossed all the sparks of hatred leap into the air'); yet he repudiated the chance to describe a woman's beauty by superciliously directing his reader: 'piensa en la mujer más hermosa que has visto en tu vida y aplica a Lorenza su hermosura. Así me evitarás y te evitarás una larga descripción' ('think of the most beautiful woman you have ever seen and apply her beauty to Lorenza. In this way you will save me and save yourself a long description').[47] Apart from breaking the reader's concentration, a command such as this interrupts the continuity of what is after all a novel; it also displays contempt for one of the most venerable of literary motifs in a work studded with the clichés of filmed melodramas.

Huidobro's addresses to the reader are a symptom of the self-consciousness which makes *Cagliostro* unsatisfying and unsuccessful as a novel. Because it constitutes his 'answer to the question whether the cinematograph can influence the novel', it is as forced as a rhetorical exercise.[48] Huidobro took himself too seriously, and his novel is, inevitably, as humourless and shallow as the films that suggested its scenes and situations. What Huidobro lacked in *Cagliostro* was the fantasy, the elfin humour, and sensitivity with which Benjamín Jarnés used films and cinema-going as motifs in some of his novels.

Like Ayala, Jarnés was intrigued by the effects films exercise on the minds of an audience; as a member of that audience he himself hoped to find on the screen 'many dreams which, out of idleness or incompetence, I did not write'.[49] Films activated Jarnés's imagination and sensibility to such a degree that he included himself among 'the first category of spectators, those who dream and sometimes record their dreams in poems, in fables, in stories, in dramatic farces'.[50] In 1930 he boldly and fancifully modified the story of Vivien and Merlin by composing a new fable in which Vivien enchants the Knights of the Round Table with 'esa máquina endiablada' ('that devilish machine'), which becomes an essential factor in his reworking of an ancient story.[51] It is not surprising that one contemporary critic felt on reading *Viviana y Merlín* 'the sensation of a marvellous film'.[52] Vivien's seduction of Merlin with her 'magic box' must be rated as fantastic a scene as ever devised for a film. Ingeniously, Jarnés spanned the centuries as Vivien's magic box appears to Merlin as 'el monstruo, dando resoplidos' ('the snorting monster') whose eyes—'dos ojos enormes de dragón' ('two huge dragon's eyes')—suddenly light up; he then justified his adventurous anachronism with the explanation:

> No, no es diabólico artilugio; es un hallazgo del hombre, que no se contó entre las profecías de Merlín. Porque Viviana no tiene edad ninguna y escoge de cualquier época sus medios de seducción y de transporte.*[53]

Viviana y Merlín alone supports Jarnés's contention that 'the influence of the cinema on contemporary literature cannot be

---

* No, it is not a devilish artefact; it is a man-made invention, which was not included among Merlin's prophecies. For Vivien is ageless and chooses from any century her means of seduction and transportation.

denied'.[54] Although original and imaginative, his reworking of a fable shows both the cinema's power to inspire new dreams and revise old ones, and his awareness of the limitations of that power. The cinema certainly inspired him to dream, but he felt obliged to contain his dreams within conventional narrative frameworks. Jarnés the novelist revealed the same measure, the same control, as Jarnés the critic, who affirmed that 'We can find poetry as much in films as in music, in painting, in literal commentary or in stone'.[55] Jarnés refused to let the cinema shape and dominate his novels, using it rather to devise scenes and tableaux which, assimilated into their structure, contribute to their texture and to their humour. In *Paula y Paulita* the narrator accompanies Paula to a special cinema programme in honour of a holidaying bishop; his promise to her that 'Nos sumergiremos en esa tina de purificación' ('We shall submerge ourselves in that purifying bath') introduces a note of irony which modulates Jarnés's description of the bishop and of the programme chosen for him, whose unexceptionable dullness and irreproachable purity are captured in the author's repeated use of the adjective 'white':

El teatrillo se ha convertido en un templo. Recogimiento, diálogos susurrados. De pronto, el palco vecino se convierte en un púlpito.

El obispo de Antinópolis se adelanta sonriendo hasta la barandilla y contempla tiernamente a los espectadores. Sorprendo en él un ademán inequívoco: automáticamente, su mano se iba a alzar para bendecir al público; pero se contiene. Después lee el programa que le ofrece el familiar, con el mismo gesto de ofrecerle el manípulo. Y toda la faz de su ilustrísima va cayendo en un hondo reposo. El programa es tan lindo y tan blanco como el lecho de una colegiala.*[56]

By informing the narrator that the special programme 'Es una sesión blanca' ('is an inoffensive session'), Paula had prepared him and us for its contents. And in devising items at once decorous and dull, Jarnés put his tongue firmly in his cheek as

---

* The little theatre has become a church. Propriety, whispered conversations. Suddenly, the adjacent box becomes a pulpit.

The bishop of Antinopolis advances smilingly to the hand-rail and looks down tenderly on the audience. I see him making an unambiguous gesture; automatically, his hand was about to rise in order to bless the gathering; but he contains himself. Then he reads the programme which his relative offers him with the same expression he would use to give him the maniple. And the face of the bishop settles into a deep repose. The programme is as pretty and as white as a schoolgirl's bed.

he set the smug, condescending bishop face to face with anodyne films in order to create a situation gently satiric of the bishop and of the programme in his honour, which comprises:

Primero. Sinfonía, Schubert.
Segundo. Información gráfica de la beatificación de los mártires de Esmirna.
Tercero. *Imelda de Lambertini.* Poema cinematográfico en blanco mayor.
Cuarto. *La oración de una madre.* Cinedrama en tres jornadas.*[57]

Paula's conjecture that 'Quizá el público bostece un poco' ('Perhaps the audience will yawn a little') permits the narrator's ironic rejoinder that the evening is 'extraordinary' because of the presence of a bishop; his presence ensured a programme whose sanctimonious tedium was a mildly ironic comment on the Catholic Church.

Jarnés inserted a visit to the cinema into his novel *Locura y muerte de nadie* (1929), but this time the specific purpose of the visit—to see a newsreel of the scene of a murder the protagonists had actually witnessed—injects into the episode something far more disturbing than irony. In this novel Jarnés directed his irony against those who tried to 'reproducir exactamente el contorno exterior de una estrella de moda' ('reproduce exactly the external appearance of a current star') or against magazine articles such as 'La ciencia del beso' and 'Besos cinematográficos'. It was with such essays in mind that he wrote mockingly of the Tres Hermanas Argelinas (Three Algerian Sisters) appearing in a night club, who 'coinciden acaso en el modo de besar, que aprendieron en la misma revista de cinema' ('by chance coincide in their manner of kissing, which they learned from the same cinema magazine').[58]

Much more disconcerting than these pricks of irony is the episode of the murder of two municipal employees, not merely because it illustrates the social and political unrest in Spain in the 1930s, but because newsreel cameramen arrive immediately to film the scene of the crime and the crowd's reaction to it.

* First. A symphony by Schubert.
Second. Newsreel of the beatificacion of the martyrs of Smyrna.
Third. *Imelda de Lambertini.* A cinematographic poem with white as the dominant note.
Fourth. *A Mother's Prayer.* A cinematic drama in three acts.

From his balcony Arturo, Jarnés's protagonist, sees the crowd's seething indignation and spontaneous anger evaporate before the cameras; the balcony allows him to look down literally and metaphorically on the throng as it is suddenly desensitized to the murders by the prospect of the cheap and ephemeral fame of a newsreel. Jarnés's finely observed and beautifully paced passage, as he describes the crowd composing itself for the cameras, is a restrained, oblique comment on man's callousness, the superficiality of his emotions, and his vainglorious pursuit of celluloid immortality:

De pronto, unos hombres audaces surcan las olas con un frágil esquife cargado de imágenes. Son operadores. Van a recoger, a prender en sus cintas aquella espléndida fiebre humana. Se instalan en un ángulo de la plaza, luego en otro. Aquella multitud no perecerá, no se destruirá al disgregarse. Giran los manubrios. Las gentes se dan cuenta. Se rehacen. Comienza en ellas a perderse la espontaneidad. Se preparan a cruzar por la pantalla. Una muchacha se adereza el pelo, otra se fija escrupulosamente un clavel, aquélla se abre algo más el escote. Algún mozuelo se engalla, enciende un puro, se ladea el sombrero. La muchedumbre recibe de golpe esta profunda impresión: ¡También ella es espectáculo! Y se dispone a serlo. Se inventan sonrisas, se avivan miradas, se atusan rizos, se ensayan posturas. Se olvida de que se prepara para un espectáculo donde cada espectador puede ser un personaje.*[59]

Jarnés's astuteness in imagining the scene filmed enabled him to follow up the episode by making Arturo, Matilde, and Juan Sánchez visit a cinema to see the newsreel. Having made a point about human vanity, Jarnés now hammered it home in an elegant exercise in parallelism which embraces narrative structure, metaphoric language, and moral attitude. As a vantage

* Suddenly, several bold men plough through the waves of people with a fragile skiff laden with pictures. They are cameramen. They are going to record, to capture on their reels of film that splendid human fever. They set themselves up in one corner of the square, then in another. That crowd will not perish, will not be destroyed when it disperses. The handles turn. The people realize that they are being filmed. They reorganize themselves. They begin to lose their spontaneity. They prepare to walk in front of the cameras. One girl straightens her hair, another fastidiously pins a carnation to her dress, and another opens her dress to show a little more of her bosom. One youth struts like a cock, lights a cigar, tilts his hat to one side. The crowd suddenly realizes with startling clarity that it too is a spectacle. And that is what it sets itself to be. Smiles are forced, looks are made to appear earnest, curls are twirled, postures are rehearsed. They forget that they are preparing themselves for a spectacle in which every spectator can figure as an actor.

point from which to observe and judge people, the box Arturo and his friends occupy in the cinema matches the balcony of his house; close-ups in the newsreel balance the individual scenes isolated by Arturo's binoculars; and the cameramen's passage through the crowd is paralleled by the marine metaphors of Arturo's entry into the darkened cinema, whose rows of seats are likened to waves:

La ondulación de las butacas, que avanza en filas simétricas hacia la ribera clara, es apenas perceptible gracias a esas diminutas linternas que andan buscando entre las ondas negras algún espacio náufrago. Pronto, aguzadas las pupilas, se va viendo en lo sumo de cada onda la pálida espuma de los rostros.*[60]

Having constructed his parallel framework of city square and cinema screen, balcony and box, Jarnés established one more correspondence when he confronted one crowd—in the Russian film being shown—with another—the one seated in the cinema. The importance for Jarnés of this confrontation is apparent in his insistence on two crowds in three consecutive paragraphs:

Arturo va repartiendo sus miradas entre ambos espectáculos, entre ambas muchedumbres. En la pantalla la muchedumbre elaborada; frente a ella, la muchedumbre en estado nativo.

Multitud expresiva y multitud en estado nativo. Multitud armónica y multitud simétrica, repartida en filas, diseminada en palcos, sin realidad apenas.

Un haz de fisonomías sin sentido colectivo, frente a una armonizada muchedumbre, a la que no comprenden.†[61]

When the newsreel succeeds the film, the 'symmetrical multitude' which failed to understand or identify itself with the artistically composed crowd of the Russian film has the chance

---

* The undulation of the seats, advancing in symmetrical rows towards the illuminated shore, is barely visible thanks to those minute torches which seek some shipwrecked space amid the black waves. Soon, our eyes, now accustomed to straining in the darkness, make out at the crest of every wave the pallid foam of people's faces.

† Arturo divides his attention between the two spectacles, between two multitudes. On the screen the carefully composed multitude; facing it, the crowd in its raw state.

An expressive crowd and a crowd in its raw state. A symphonic crowd and a symmetrical crowd, divided into rows, scattered in balconies, almost bereft of reality.

A surface of faces without any collective meaning, facing a harmonized crowd, which they do not understand.

to recognize itself. The eagerness with which 'Juan Sánchez del palco' ('Juan Sánchez of the box') watches his struggle to occupy 'el primer puesto en la masa anónima' ('the front position in the anonymous mass') and sees himself dominate the screen is censured by Jarnés's allusion to a 'lamentable Juan Sánchez'; hypnotized by the reflection of himself on what the author called the 'implacable' mirror, Juan Sánchez is no more than a vain and insignificant member of the collective Narcissus that is the cinema audience.[62] In *Paula y Paulita* Jarnés had written with enthusiastic overstatement that 'La pantalla derrama su mística blancura sobre todos, les hace contemplarse en ella como nerviosos narcisos' ('The screen sheds its mystical whiteness over everyone, making them contemplate themselves in it like a nervous Narcissus'); in *Locura y muerte de nadie* he hardened his attitude, which became openly critical of the 'plástica inmortalidad' promised by the camera:

La muchedumbre sigue con avidez contemplándose a sí misma. Todos los espectadores son un solo Narciso, un Narciso descomunal que se mira estremecer en el agua neutral de la pantalla. A unos ojos desorbitados de allá, corresponden otros ojos desorbitados de acá.*[63]

In replacing Narcissus's fountain with a cinema screen, Jarnés modernized the classic theme of self-contemplation and at the same time modified it to accommodate his poised criticism of human vanity. His ability to take a fresh and not entirely deferential look at a venerable theme of literature or art is displayed again in *Escenas junto a la muerte* (1931). When the narrator expressed his desire to go to the cinema to see *Charlot en Zalamea* because 'dicen que está muy bien' ('they say it is very good'), Jarnés prepared us impishly for his fifth chapter, 'Charlot en Zalamea (Film)', which is purportedly his account of a film that bridges the seventeenth and the twentieth centuries.[64] A film of *El alcalde de Zalamea* was made in 1914; and Jarnés had already joined in his compatriots' veneration of Chaplin with his own tribute to 'Charlot' in *Ejercicios* (1927). By imagining an encounter between Chaplin and Calderón de la Barca's

---

* The crowd continues to watch itself avidly. All the spectators are a single Narcissus, a monstrous Narcissus who watches himself tremble in the neutral water of the screen. Eyes staring on the screen are matched by eyes staring from the seats.

character Pedro Crespo, Jarnés devised an ingenious way of re-examining the drama *El alcalde de Zalamea* and thereby confronting two worlds, two centuries, two genres, and two moral climates. The plot of his 'film' is thus as fanciful as that of an actual film like *A Yankee at King Arthur's Court* (1949) or of a possible one like *Calderón in California*.

Chaplin and Pedro Crespo come face to face immediately. The drum-beats which herald the arrival of Chaplin and his troupe summon Crespo, ever zealous in the exercise of his mayoral duties. Instead of encountering the soldiers he feared, he finds himself 'asombrado ante un diminuto bigote, ante unos gruesos zapatones, ante un bastoncillo nervioso, ante un extraño sombrero'.*[65] In the rapid exchange between them, Jarnés set the unsophisticated vitality of slapstick films against the solemnity of Calderón's *autos sacramentales*, the artistic integrity of Chaplin against Crespo's use of authority. By making Crespo justify censorship with the most famous words he utters in the play, Jarnés mocked not only Crespo's reasons and Calderón's words, but revealed his preoccupation with censorship; that preoccupation he was to display more explicitly in 1935 in the inquiry organized by the magazine *Nuestro Cinema*:

—¿Quién eres?
—Charlot.
—¿Y esos?
—Mis amigos.
—¿Bufones?
—Artistas.
—¿Qué queréis?
—Representar.
—¿Autos sacramentales?
—Farsas que yo invento.
—¿Morales?
—Alegres. Traemos con nosotros la alegría. Hemos expulsado a Pierrot por cursi y a Tristán por llorón.
—Sois el mismo demonio. ¡Largo de aquí!
Charlot vuelve la espalda, hace callar al tambor y se va, calle adelante. A los veinte pasos Pedro Crespo le llama.
—Oye.

---

* astonished before a diminutive moustache, before some large, heavy shoes, before a nervous little cane, before a strange hat.

—Diga, alcalde.

—Llama a tu gente. Representaréis en mi casa. Si me parece bien, daréis la función en la plaza.

—¿Censura? ¿Por qué?

—¿Soy aquí el representante del honor, que es patrimonio del alma, y el alma solo es de Dios.*[66]

Chaplin's first impulse is to leave, but it is checked by the appearance of Isabel, Crespo's daughter, who, like the beautiful heroines of Chaplin's films, makes his heart triumph over his head. Isabel's role is a key one in Jarnés's fantasy; by a look she encourages the comic to stay, and by staying he ends up in prison, for Crespo cannot accept as art the farce presented by Chaplin under the title *Sotabanco (Garret)*, which subverts all the values he held sacred and constant. His refusal to deem as anything but immoral 'una ramera generosa y un hampón honrado' ('a generous whore and an honest scoundrel') impels him to imprison the comic; it is Isabel who engineers his escape but only after El Trujamán (The Interpreter) has told him—in a precise reminiscence of Calderón's play—of Crespo's execution by garrotte of 'a captain' and—a new fact introduced by Jarnés—of Isabel's flight from the convent in which her father

---

* —Who are you?

—Charlie Chaplin.

—And who are they?

—My friends.

—Buffoons?

—Artists.

—What do you want?

—To put on a show.

—*Autos sacramentales?*

—Farces that I make up.

—Are they moral?

—They are gay. We bring gaiety with us. We have expelled Pierrot for being pretentious and Tristan for being a cry-baby.

—You are the devil himself. Clear off!

Chaplin turns his back, silences the drummer, and moves off up the street. After only twenty paces Crespo calls him.

—Listen.

—Yes, mister mayor?

—Call back your people. You shall put on a show in my house. If I think it is suitable, you will put it on in the public square.

—Censorship? Why?

—Here I am the representative of honour, which is the patrimony of the soul, and the soul belongs only to God.

had put her because 'se negó a cumplir los cánones' ('she refused to obey the rules').[67]

In imagining a sequel to the violent events dramatized by Calderón, particularly the captain's rape of Isabel and his execution, Jarnés offered an alternative version of the events which leads us to revise our attitudes to Isabel, Crespo, and the unfortunate Don Alvaro. As Isabel and Chaplin flee through the forest, she stops first to seek her honour, which, as she reminds her companion in Calderonian terms, 'Es la joya más rica' ('is the richest jewel'), and then to feverishly touch the ground where she lost her virginity to the passionate Don Alvaro, whose 'voz de barítono tremolaba de fiebre, desfallecía, ronca y dulce al mismo tiempo . . .' ('baritone voice fluttered with fever, died away in his throat, hoarse and gentle at the same time . . .').[68] In Jarnés's Isabel we see not the wronged and avenged heroine of *El alcalde de Zalamea* but a woman unhinged by sexual arousal and by the remorse which followed it. Devotees of Calderón's play may find it difficult to recognize their heroine in the woman who confesses that 'Escandalicé el convento con mis suspiros y mis ataques' ('I scandalized the convent with my sighs and my nervous fits'); and Chaplin's sensible advice to her brother when he catches up with them—'coge a tu hermana y métela en una clínica hasta que se case . . . o cosa análoga' ('take hold of your sister and put her in a clinic until she gets married . . . or something of the sort')—is justified by the symptoms she had already confided in him:

Recorría semidesnuda los pasillos, llamaba a las puertas de las celdas, fingía cartas de amor que me llegaban escondidas en libros de devoción . . . *[69]

Jarnés showed scant respect for Calderón, whom he derided first in Isabel's recollection that she had to narrate her misfortune 'in verse' and then in Chaplin's reply to her brother's indignant protest that 'Un vagabundo ha raptado a mi hermana' ('A tramp has abducted my sister'):

—Mira, Juan, eso ya me va cansando un poco. Tu hermana se deja raptar con una inexplicable facilidad. Bueno es urdir y aceptar un

---

* I would wander half naked through the corridors, I would knock on the doors of the cells, I would pretend to receive love letters hidden in books of devotion . . .

primer rapto para que luego se luzca un dramaturgo, pero esto ya es abusar de mí.*⁷⁰

Crespo's lack of humanity and the austere moral values of his creator were indicted by Jarnés when he made Don Lope describe the former as 'brutal' and muse, in the final words of the piece, as Chaplin makes his exit: '—¡Pobre muchacho! ¡Tan inteligente! ¡Pedro Crespo hubiera acabado con él!'†⁷¹

Chaplin's incursion into seventeenth-century society enabled Jarnés to question its moral code and to reassess a play he refused to venerate. For Jarnés the ideal standards of humanity, compassion, and understanding are set by Chaplin, who is the solitary observer mirroring the weaknesses and foibles of others:

El mundo pasa y le deja en la cuneta, como a un espíritu extraño. Charlot representa el sentido profundo de lo cómico en el hombre, y ningún grupo humano es capaz de soportar tan formidable espejo.‡⁷²

To write a new version of an established classic is to challenge its standing and the premises on which its reputation is founded. What Jarnés did in 'Charlot en Zalamea' was to set against the inhumanity of Crespo and his creator the humanity of Chaplin, whose role as a warm but lonely observer of life is one that he himself adopted. Jarnés's tribute to Chaplin as 'un prestidigitador de emociones' ('a conjuror of emotions') is justified by the antipathy he clearly felt for Pedro Crespo and Calderón.⁷³ Vanity and cruelty are timeless and universal human failings; the cinema enabled Jarnés to present them in a new situation and in a new narrative framework.

---

* —Look here, Juan, I am getting slightly weary of all that. Your sister lets herself be abducted with inexplicable ease. It's all very well to scheme and accept the first abduction so that a dramatist may then show off his skills, but this is really taking advantage of me.

† —Poor lad! And so intelligent! Pedro Crespo would have done away with him!

‡ The world goes by and leaves him stranded in the ditch, as if he were a strange spirit. Chaplin represents the profound sense of the comic in man, and no human group is capable of enduring such a formidable mirror.

CONCLUSION

THE END OF A DREAM

WRITTEN in 1920, Pedro Salinas's poem 'Cinematógrafo' celebrated the entry of moving pictures into the consciousness of many Spanish writers; published in 1936, Andrés Carranque de Ríos's novel of the same title assailed the failure of the Spanish film-makers to create an industry that matched the standards set by foreign competitors. José Sancho, the owner of the seedy 'Academia-Film' and amateurish film director, Rocamora, the proprietor of 'Films Rocamora', and Poch, the hard-headed Valencian businessman, embodied in *Cinematógrafo* the technical ignorance, the abject tastes, and unscrupulous practices of philistines concerned not with quality but with quick financial gain. Elaborating on Castanys's jibe that a guitar, cape, and torero hat were essential ingredients 'for a national production', Carranque de Ríos derided the Spanish film industry by attributing to Rocamora the films *Un bandido andaluz, Maldición gitana, El amor de un torero*, and *La tragedia del torero*.[1] As he acidly pointed out, 'De técnica cinematográfica el señor Rocamora sabía bien poca cosa. Todo lo hacía por lo que leía en las revistas de cine' ('Sr Rocamora knew very little about cinematographic technique. He did everything according to what he read in the cinema magazines').[2] One of Rocamora's actors proposed a solution to inferior acting and inexpert directing when he stated that 'nosotros debemos ver cómo trabajan los artistas extranjeros' ('we must see how foreign artists work').[3] Happily for Spanish literature of the 1920s and 1930s, that is precisely what so many Spanish writers did.

The writers who have figured most prominently in this book were, mercifully, disdainful of Spanish films and of the actors who appeared in them, who hardly warranted a mention in their works. Impervious to the narrowly national allure of an imagined film like *Maldición gitana* or of actual ones like *Amor gitano* and *Venganza gitana*, they found in the cinema a stimulus that transcended the boundaries of country and language. One can only be profoundly thankful that the call for restrictive quotas made by a resentful Spanish film industry did not staunch the flow of foreign films and so starve of sustenance minds that were active, impressionable, and talented. In providing writers with what E. H. Gombrich has called a 'visual vocabulary', films broadened the range of their expression and added new depth and dimensions to their works.[4] The works I have considered in the preceding chapters show that poems, plays, stories, and novels do not have to be 'doped with literary borrowings', to use a memorable phrase of Henry Miller. What writers saw on the cinema screen harmonized with what they read on the printed page, and scenes and sequences and stars of films complemented so naturally the imprint left by wide reading that in Jarnés's 'film' Chaplin coexists with Calderón de la Barca's Pedro Crespo and in Alberti's *Yo era un tonto y lo que he visto me ha hecho dos tontos* the silent screen comics move easily in the world of *Alice in Wonderland* and anonymous, popular songs.

Without the inspiration provided by the cinema Spanish literature of the 1920s and 1930s would have been poorer, and no study of it can afford to overlook the essential fact that the experience of watching films made writers pick up their pens and write. Our understanding of Spanish literature of those years is complete only when we recognize the fertilization of words by images and measure the enrichment of theme, emotion, and technique brought by the cinema. In 1936, the year that marked the end of so many illusions, the door of the dream-house closed; those who love and enjoy Spanish literature must give thanks that so many Spanish writers stepped inside.

NOTES

INTRODUCTION

1. 'Un cine sencillo', *Los Muchachos*, no. 98 (26 Mar. 1916), pp. 7–9.
2. 'Secretos del cine', *Los Muchachos*, no. 69 (5 Sept. 1915), pp. 13–14.
3. Ricardo Acevedo, 'En el cine (Cuento)', *Los Muchachos*, no. 229 (29 Sept. 1918), p. 13.
4. See for example: Bacarisse, 'El cronista del cinematógrafo', *España*, no. 294 (18 Dec. 1920), pp. 15–16; Juan Piqueras, '"Kuhle Wampe" y el cine proletario', *Octubre*, no. 1 (1933), pp. 20–1.
5. J. P. González Martín, 'La prosa de Rafael Alberti', *Insula*, no. 310 (Sept. 1972); José-Carlos Mainer, *La edad de plata (1902–1931). Ensayo de interpretación de un proceso cultural* (Barcelona, 1975), p. 196.
6. Robert Richardson, *Literature and Film* (Bloomington, 1969), p. 3.
7. *La Révolution Surréaliste*, no. 3 (15 Apr. 1925), p. 7.
8. Charlotte Becker, 'Lillian Gish', *Motion Picture Classic*, vol. IX (Jan. 1920), no. 5, p. 55.

CHAPTER I

1. Laurie Lee, *As I Walked Out One Midsummer Morning* (Harmondsworth, 1971), pp. 93–4.
2. Juan Antonio Cabero, *Historia de la cinematografía española* (Madrid, 1949), pp. 24–5.
3. María Teresa León, *Memoria de la melancolía* (Buenos Aires, 1970), p. 97.
4. Rogelio Sinán, 'Nocturno sintético', *La Gaceta Literaria*, no. 68 (15 Oct. 1929); Giménez Caballero, *Julepe de menta* (Madrid, 1929), p. 25.
5. Giménez Caballero, *Julepe de menta*, p. 29.
6. Ortega y Gasset, *Obras completas*, 4th ed. (Madrid, 1957), vol. III, p. 66.
7. Angel Marsá, 'Elogio sentimental del cine', *El Cine*, no. 572 (31 Mar. 1923), p. 3.
8. Gómez de la Serna, 'El hijo surrealista', *Revista de Occidente*, vol. XXX (1930), no. LXXXVII, p. 29.
9. Reported in *Nuestro Cinema*, no. 10 (Mar. 1933), p. 143.
10. Mildred Constantine and Alan Fern, *Revolutionary Soviet Film Posters* (Baltimore and London, 1974), p. 2.
11. 'News and Notes', *Pictures and Picturegoer*, no. 223 (18–25 May 1918), p. 482.
12. Rafael Gil, 'Cinema documental y educativo', *Popular Film*, Año VI (3 Sept. 1931), no. 264; A. Casinos Guillén, 'Laboremos por un cinema infantil educativo', *Popular Film*, Año VIII (28 Sept. 1933), no. 372; L. Fernández Cancela, 'El cine educativo', *Cinegramas*, Año I (25 Nov. 1934), no. 11; Pérez Bellver, 'Películas educativas', *Films Selectos*, Año

VI (5 Oct. 1935), no. 259, p. 3; Casinos Guillén, 'Notas y noticias del cinema educativo', *Popular Film*, Año XI (12 Nov. 1936), no. 533.

13. Giménez Caballero, '¿Qué es cinema educativo?', *La Gaceta Literaria*, no. 115 (1 Oct. 1931).

14. Mateo Santos, 'El cine como instrumento pedagógico', *Popular Film*, Año VI (5 Feb. 1931), no. 234; Mariana Hoffmann, 'Influencia del cinema en la imaginación de los niños', *Popular Film*, Año VII (3 Mar. 1932), no. 290.

15. '¿Qué opina usted del cine y cuáles son sus estrellas favoritas? Encuesta dirigida por Don Piñor', *Juventud*, Año II (1 Feb. 1929), no. 13.

16. Luis Gómez Mesa, *Autenticidad del cinema (Teorías sin trampa)* (Madrid, 1936), p. 38; Jarnés, 'Literatura y cinema', *Films Selectos*, Año IV (17 June 1933), no. 140, p. 3.

17. César M. Arconada, 'Hacia un cinema proletario', *Nuestro Cinema*, nos. 8–9 (Jan.–Feb. 1933), pp. 92–4; Piqueras, '"Kuhle Wampe" y el cine proletario', *Octubre*, no. 1 (1933), pp. 20–1.

18. Juan M. Plaza, 'Posibilidades sociales del cinema', *Nuestro Cinema*, nos. 8–9 (Jan.–Feb. 1933), pp. 90–2; F. Martínez González, 'Apuntes sobre cinema social', *Popular Film*, Año VIII (23 Feb. 1933), no. 341; A. Consiglio, 'Función social del cinema', *Popular Film*, Año IX (18 Jan. 1934), no. 388.

19. Casinos Guillén, 'Literatura y cinema', *Popular Film*, Año VIII (11 May 1933), no. 352.

20. Cabero, *Historia de la cinematografía española*, p. 247.

21. 'We Hear that —', *Pictures and Picturegoer*, vol. XIII (16–23 June 1917), no. 175, p. 6.

22. Juan del Sarto, 'Estética y ritmo de Johnny Weismuller y Maureen Sullivan', *Cinegramas*, Año I (28 Oct. 1934), no. 7; 'La ciencia del beso', *La Pantalla*, Año II (24 Feb. 1928), no. 9, p. 141.

23. Gómez-Mesa, '"El acorazado Potemkin" en la sesión 21ª. del Cineclub', *La Gaceta Literaria*, no. 106 (15 May 1931).

24. Buñuel, *L'Age d'or. Un chien andalou* (London, 1968), pp. 28, 56.

25. C. Fernández Cuenca, 'Besos cinematográficos', *La Pantalla*, Año II (14 Oct. 1928), no. 42, p. 679; M. R. Rubí, 'Cómo besan los ases de la pantalla. Clases e importancia de los besos', *Films Selectos*, Año I (1 Nov. 1930), no. 5; Doris Falberg, 'Los besos cinematográficos', *El Cine*, Año XVI (23 June 1927), no. 793; J. Sacedón, 'Los besos cinematográficos', *¡Tararí!*, Año II (31 Dec. 1931), no. 48; J. B. Valero, 'El beso en el cine', *Films Selectos*, Año IV (10 June 1933), no. 139; 'El nuevo arte del beso', *Popular Film*, Año IX (11 Jan. 1934), no. 387; F. Ferrari Billoch, '¿Sabría usted besar para el celuloide?', *Cinegramas*, Año II (6 Jan. 1935), no. 17.

26. 'Secretos del cine', *Los Muchachos*, no. 69 (5 Sept. 1915), pp. 13–14; 'Cine sencillo', *Los Muchachos*, no. 98 (26 Mar. 1916), pp. 7–9; J. Arqués, 'Delicias del cine', *Charlot*, no. 15 (3 June 1916). See too the comic strips under the title 'Cinematografía de Los Muchachos' published in *Los Muchachos*, no. 5 (14 June 1914) and no. 67 (22 Aug. 1915).

27. Apollinaire, 'Antes del cinema, Cohete-señal, Océano de tierra', *Grecia*,

no. 12 (Apr. 1919), pp. 11–12; Torre, 'Friso ultraísta. Film', *Grecia*, no. 16 (20 May 1919); Garfias, 'Cinematógrafo', *Grecia*, no. 17 (30 May 1919).

28. Bacarisse, 'Crónica de cinematógrafo. Cervantes y Julio Verne', *España*, no. 295 (25 Dec. 1920), pp. 14–15; 'Kinéscopo. Teddy, o el héroe cómico', *España*, no. 300 (29 Jan. 1921), pp. 10–11.

29. 'Boletín del Cineclub. Ramón Gómez de la Serna, Jazzbandismo', *La Gaceta Literaria*, no. 52 (15 Feb. 1929); 'Palabras de Pío Baroja en torno a "Zalacaín el aventurero"', *La Gaceta Literaria*, no. 53 (1 Mar. 1929); 'Palabras del doctor Marañón en el Cineclub acerca de la vanguardia y el cinematógrafo', *La Gaceta Literaria*, no. 83 (1 June 1930).

30. Buñuel, 'La dama de las camelias', *La Gaceta Literaria*, no. 24 (15 Dec. 1927).

31. Buñuel, 'Metrópolis', *La Gaceta Literaria*, no. 9 (1 May 1927); Maurois, 'La Poésie du cinéma', in Maurois *et al*, *L'Art cinématographique*, vol. III (Paris, 1927), pp. 1–37.

32. 'Luis Buñuel, en Madrid', *La Gaceta Literaria*, no. 27 (1 Feb. 1928); 'Una organización. Cinema para minorías', *La Gaceta Literaria*, no. 41 (1 Sept. 1928).

33. Giménez Caballero, 'Convocatoria a los cineastas. Cineclub Español (C. E.)', *La Gaceta Literaria*, no. 43 (1 Oct. 1928).

34. 'Noticias del Cineclub', *La Gaceta Literaria*, no. 52 (15 Feb. 1929).

35. Quoted by J. F. Aranda, *Luis Buñuel. Biografía crítica* (Barcelona, 1969), p. 86.

36. 'Buñuel y Dalí en el Cineclub', *La Gaceta Literaria*, no. 51 (1 Feb. 1929).

37. Piqueras, 'Boletín del Cineclub', *La Gaceta Literaria*, no. 72 (15 Dec. 1929).

38. 'Historia del Cineclub Español', *La Gaceta Literaria*, no. 105 (1 May 1931); Giménez Caballero, 'Muerte y resurrección del Cineclub', *La Gaceta Literaria*, no. 121 (15 Jan. 1932).

39. Carlez, 'Sombra y sonido', *Impresiones*, Año II (23 Jan. 1930), no. 21.

40. J. G. de Ubieta, 'El "cine de minorías" en España', *Popular Film*, Año VIII (23 Mar. 1933), no. 345.

41. Arconada, 'Boletín del Cineclub. Sesión inaugural', *La Gaceta Literaria*, no. 49 (1 Jan. 1929); Giménez Caballero, 'El Cineclub, la Vanguardia y los tacones', *La Gaceta Literaria*, no. 51 (1 Feb. 1929).

42. 'El Cineclub en el resto de España', *La Gaceta Literaria*, no. 47 (1 Dec. 1928); 'Respuestas Cineclub', *La Gaceta Literaria*, no. 48 (15 Dec. 1928).

43. Juan Medina, 'Revisión de Cineclubs', *Popular Film*, Año VIII (20 July 1933), no. 362.

44. A. R., 'El Cineclub. Tercera sesión', *La Gaceta Literaria*, no. 53 (1 Mar. 1929).

45. 'Cineclub. Lista de inscripciones', *La Gaceta Literaria*, no. 48 (15 Dec. 1928).

46. Piqueras, 'Boletín del Cineclub. La sexta sesión', *La Gaceta Literaria*, no. 58 (15 May 1929).

47. Piqueras, 'Influencia del Cineclub en los programas del cinema público', *La Gaceta Literaria*, no. 63 (1 Aug. 1929).
48. 'El Cineclub. La próxima sesión: Lo cómico en el cinema', *La Gaceta Literaria*, no. 56 (15 Apr. 1929).
49. 'Organización del "Cineclub"', *La Gaceta Literaria*, no. 48 (15 Dec. 1928).

CHAPTER 2

1. Alexander Walker, *Sex in the Movies* (Harmondsworth, 1968), p. 124; J. D. Williams, 'The Influence of the Screen', in Gerald Fort Buckle, *The Mind and The Film. A Treatise on the Psychological Factors in the Film* (London, 1926), p. xi.
2. Ariane Marie Povzner, *La Filmophagie* (Paris, 1967); mentioned by Paul Ilie, 'Surrealism and Cinema', *Diacritics*, Winter 1972, p. 58.
3. Fred W. Phillips, 'The Therapeutic Value of the Movies', *Motion Picture Classic*, vol. IV (Mar. 1917), no. 1, p. 59.
4. Chester W. Cleveland, 'Greenroom Blottings ...', *Motion Picture Classic*, vol. V (Nov. 1917), no. 3, p. 80.
5. Armando, 'Very Wild Western. The Dance Hall', *Motion Picture Classic*, vol. XXVII (June 1928), no. 4, pp. 34–5; Fred Pullin, 'Scenes We Are Sick Of', *Pictures and Picturegoer*, no. 253 (14–21 Dec. 1918), p. 609; Picatostes, 'Y la vanguardia le volvió loco', *Siluetas*, Año I (1 Feb. 1930), no. 5, p. 15.
6. Helena Millais, 'America as seen on the Films', *Pictures and Picturegoer*, no. 237 (24–31 Aug. 1918), p. 211.
7. 'Picture Pin-Pricks', *The Picturegoer*, no. 43 (July 1924), p. 7.
8. F. J. S., 'Double Exposures', *Motion Picture Classic*, vol. VII (Sept. 1918), no. 1, p. 62.
9. Jardiel Poncela, 'El cine a través del humorismo. Aforismos, máximas y mínimas de las películas del oeste', *La Pantalla*, Año III (24 Feb. 1929), no. 56, p. 936.
10. Castanys, 'Elementos indispensables para la realización de un film', *Films Selectos*, Año VII (16 May 1936), no. 291, p. 17.
11. Valentí Castanys, *Barcelona-Hollywood (Ràdio-Cinéma-Sonor)* (Barcelona, 1935), pp. 50, 67.
12. Castanys, *Barcelona-Hollywood*, p. 62.
13. Castanys, *Barcelona-Hollywood*, p. 14.
14. Espina, *Pájaro pinto* (Madrid, 1927), pp. 7, 120.
15. Ibid., pp. 125–6.
16. Gómez de la Serna, *Obras completas* (Barcelona, 1956), vol. I, pp. 1833, 1831.
17. Hart Crane, *The Great Western Plains* (1922), in Brom Weber (ed.), *The Complete Poems and Selected Letters of Hart Crane* (London, 1968), p. 150; Gómez de la Serna, *Obras completas*, vol. I, p. 1864.
18. Gómez de la Serna, *Obras completas*, vol. I, pp. 1872, 1866, 1860.
19. Ibid., pp. 1852, 1841.
20. Ibid., pp. 1829, 1866.

21. *The Collected Works of Nathaniel West* (Harmondsworth, 1975), p. 146.
22. Fernando Vela, *El arte al cubo* (Madrid, 1927), p. 63; Unamuno, 'La literatura y el cine', in *Obras completas*, vol. XI (Madrid, 1958), p. 535.
23. Unamuno, *Obras completas*, vol. II, p. 908.
24. Unamuno, 'La literatura y el cine', in *Obras completas*, vol. XI, p. 532; Gómez de la Serna, *Obras completas*, vol. I, p. 1890.
25. Gómez de la Serna, *Obras completas*, vol. I, p. 1829.
26. *The Collected Works of Nathaniel West*, p. 99.
27. Jean Cocteau, 'No hay en el mundo un rincón sin "cine"', *La Prensa* (Santa Cruz de Tenerife), 11 April 1933; José Castellón Díaz, 'Cines. Generalidades', *Nuestro Tiempo*, no. 1 (1935).
28. Mariana Hoffmann, 'Influencia del cinema en la imaginación de los niños', *Popular Film*, Año VII (3 Mar. 1932), no. 290.
29. Ricardo Acevedo, 'En el cine (Cuento)', *Los Muchachos*, no. 229 (29 Sept. 1918), p. 13.
30. Howard Rosenberg, 'TV-Inspired Crime is Indicted', *Los Angeles Times*, 5 May 1978.
31. Pedro de Répide, 'La infancia y el cine', *Hespérides*, Año II (10 July 1927), no. 80.
32. 'Film as an argument for censorship, judge says', *The Times*, 24 July 1973.
33. *Pictures and Picturegoer*, no. 183 (11–18 Aug. 1917), p. 196; Walker, *Sex in the Movies*, pp. 257–8.
34. R. Martínez de la Riva, 'La censura cinematográfica', *Hoy (Diario republicano de Tenerife)*, 14 July 1935.
35. Maeztu, 'La semana contra el "cine inmoral"', *Gaceta de Tenerife*, 17 May 1935.
36. Eisenstein, 'Código de conducta moral del cinema norteamericano', *Octubre*, no. 6 (Apr. 1934), p. 28.
37. 'Inga', 'El cine y la propaganda de guerra', *Octubre*, no. 2 (July–Aug. 1933), p. 31.
38. F. M., 'Cinema: espejo del mundo', *Octubre*, no. 1 (1933), pp. 23–4.
39. Maeztu, *Autobiografía* (Madrid, 1962), p. 332.
40. *The Film Daily Year Book and Weekly Film Digest* (New York, 1928), p. 979; *The Film Daily Year Book of Motion Pictures and Weekly Film Digest* (New York, 1935), p. 1076; *The Film Daily Year Book of Motion Pictures and Weekly Film Digest* (New York, 1930), p. 1045.
41. Maeztu, 'La semana contra el "cine inmoral"', *Gaceta de Tenerife*, 17 May 1935.
42. Giménez Caballero, 'Cineclub en la Universidad', *La Gaceta Literaria*, no. 82 (15 May 1932).
43. 'Se prohibe la proyección de la película "La Edad de Oro"', *Gaceta de Tenerife*, 15 June 1935.
44. Giménez Caballero, 'Cinema. Las tripas del silencio español', *La Gaceta Literaria*, no. 119 (1 December 1931); 'El pleito surrealista. "Gaceta de Tenerife" falsea la verdad', *La Tarde* (Santa Cruz de Tenerife), 15 June 1935.

45. 'Una carta. Sobre la prohibición de ser proyectada la película "La Edad de Oro"', *Gaceta de Tenerife,* 16 June 1935.
46. 'La Edad de Oro', *Gaceta de Tenerife,* 14 June 1935.
47. 'La "Gaceta" y nosotros', *El Noticiario* (Santa Cruz de Tenerife), 24 June 1935.

CHAPTER 3

1. Unamuno, 'La literatura y el cine', in *Obras completas,* vol. XI, p. 535.
2. 'Palabras del doctor Marañón en el Cineclub acerca de la vanguardia y el cinematógrafo', *La Gaceta Literaria,* no. 83 (1 June 1930).
3. 'Una encuesta sobre el cine sonoro', *La Gaceta Literaria,* no. 69 (1 Nov. 1929); 'Enrique Jardiel Poncela contesta a veintidós preguntas que le hace ¡*Tararí!*', ¡*Tararí!,* Año I (1 Nov. 1930), no. 3, p. 12; Agustín Espinosa, 'Un coleccionista en el cine', *La Tarde* (Santa Cruz de Tenerife), 14 Feb. 1933.
4. Castanys, 'Elementos indispensables para la realización de un film', *Films Selectos,* Año VII (16 May 1936) no. 291; J. Hesse, 'Los "talkies" y el cine español', *Popular Film,* Año I (1 Feb. 1930), no. 5.
5. M. Santos, '¿Dónde está el cine español?', *Popular Film,* Año IX (8 Mar. 1934), no. 393; Santos, 'Hay que defender el cine español', *Popular Film,* Año IX (18 Oct. 1934), no. 426; See too Jaime de Sort, 'El inexplicable fracaso de los cineastas españoles. En pro de la cinematografía española', *Sparta,* Año I (19 Nov. 1932), no. 3; M. Santos, 'Nuestro cinema exige una película genuinamente española', *Popular Film,* Año IX (20 Sept. 1934), no. 423; Ramón Mora Masip, 'Lo que le falta al cine español', *Popular Film,* Año XI (2 Jan. 1936), no. 489.
6. *The Film Daily Year Book of Motion Pictures and Weekly Film Digest* (New York, 1930), p. 1045.
7. José M. Benítez Toledo, 'Teatro y cine', *Hespérides,* Año II (10 July 1927), no. 80.
8. Juan M. Plana, '¿Cinema o teatro?', *Popular Film,* Año VIII (23 June 1932), no. 306; R. Villán, '¿Cine o teatro?', *Popular Film,* Año X (31 Oct. 1935), no. 480.
9. E. Lafuente, 'Teatro y cinema', *La Gaceta Literaria,* no. 43 (1 Oct. 1928); E. Vera, 'Eternos rivales. Cinema y teatro', *Cinema,* Dec. 1932; Domingo de Fuenmayor, 'El pleito eterno. ¿Cine? ¿Teatro?', *Films Selectos,* Año IV (25 Feb. 1933), no. 124, p. 9; Pérez Bellver, 'Cine y teatro', *Films Selectos,* Año I (23 Feb. 1935), no. 227; M. Nieto Muñoz, 'El teatro ante el cinema', *Popular Film,* Año X (25 July 1935), no. 466.
10. Carlos Fortuny, 'Diálogos de la vida moderna. El teatro y el cine', ¡*Tararí!,* Año I (25 Dec. 1930), no. 10.
11. Rafael Marquina, 'La literatura y el cine. II', *La Pantalla,* Año II (9 Dec. 1928), no. 49, p. 823.
12. Hugo Munsterberg, *The Photoplay. A Psychological Study* (London and New York, 1916), p. 196.
13. Henry Albert Phillips, 'Three More Authors Consider the Films', *Motion Picture Classic,* vol. XXIV (Oct. 1926), no. 2, p. 77.

14. Lorenzo Conde, 'Retórica cinematográfica', *Films Selectos*, Año V (23 June 1934), no. 193, p. 3.
15. F. Carrasco de la Rubia, '¿Qué es cine? ¿Qué es teatro?', *Popular Film*, Año IX (29 Dec. 1934), no. 432.
16. F. Hernández Girbal, 'Al cine español le estorban los autores teatrales', *Cinegramas*, Año I (14 Oct. 1934), no. 5.
17. Manuel and Antonio Machado, *Obras completas* (Madrid, 1962), p. 415.
18. Valle-Inclán, *Obras escogidas* (Madrid, 1958), pp. 1089, 1072, 1075.
19. Valle-Inclán, *Luces de bohemia*, 3rd ed. (Madrid, 1971), p. 70.
20. 'Don Ramón del Valle Inclán y el cine', *El Cine*, Año XI (4 Feb. 1922), no. 512, p. 4; partly reproduced as 'Valle-Inclán y su opinión sobre el "cine"', *El Bufón*, no. 1 (15 Feb. 1924). The stage direction quoted from *Las galas del difunto* is found in Valle-Inclán, *Obras escogidas*, p. 1073.
21. Epstein, *Le Cinématographe vu de l'Etna* (1926); quoted by Pierre Leprohon, *Jean Epstein* (Paris, 1964), p. 36.
22. Valle-Inclán, *Luces de bohemia*, 3rd ed., pp. 16, 98.
23. Valle-Inclán, *Obras escogidas*, p. 812.
24. Valle-Inclán, *Luces de bohemia*, 3rd ed., p. 36.
25. Valle-Inclán, *Obras escogidas*, pp. 840, 878.
26. Ibid., p. 1199; *Luces de bohemia*, 3rd ed., p. 20.
27. Ibid., pp. 832, 873–4.
28. Valle-Inclán, *Luces de bohemia*, 3rd ed., pp. 99, 102.
29. In Federico Navas, *Las esfinges de Talía o encuesta sobre la crisis del teatro* (El Escorial, 1928), p. 51.
30. 'Don Ramón de Valle Inclán y el cine', *El Cine*, Año XI (4 Feb. 1922), no. 512, p. 4.
31. Benavente, *Teatro*, vol. 37 (Madrid, 1931), p. 109.
32. *Arte y cinematografía*, no. 279 (June 1924).
33. 'Benavente y el cine', *El Cine*, Año XIII (27 Nov. 1924), no. 659.
34. J. Pérez Domenech, 'Hablan los autores jóvenes. Claudio de la Torre asegura que el cine es el mejor invento literario', *La Prensa* (Santa Cruz de Tenerife), 11 June 1933.
35. *Arte y cinematografía*, no. 276 (March 1924); *Popular Film*, Año IX (18 Jan. 1934), no. 388.
36. R. Martínez de la Rosa, 'Lo que dice Blasco Ibáñez. No existe actualmente el cinematógrafo universal', *El Cine*, Año XIII (8 May 1924), no. 630.
37. Henry Albert Phillips, 'Four More Authors Discuss the Films', *Motion Picture Classic*, vol. XXIV (July 1926), no. 5, p. 24.
38. F. H. G., 'Los que pasaron por Hollywood. Gregorio Martínez Sierra', *Cinegramas*, Año II (2 June 1935), no. 38.
39. W. Fernández Flórez, 'Una aventura de cine', *La Pantalla*, Año I (18 Nov., 25 Nov., 2 Dec. 1927), nos. 1, 2, 3; A. Insúa, 'Los vencedores de la muerte. Película novelesca', *La Pantalla*, Año II (24 Feb., 2 Mar., 9 Mar. 1928), nos. 9, 10, 11.
40. '¿Qué opina usted del cine?', *La Pantalla*, Año I (18 Nov. 1927), no. 1, p. 2. See too Azorín, 'El "cine" y el teatro', *ABC*, 26 May 1927; reprinted in *Obras completas*, vol. IX, 2nd ed. (Madrid, 1963), pp. 105–8.

41. See J. L. Salado, 'Conversación con Palacio Valdés acerca de "La hermana San Sulpicio"', *La Pantalla*, Año II (17 Feb. 1928), no. 8, p. 118.
42. '¿Qué opina usted del cine?', *La Pantalla*, Año I (9 Dec. 1927), no. 4, p. 50.
43. Baroja, 'Nuestros novelistas y el Cinema', *La Gaceta Literaria*, no. 24 (15 Dec. 1927).
44. Irene Polo, 'Pío Baroja nos confiesa que su ideal sería escribir argumentos de película', *Films Selectos*, Año II (21 Nov. 1931), no. 58, p. 5.
45. Guzmán Merino, '"Cita de ensueños". III', *Popular Film*, Año XI (6 Aug. 1936), no. 519.
46. Pérez Bellver, 'Novelas filmadas', *Film Selectos*, Año VI (19 Jan. 1935), no. 222; G. Gómez de la Mata, 'Literatura en el cine', *Films Selectos*, Año I (13 Apr. 1935), no. 234, p. 5.
47. A. D. Emerson, 'Should Novels be Filmed?', *Pictures and Picturegoer*, no. 226 (18–15 July 1918).
48. E. W. White, *Parnassus to Let* (London, 1928), p. 15.
49. André Obey, 'Musique et cinéma: deux mamelles', *Le Crapouillot*, 16 Mar. 1923, p. 20.
50. Gloria Bello, 'De la adaptación de diversos géneros de novela a la pantalla', *Popular Film*, Año VII (17 Nov. 1932), no. 327; María Luisa Clement, 'Novelas cinematografiables', *Films Selectos*, Año V (28 Apr. 1935), no. 185, p. 5.
51. Lorenzo Conde, 'Retórica cinematográfica', *Films Selectos*, Año V (23 June 1934), no. 193, p. 3; A. Orts-Ramos, 'Goethe y el cinematógrafo', *Films Selectos*, Año III (11 June 1932), no. 87, p. 5; Antón Guilio Bragaglia, 'El "Orlando furioso", poema cinematográfico', *Popular Film*, Año VII (15 Sept. 1932), no. 318. Bragaglia continued his essay in no. 319 (22 Sept.), no. 320 (29 Sept.), no. 321 (6 Oct.); the remarks I quoted appear in nos. 319 and 321.
52. Rafael Gil, 'Literatura en el cinema y cinema en la literatura', *Popular Film*, Año XI (6 Aug. 1936), no. 519.
53. Jarnés, 'Literatura y cinema', *Films Selectos*, Año IV (17 June 1933), no. 140, p. 3.
54. Torre, *Literaturas europeas de vanguardia* (Madrid, 1923), p. 386.

CHAPTER 4

1. Maurois, 'La Poésie du cinéma', in Maurois *et al*, *L'Art cinématographique*, vol. III (Paris, 1927), p. 33; Arconada, 'La poesía en el cinema', *Nuestro Cinema*, Segunda época, no. 1 (Jan. 1935).
2. Maurois, 'La Poésie du cinéma', in Maurois *et al*, *L'Art cinématographique*, vol. III, pp. 30, 35; Emile Vuillermoz, 'La Musique des images', in Maurois *et al*, *L'Art cinématographique*, vol. III, p. 63.
3. J. Palau, 'Precisiones sobre el ritmo', *Films Selectos*, Año III (17 Dec. 1932), no. 114.
4. F. Caravaca, 'Rivas-Cheriff, animador del Teatro Escuela de Arte, opina sobre el ritmo y la poesía en el "cinema"', *Films Selectos*, Año VI (28 Dec. 1935), no. 271, p. 9.

5. Cocteau, 'El arte y la revolución: el "cine", poesía de hoy', *La Prensa* (Santa Cruz de Tenerife), 16 Feb. 1933; Fernando Vela, *Desde la ribera oscura (Sobre una estética del cine)* (Madrid, 1925), p. 217.

6. Marquina, 'La poesía en el cinematógrafo', *La Pantalla*, Año III (21 July 1929), no. 76, p. 1258; 'Un cineasta francés. Algunas ideas de Jean Epstein', *La Gaceta Literaria*, no. 43 (1 Oct. 1928).

7. Arconada, 'La poesía en el cinema', *Nuestro Cinema*, Segunda época, no. 1 (Jan. 1935); Arconada, 'Boletín del Cineclub. Sesión inaugural', *La Gaceta Literaria*, no. 49 (1 Jan. 1929).

8. Marquina, 'La poesía en el cinematógrafo', *La Pantalla*, Año III (21 July 1929), no. 76, p. 1258.

9. Marquina, 'La poesía en el cinematógrafo', *La Pantalla*, Año III (21 July 1929), no. 76, p. 1258.

10. Torre, 'El cinema y la novísima literatura: sus conexiones', *Cosmópolis*, no. 33 (1921), pp. 403-4.

11. Torre, 'Cinema', *Revista de Occidente*, vol. XII (1926), no. XXXIV, p. 120.

12. Piqueras, 'Influencias del Cineclub en los programas del cinema público', *La Gaceta Literaria*, no. 63 (1 Aug. 1929).

13. Anon., 'Noticiario', *La Gaceta Literaria*, no. 24 (15 Dec. 1927).

14. Epstein, *La Poésie d'aujourd'hui. Un nouvel état d'intelligence* (Paris, 1921), pp. 171, 173.

15. Ibid., p. 173.

16. Carlos Vinafán, 'A Lulú Alvarez. Naciente "estrella" de Hollywood', *Popular Film*, Año VII (25 Aug. 1932), no. 315.

17. Leandro Rivera Pons, 'Mary Pickford', *Popular Film*, Año X (27 June 1935), no. 462; 'Mimí Jordán', *Popular Film*, Año X (25 July 1935), no. 466.

18. A. Suárez Guillén, 'Fritz Lang, el poeta moderno de la cinematografía', *La Pantalla*, Año III (28 July 1929), no. 77, p. 1268; J. Castellón Díaz, 'El genio de Eisenstein', *Popular Film*, Año VII (24 Mar. 1932), no. 293.

19. Epstein, *Le Cinématographe vu de l'Etna*; quoted by Pierre Leprohon, *Jean Epstein*, p. 36.

20. Alberti, *La arboleda perdida. Libros I y II de memorias* (Buenos Aires, 1959), p. 283.

21. J. Mitry, 'Le Présent et l'avenir du film. Rêves et réalités. Abel Gance', *Le Théâtre et Comoedia Illustré*, 27ᵉ. année (1 May 1924), no. 33.

22. Alberti, 'El "Potemkin" en Brujas', *El Sol*, 19 Apr. 1932; reprinted in Alberti, *Prosas encontradas 1924-1942*, 2nd ed. (Madrid, 1973), pp. 93-7.

23. Lorca, 'Trip to the Moon. A Filmscript,' *New Directions*, vol. 18 (1964), pp. 35, 40.

24. Frank D. McDonnell, *The Spoken Seen. Film and the Romantic Imagination* (Baltimore, 1975), p. 4.

25. Vela, 'Desde la ribera oscura (Sobre una estética del cine)', *Revista de Occidente*, vol. VIII (1925), no. XXIII, p. 226.

26. William Carlos Williams, *Selected Poems*, ed. Charles Tomlinson (Harmondsworth, 1976), p. 185.

27. Ayala, *Indagación del cinema* (Madrid, 1929), p. 62.

28. See Margharita Morreale, 'Quevedo y el Bosco. Una apostilla a "Los Sueños"', *Clavileño*, vol. VII (1956), no. 40, pp. 40–4.

29. See Ian R. J. Jack, *Keats and the Mirror of Art* (Oxford, 1967).

30. E. H. Gombrich, *Art and Illusion. A Study in the Psychology of Pictorial Representation* (London and New York, 1960), p. 181.

31. Altolaguirre, 'Elogio del cine', *Nivel*, no. 43 (25 July 1962).

32. José Moreno Villa, *La música que llevaba (1913–1947)* (Buenos Aires, 1949), p. 247.

33. Moreno Villa, *La música que llevaba*, p. 222.

34. Ibid., p. 227.

35. Ildefonso Manolo Gil, *Borradores. Primeros versos* (Madrid, 1931), p. 37.

36. Dalí, 'Poema', *La Gaceta Literaria*, no. 28 (15 Feb. 1928).

37. Dalí, *Babaouo* (Paris, 1932), p. 28.

38. Dalí, 'Abrégé d'une histoire critique du cinéma', in *Babaouo*, p. 11.

39. Buñuel, 'Pájaro de angustia', *Hélix*, no. 4 (May 1929), p. 5.

40. Ado Kyrou, *Luis Buñuel* (Paris, 1962), p. 15.

41. J. F. Aranda, *Luis Buñuel. Biografía crítica* (Barcelona, 1969), pp. 75–6.

42. Buñuel, 'Une girafe', *Le Surréalisme au Service de la Révolution*, no. 6 (1933), pp. 34, 35.

43. Aranda, *Luis Buñuel*, p. 286.

44. Carlos Vinafán, 'A Lulú Alvarez. Naciente "estrella" de Hollywood', *Popular Film*, Año VIII (25 Aug. 1932), no. 315; Leandro Rivera Pons, 'Mimí Jordán', *Popular Film*, Año X (25 July 1935) no. 466; Rivera Pons, 'Lilian Harvey', *Popular Film*, Año X (25 Apr. 1935), no. 453; Jaime Salas, 'Comentarios poéticos a un film. "Chu Chin Chow"', *Cinegramas*, Año II (29 Jan. 1935), no. 19.

45. Ned Hungerford, 'To Theda Bara', *Motion Picture Classic*, vol. IX (Oct. 1919), no. 2, p. 60.

46. Hart Crane, *The Bridge*, in *The Complete Poems and Selected Letters of Hart Crane*, ed. Brom Weber (London, 1968), p. 45.

47. Ayala, *Indagación del cinema*, p. 177.

48. Rafael Laffón, 'Programa mínimo', *La Gaceta Literaria*, no. 41 (1 Sept. 1928).

49. Moreno Villa, *La música que llevaba*, p. 270.

50. Gutiérrez Albelo, 'Minuto a Brigitte Helm', *Gaceta de Arte*, no. 11 (Dec. 1932), p. 3.

51. Pedro Garfias, 'Cinematógrafo', *Grecia*, no. XVII (30 May 1919).

52. J. Rivas Panedas, 'Poema cinemático. Un ladrón', *La Gaceta Literaria*, no. 27 (1 Feb. 1928).

53. R. Blanco-Fombona, 'Cine', *La Gaceta Literaria*, no. 41 (1 Sept. 1928).

54. Torre, 'Poème dadaïste. Roues', in M. Sanouillet (ed.), *391. Revue publiée de 1917 à 1924 par Francis Picabia*, vol. I (Paris, 1960), p. 101.

55. Torre, 'El cinema y la novísima literatura: sus conexiones', *Cosmópolis*, no. 33 (1921), p. 404; 'Friso ultraísta. Film', *Grecia*, no. XVI (20 May 1919).

56. Torre, 'Cinema', *Revista de Occidente*, vol. XII (1926), no. XXXIV, p. 120.

57. Torre, 'Fotogenia', in *Hélices. Poemas 1918–1922* (Madrid, 1923), pp. 102–3.
58. Torre, 'En el cinema', in *Hélices*, pp. 104–5.
59. Nancy Nadin, 'If Life resembled the Movies', *The Picturegoer*, no. 4 (Apr. 1927), p. 46.
60. Torre, 'El 7°. episodio', in *Hélices*, p. 108.
61. See Kalton C. Lahue, *A History of the Moving Picture Serial* (Norman, Oklahoma, 1964), pp. 190–1.
62. Torre, 'Color', in *Hélices*, p. 101; 'Charlot', in *Hélices*, pp. 106–7.
63. Leopoldo de Luis, *Vicente Aleixandre* (Madrid, 1970), p. 38.
64. See C. B. Morris, *Surrealism and Spain 1920–1936* (Cambridge, 1972).
65. Aleixandre, 'Renacimiento', *Litoral*, no. 8 (May 1929); 'Noche: órbita política' (1927), *Insula*, no. 329 (Apr. 1974).
66. Aleixandre, *Obras completas* (Madrid, 1968), p. 270.
67. Ibid., pp. 91–2.
68. Ibid., p. 268.
69. Ibid., pp. 356.
70. Salinas, *Poesías completas* (Madrid, 1955), p. 326.
71. Salinas, 'Amsterdam' (*Fábula y signo*), in *Poesías completas*, p. 101; Eugène Deslaw, 'Después de mis primeros films', *La Gaceta Literaria*, no. 55 (1 Apr. 1929); *The Museum of Modern Art Film Index. Vol. I: The Film as Art* (New York, 1976), p. 643.
72. Salinas, 'Cinematógrafo', in *Poesías completas*, pp. 68–71.
73. Salinas, 'Far West', in *Poesías completas*, pp. 59–60.

CHAPTER 5

1. Alberti's recital was announced in 'La próxima sesión: Lo cómico en el Cinema', *La Gaceta Literaria*, no. 56 (15 Apr. 1929), and reported in Piqueras, 'Boletín del Cineclub. La sexta sesión', *La Gaceta Literaria*, no. 58 (15 May 1929).
2. Alberti, *La arboleda perdida*, p. 279.
3. Alberti, 'El "Potemkin" en Brujas', *El Sol*, 19 Apr. 1932; 'Se reciben bahías', *El Sol*, 18 Aug. 1931; reprinted in Alberti, *Prosas encontradas 1924–1942*.
4. Alberti, 'El "Potemkin" en Brujas', in Alberti, *Prosas encontradas 1924–1942*, 2nd ed., p. 96. For an account of the industrial and agricultural unrest in Andalusia, see Manuel Tuñón de Lara, *Luchas obreras y campesinas en la Andalucía del siglo XX. Jaén (1917–1920). Sevilla (1930–1932)* (Madrid, 1978).
5. María Teresa León, *Memoria de la melancolía*, p. 47.
6. Ibid., p. 121.
7. 'Rafael Alberti à l'agrégation d'espagnol. Un entretien avec Pablo Vives', *Les Lettres Françaises*, no. 901 (16–22 Nov. 1961), p. 4.
8. Alberti, *La arboleda perdida*, p. 283.
9. Ibid., p. 284.
10. Ibid., p. 284.
11. Ibid., p. 284.

12. Ibid., p. 284.
13. Ibid., p. 239.
14. 'Rafael Alberti à l'agrégation d'espagnol. Un entretien avec Pablo Vives', *Les Lettres Françaises*, no. 901 (16–22 Nov. 1961), p. 4.
15. J. L. Salado, 'Rafael Alberti, de niño, quería ser pintor', *Cervantes*, vol. VII (Mar.–Apr. 1934), p. 40.
16. Juan Ramón Jiménez, 'Acento. Satanismo inverso', *La Gaceta Literaria*, no. 98 (1931).
17. For a brief entry on Nick Carter, see *The Penguin Companion to Literature. U.S.A. and Latin America* (London, 1971), p. 53. Under the title 'Nick Carter (1ª Serie)', the following episodes of a serial were announced in *El Cine*, Año IV (30 Jan. 1915), no. 159: 1. La acechanza; 2. Las joyas robadas; 3. El buen doctor; 4. El emparedado vivo de Black Manor. *El Cine* also announced the film *Aventura de Nick Carter* in Año XI (13 May 1922), no. 526, p. 8.
18. Piqueras, 'Boletín del Cineclub. La sexta sesión', *La Gaceta Literaria*, no. 58 (15 May 1929).
19. Alberti, *La arboleda perdida*, p. 279.
20. C. A. Pérez, 'Rafael Alberti: Sobre los tontos', *Revista Hispánica Moderna*, vol. XXXII (1966), pp. 208–9, 216.
21. Domenchina, *Crónicas de 'Gerardo Rivera'* (Madrid, 1935), p. 245.
22. Bergamín, 'De veras y de burlas', *La Gaceta Literaria*, no. 71 (1 Dec. 1929).
23. Anon., '¡El tonto de Rafael!', *Lola*, no. 5 (Mar. 1928); Jiménez, *Cartas (primera selección)* (Madrid, 1962), p. 273.
24. A photograph of Gómez de la Serna 'de falso negro' appeared in *La Gaceta Literaria*, no. 52 (15 Feb. 1929).
25. Pedro G. Arias, 'Una conferencia en el Lyceum Club. (Impronta literaria)', *La Gaceta Literaria*, no. 90 (15 Sept. 1930).
26. José Díaz Fernández, *La Venus mecánica* (Madrid, 1929), pp. 163–4.
27. 'Un "suceso" literario. La conferencia de Rafael Alberti', *La Gaceta Literaria*, no. 71 (1 Dec. 1929).
28. 'Las musas de vanguardia se rebelan contra su poeta. Una conferencia de Rafael Alberti, una paloma, un galápago, una zapatilla y unos insultos', *Heraldo de Madrid*, 11 Nov. 1929.
29. Alberti, *Poesía 1924–1967* (Madrid, 1972), p. 413.
30. Alberti, 'Carta de Maruja Mallo a Ben Turpin' and 'Charles Bower, inventor', *La Gaceta Literaria*, no. 65 (1 Sept. 1929).
31. M. G., 'Greta Garbo', *Popular Film*, Año VIII (1 June 1933), no. 355.
32. Jacques Baroncelli, *Pantomime. Musique. Cinéma* (Paris, 1915), p. 10.
33. J. L. Salado, 'Rafael Alberti, de niño, quería ser pintor', *Cervantes*, vol. VII (Mar.–Apr. 1934), p. 40.
34. *The Film Daily Year Book of Motion Pictures and Weekly Film Digest* (New York, 1934), p. 116.
35. *Motion Picture Classic*, vol. XXVI (Jan. 1928), no. 5. Bowers's death in November 1946 was reported in *The New York Herald Tribune* (27 Nov.) in an obituary article entitled 'Charles Bowers Dies; Pioneer in Film Cartoons'.

36. Alberti, *Poemas escénicos (primera serie)* (Buenos Aires, 1962), p. 7.
37. Luis Gómez Mesa, 'Sobre la pantalla cómica', *La Gaceta Literaria*, no. 108 (15 June 1928).
38. Huidobro, 'Harold Lloyd', *La Gaceta Literaria*, no. 43 (1 Oct. 1928).
39. John McCabe, *Mr. Laurel and Mr. Hardy* (London, 1962), p. 52.
40. A. Casinos Guillén, 'Parejas que triunfan', *Popular Film*, Año VII (14 Apr. 1932), no. 296, p. 4.
41. Rosa Chacel, *Estación, ida y vuelta* (Madrid, 1930), p. 191; Gerald Mast, *The Comic Mind. Comedy and the Movies* (London, 1974), p. 151.
42. Adam Reilly, *Harold Lloyd. The King of Daredevil Comedy* (New York, 1977), p. 172.
43. Alberti, 'Five o'clock tea' and 'Falso homenaje a Adolphe Menjou', *La Gaceta Literaria*, no. 66 (15 Sept. 1929).
44. See C. B. Morris, 'Some Literary Sources in Alberti's *Yo era un tonto*', *The Malahat Review*, no. 47 (July 1978), pp. 173–80.
45. Manuel Bayo, *Sobre Alberti* (Madrid, 1974), p. 20.
46. Díaz Fernández, *La Venus mecánica*, p. 32.
47. Luis Pancorbo, 'Rafael Alberti: Más años fuera que dentro de España. Entrevista con el poeta en Roma', *Revista de Occidente*, no. 148 (July 1976), p. 74.
48. Federico Bravo Morata, *La Dictadura. I (1924 a 1927)* (Madrid, 1973), p. 38.
49. J. A. Cabero, 'Crónica cinematográfica', *Heraldo de Madrid*, 6 Feb. 1929.
50. 'Girl to Renew Wallace Beery Suit', *New York Times*, 14 Aug. 1928; 'Las musas de vanguardia se rebelan contra su poeta. Una conferencia de Rafael Alberti, una paloma, un galápago, una zapatilla y unos insultos', *Heraldo de Madrid*, 11 Nov. 1929. The lawsuit against Beery was reported in Spain in 'Cinegramas', *La Pantalla*, Año II (11 Nov. 1928), no. 45, p. 767.

CHAPTER 6

1. 'Cartas de Luis Cernuda (1926–1929)', *Insula*, no. 207 (Feb. 1964).
2. Cernuda, 'Anotaciones', *La Verdad*, no. 59 (1 Oct. 1926).
3. Cernuda, 'Historial de un libro (La Realidad y el Deseo)', *Papeles de Son Armadans*, Año IV, vol. XII (1959), no. XXXV, p. 135; reprinted in Cernuda, *Poesía y literatura* (Barcelona, 1960), pp. 231–80.
4. See *La Pantalla*, Año II (14 Oct. 1928), no. 42, p. 693; Año III (26 May 1929), no. 68, p. 1123.
5. Cernuda, *Perfil del aire* (Málaga, 1927), p. 50.
6. Ibid., p. 31.
7. See José María Capote Benot, 'Relación de la biblioteca', in *El período sevillano de Luis Cernuda* (Madrid, 1971), pp. 151–60.
8. Cernuda, 'El indolente', *La Verdad*, no. 56 (18 July 1926).
9. Cernuda, 'Historial de un libro', in *Poesía y literatura*, pp. 261–2.
10. 'Cartas de Luis Cernuda (1926–1929)', *Insula*, no. 207 (Feb. 1964); also in Capote Benot, *El período sevillano de Luis Cernuda*, p. 31.
11. See Capote Benot, *El período sevillano de Luis Cernuda*, pp. 31–3.

12. Margaret Farrand Thorp, *America at the Movies* (New Haven, 1939), p. 5; quoted by George Bluestone, *Novels into Film. The Metamorphosis of Fiction into Cinema* (Berkeley and Los Angeles, 1973), p. 39.

13. Cernuda, 'Historial de un libro', in *Poesía y literatura*, p. 247.

14. 'El Cineclub. La quinta sesión del Cineclub', *La Gaceta Literaria*, no. 56 (15 Apr. 1929).

15. 'Segunda encuesta de Nuestro Cinema', *Nuestro Cinema*, Segunda época, Año IV (Aug. 1935), no. 17.

16. Carlos Morla Lynch, *En España con Federica García Lorca* (Madrid, 1958), p. 312.

17. See C. B. Morris, *Surrealism and Spain 1920–1936*, p. 259; under the title 'Sketch de la pintura moderna', a brief summary of this talk appears in Lorca, *Obras completas*, 20th ed., vol. I, pp. 1071–2.

18. See Helen F. Grant, 'Una "aleluya" erótica de Federico García Lorca', in *Actas del primer congreso internacional de hispanistas* (Oxford, 1964), pp. 307–14.

19. See Morris, *Surrealism and Spain 1920–1936*, plates 3 and 5.

20. See C. B. Morris, '"Bronce y sueño": Lorca's Gypsies', *Neophilologus*, vol. LXI (1977), pp. 227–44.

21. Herschel Brickell, 'Spanish Poet in New York', *The Virginia Quarterly Review*, vol. XXI (July 1945), no. 3, p. 392.

22. Richard Diers, 'Introductory Note' to Lorca, 'Trip to the Moon. A Filmscript', trans. Bernice G. Duncan, *New Directions*, vol. 18 (1964), p. 34. The filmscript, which is known only in this English translation, appears on pp. 35–41; the Spanish original is in the possession of Emilio Amero.

23. David Gershator, 'Federico García Lorca's *Trip to the Moon*', *Romance Notes*, vol. 9 (1968–9), p. 214.

24. The *New York Times* reported the annual orphans' outing to Coney Island; see for example the issues of 8 June 1911 and 8 June 1927.

25. Federal Writers' Project, *New York City Guide* (New York, 1939), p. 475.

26. Lorca, *Autógrafos I: Facsímiles de ochenta y siete poemas y tres prosas.* Prólogo, transcripción y notas por Rafael Martínez Nadal (Oxford, 1975), p. 205.

27. Peter Lyon, 'The Master Showman of Coney Island', *American Heritage*, vol. IX (June 1958), no. 4, p. 92. On page 15 of his article, which occupies pp. 14–20 and 92–5, Lyon reproduced an engraving of a group of people watching 'A trip to the moon, in the world famous air ship "Luna" '. Thompson's A Trip to the Moon is also mentioned in Federal Writers' Project, *New York City Guide*, pp. 474–5, and in Edo McCullough, *A Sentimental Journey into the Past* (New York, 1957), p. 302.

28. John F. Kasson, *Amusing the Millions. Coney Island at the Turn of the Century* (New York, 1978), p. 61.

29. José Mª. Caparrós Lera, *El cine republicano español 1931–1939* (Barcelona, 1977), p. 198.

30. Valle-Inclán, *Obras escogidas*, p. 881.

31. See Morris, '"Bronce y sueño": Lorca's Gypsies', *Neophilologus*, vol. LXI (1977), p. 242.
32. Lorca, *El público y Comedia sin título. Dos obras teatrales póstumas* (Barcelona, 1978), p. 321.

CHAPTER 7

1. Jarnés, *Viviana y Merlín* (Madrid, 1930), pp. 69, 71.
2. Rafael Gil, 'Benjamín Jarnés y el cine', *Films Selectos*, Año VII (25 July 1936), no. 301, p. 5.
3. Wayne Barga, 'Movie Books. Studios Find Gold Mine in Novelizations', *Los Angeles Times*, 25 Apr. 1978.
4. A. Durán, 'Conversaciones con Gabriel García Márquez', *Revista Nacional de Cultura*, vol. XXIX (1968), no. 185, p. 25.
5. Blasco Ibáñez, *Obras completas*, vol. I, 5th ed. (Madrid, 1964), p. 579.
6. Rosa Chacel, *Estación, ida y vuelta*, pp. 186, 191.
7. Francisco Ayala, 'Tipo de arte del cinema', in *Indagación del cinema*, pp. 25–6.
8. Jarnés, 'Literatura y cinema', *Films Selectos*, Año IV (17 June 1933), no. 140, p. 3; André Levinson, 'Pour une poétique du film', in Maurois *et al*, *L'Art cinématographique*, vol. IV, p. 70.
9. Víctor Fuentes, 'La narrativa española de vanguardia (1923–1931): un ensayo de aproximación', *The Romanic Review*, vol. LXIII (1972), p. 215.
10. Antonio Espina, *Pájaro pinto*, p. 17.
11. Díaz Fernández, *La Venus mecánica*, p. 34.
12. Jarnés, *Paula y Paulita* (Madrid, 1929), p. 120.
13. Jarnés, *Escenas junto a la muerte* (Madrid, 1931), p. 152.
14. Díaz Fernández, *La Venus mecánica*, p. 117.
15. Ibid., pp. 35, 45–6, 169–70.
16. Ibid., pp. 310, 190.
17. Ibid., pp. 72–3.
18. Espina, *Pájaro pinto*, p. 118.
19. Ayala, *Indagación del cinema*, p. 25.
20. Ayala, *Cazador en el alba y otras narraciones*, 2nd ed. (Barcelona, 1971), pp. 47, 69.
21. Ibid., p. 76.
22. Ibid., p. 97.
23. Valle-Inclán, *Luces de bohemia*, 3rd ed., p. 106.
24. Ayala, *Cazador en el alba*, 2nd ed., pp. 96–7.
25. Ibid., p. 97.
26. Ibid., pp. 97–8.
27. Ibid., p. 98.
28. Ibid., p. 96.
29. Ayala, 'Greta Garbo', in *Indagación del cinema*, pp. 135, 136, 137.
30. Ayala, *Cazador en el alba*, 2nd ed., p. 110; Arconada, 'Posesión lírica de Greta Garbo', *La Gaceta Literaria*, no. 37 (1 July 1928). See too Arconada, *Vida de Greta Garbo y otros escritos* (Madrid, 1974).

31. Ayala, *Cazador en el alba*, 2nd ed., p. 107.
32. Ayala, 'Los noticiarios', in *Indagación del cinema*, p. 70.
33. Ayala, *Cazador en el alba*, 2nd ed., pp. 108–9.
34. Ibid., p. 109.
35. Ibid., pp. 109, 110.
36. Ibid., p. 113.
37. Ayala, 'Efecto cómico del ralentí', in *Indagación del cinema*, pp. 63, 62; *Cazador en el alba*, 2nd ed., p. 113.
38. Chacel, *Estación, ida y vuelta*, p. 191.
39. Ibid., pp. 113–14.
40. Ibid., pp. 184, 185.
41. Huidobro, 'Preface' to *Mirror of a Mage*, trans. Warre B. Wells (London, 1931), p. 17.
42. Huidobro, *Cagliostro. Novela-Film*, 2nd ed. (Santiago de Chile, 1942), pp. 44–5, 54–5.
43. Huidobro, 'Preface' to *Mirror of a Mage*, p. 19.
44. Huidobro, *Cagliostro*, 2nd ed., pp. 114, 116.
45. Huidobro, 'Preface' to *Mirror of a Mage*, p. 17.
46. Huidobro, *Cagliostro*, 2nd ed., pp. 47, 67, 74–8.
47. Ibid., pp. 49, 39.
48. Huidobro, 'Preface' to *Mirror of a Mage*, p. 20.
49. Jarnés, *Cita de ensueños (Figuras del cinema)* (Madrid, 1936), p. 15.
50. Ibid., p. 16.
51. Jarnés, *Viviana y Merlín*, pp. 69, 74.
52. Rafael Gil, 'Literatura en el cinema y cinema en la literatura', *Popular Film*, Año XI (6 Aug. 1936), no. 519.
53. Jarnés, *Viviana y Merlín*, pp. 114, 115.
54. Jarnés, 'Literatura y cinema', *Films Selectos*, Año IV (17 June 1933), no. 140, p. 3.
55. Ibid., p. 3.
56. Jarnés, *Paula y Paulita* (Madrid, 1929), pp. 120–1.
57. Ibid., pp. 120, 121.
58. Jarnés, *Locura y muerte de nadie* (Madrid, 1929), pp. 31, 97. Articles on kissing included 'La ciencia del beso', *La Pantalla*, Año II (24 Feb. 1928), no. 9, p. 141; C. Fernández Cuenca, 'Besos cinematográficos', *La Pantalla*, Año II (14 Oct. 1928), no. 42, p. 679.
59. Jarnés, *Locura y muerte de nadie*, pp. 162–3.
60. Ibid., p. 174.
61. Ibid., pp. 174–5.
62. Ibid., pp. 182–3.
63. Jarnés, *Paula y Paulita*, p. 123; *Locura y muerte de nadie*, pp. 181–2.
64. Jarnés, *Escenas junto a la muerte*, p. 152.
65. Ibid., p. 160.
66. Ibid., pp. 160–1; see 'Segunda encuesta de Nuestro Cinema', *Nuestro Cinema*, Segunda época, Año IV (Aug. 1935), no. 17.
67. Jarnés, *Escenas junto a la muerte*, pp. 163, 165.
68. Ibid., pp. 169, 172.
69. Ibid., pp. 173, 175, 173.

70. Ibid., pp. 172, 175.
71. Ibid., pp. 176, 177.
72. Ibid., p. 163.
73. Ibid., p. 163.

CONCLUSION

1. Castanys, 'Elementos indispensables para la realización de un film', *Films Selectos*, Año VII (16 May 1936), no. 291, p. 17; Carranque de Ríos, *Cinematógrafo. Novela* (Madrid, 1936), pp. 74, 219.
2. Carranque de Ríos, *Cinematógrafo*, p. 46.
3. Ibid., p. 217.
4. E. H. Gombrich, *Art and Illusion*, p. 167.

SELECT CRITICAL BIBLIOGRAPHY

THE CINEMA AND LITERATURE

THE cinema has spawned a vast critical bibliography; however, only a minute fraction of it is devoted to the influence of films on literature or to the cinema's debt to literature. I shall therefore concentrate on these particular aspects.

A. GENERAL STUDIES AND REFERENCE WORKS

BERGE, ANDRE, 'Cinéma et littérature', *L'Art cinématographique III*, Paris, 1927.

BLUESTONE, GEORGE, *Novels into Film. The Metamorphosis of Fiction into Cinema*, Berkeley, Los Angeles and London, 1973.

DAISNE, JOHANN, *Dictionnaire filmographique de la littérature mondiale*, 2 vols., Gand, 1971–5.

EMERSON, A. D., 'Should Novels be Filmed?' *Pictures and Picturegoer*, no. 226, 8–15 June 1918.

ENSER, A. G. S., *Filmed Books and Plays. A List of Books and Plays from which films have been made, 1928–1967*, London, 1968.

EPSTEIN, JEAN, *La Poésie d'aujourd'hui. Un nouvel état d'intelligence*, Paris, 1921.

MAGNY, C. E., *The Age of the American Novel: the film aesthetic of fiction between the two wars*, trans. E. Hochman, New York, 1972.

MURRAY, EDWARD, *The Cinematic Imagination. Writers and the motion pictures*, New York, 1972.

RICHARDSON, ROBERT, *Literature and Film*, Bloomington and London, 1969.

B. ANTHOLOGIES OF SPANISH TEXTS

PEREZ MERINERO, CARLOS and DAVID, *En pos del cinema. Una antología*, Barcelona, 1974.

— *Del cinema como arma de clase: antología de Nuestro Cinema 1932–1935*, Valencia, 1975.

C. THE CINEMA AND LITERATURE IN SPAIN

ALGARO, A. del AMO, 'Mi concepto sobre la literatura en el cinema', *Popular Film*, no. 415, 26 July 1934.

ALVAR, MANUEL, 'Técnica cinematográfica en la novela española de hoy', in Alvar, *Estudios y ensayos de literatura contemporánea*, Madrid, 1971.

AYALA, FRANCISCO, 'Novela y cine en cotejo', in Ayala, *El cine. Arte y espectáculo*, Veracruz, 1966.

BELLO, GLORIA, 'De la adaptación de diversos géneros de novela a la pantalla', *Popular Film*, no. 327, 17 November 1932.

BRAGAGLIA, ANTON GIULIO, 'El "Orlando furioso", poema cinematográfico', *Popular Film*, nos. 318–21, 15 September–6 October 1932.

CLEMENT, MARIA LUISA, 'Novelas cinematografiables', *Films Selectos*, no. 185, 28 April 1934.

CORBALAN, PEDRO, 'Los escritores y el cine (1925–1933)', *Informaciones*, supplement no. 322, 12 September 1974.

GIL, RAFAEL, 'Literatura en el cinema y cinema en la literatura', *Popular Film*, no. 519, 6 August 1936.

GOMEZ DE LA MATA, G., 'Literatura en el cine', *Films Selectos*, no. 234, 13 April 1935.

GOMEZ MESA, LUIS, *La literatura española en el cine nacional 1907–1977 (Documentación y crítica)*, Madrid, 1978.

GRANADOS FERNANDEZ, JOAQUIN, 'El montaje como valoración filmoliteraria', *Revista de Literatura*, II, 1953.

GUILLEN, JORGE, 'Desde París. El séptimo arte', *La Libertad*, 19 May 1922.

GUZMAN, A., 'La paradoja de los literatos', *Popular Film*, no. 410, 21 June 1934.

JARNES, BENJAMIN, 'Literatura y cinema', *Films Selectos*, no. 140, 17 June 1933.

MAINER, JOSE-CARLOS, *La edad de plata (1902–1931). Ensayo de interpretación de un proceso cultural*, Barcelona, 1975.

MARQUINA, RAFAEL, 'La literatura y el cine', *La Pantalla*, nos. 48–53, 2 December 1928–3 February 1929.

MARTINEZ GONZALEZ, FRANCISCO, 'Breves sugestiones de literatura y cinema. Cinema-teatro-novela (Tríptico)', *Popular Film*, no. 356, 8 June 1933.

MORRIS, C. B., *The Dream-House (Silent films and Spanish poets)*, Hull, 1977.

ORTS-RAMOS, A., 'Goethe y el cinematógrafo', *Films Selectos*, no. 87, 11 June 1932.

PEREZ BELLVER, 'Novelas filmadas', *Films Selectos*, no. 222, 19 January 1935.

SERRANO DE OSMA, CARLOS, 'Literatura y cinema', *Popular Film*, no. 352, 11 May 1933.

SOLALINDE, A. G., 'Lope de Vega y el cinematógrafo', *La Gaceta Literaria*, no. 8, 15 April 1927.

TOLEDANO, M., 'El cine y la literatura. ¿Dónde empieza y dónde termina el derecho de adaptación de las obras literarias?', *Films Selectos*, no. 192, 16 June 1934.

TORRE, GUILLERMO DE, 'El cinema y la novísima literatura: sus conexiones', *Cosmópolis*, no. 33, 1921.

— 'Cinema', *Revista de Occidente*, XII, no. XXIV, 1926.

— 'Cinema y novísima literatura', *La Gaceta Literaria*, no. 43, 1 October 1928.

UNAMUNO, MIGUEL DE, 'La literatura y el cine', in *Obras completas*, vol. XI, Madrid, 1958.

D. INDIVIDUAL SPANISH WRITERS

Rafael Alberti

BERGAMIN, JOSE, 'De veras y de burlas', *La Gaceta Literaria*, no. 71, 1 December 1929.

MORRIS, C. B., 'Some literary sources in Alberti's *Yo era un tonto*', *The Malahat Review*, no. 47, July 1978.

PEREZ, C. A., 'Rafael Alberti: Sobre los tontos', *Revista Hispánica Moderna*, XXXIII, 1966.

Federico García Lorca

ALLEN, R. C., 'A commentary on Lorca's *El paseo de Buster Keaton*', *Hispanófila*, no. 48, 1973.

GERSHATOR, DAVID, 'Federico García Lorca's *Trip to the Moon*', *Romance Notes*, IX, 1968–9.

HAVARD, R. G., 'Lorca's Buster Keaton', *Bulletin of Hispanic Studies*, LIV, 1977.

HIGGINBOTHAM, VIRGINIA, 'El viaje de García Lorca a la luna', *Insula*, no. 254, January 1968.

— 'García Lorca y el cine', *García Lorca Review*, VI, 1978.

POWER, KEVIN, 'Una luna encontrada en Nueva York', *Trece de nieve*, nos. 1–2, December 1976.

Benjamín Jarnés

GIL, RAFAEL, 'Benjamin Jarnés y el cine', *Films Selectos*, no. 301, 25 July 1936.

INDEX